SUBVERSIVE WORDS

SUBVERSIVE WORDS

Public Opinion in Eighteenth-Century France

Arlette Farge

Translated by Rosemary Morris

The Pennsylvania State University Press
University Park, Pennsylvania

First Published in France as *Dire et mal dire: L'opinion publique au XVIIIe siècle*
© 1992 Éditions du Seuil

English translation © 1994 Polity Press

First published in 1995 in the United States of America and Canada by The
Pennsylvania State University Press, University Park, PA 16802

ISBN 0–271–01431–8 (cloth)
ISBN 0–271–01432–6 (paper)

Library of Congress Cataloging in Publication Data
A CIP catalog record for this book is available from the Library of Congress.

Typeset in 10 on 12 pt Sabon
by Graphicraft Typesetters Ltd, Hong Kong
Printed in Great Britain

This book is printed on acid-free paper.

It is the policy of The Pennsylvania State University Press to use acid-free paper for
the first printing of all clothbound books. Publications on uncoated stock satisfy
minimum requirements of American National Standard for Information Sciences
– Permanence of Paper for Printed Library Materials, ANSI Z39.48 – 1984.

Contents

J'ai embelli ma vie de jours que je n'ai pas vécus.
I have embellished my life with days I never knew.
Pascal Quignard

Foreword

Time: the eighteenth century. Words – light, rebellious, angry or insulting – are taking flight. Sternly, the king persecutes the word and shuts
it within prison walls. It falls exhausted into a police report or is set
down and read in an order of imprisonment. The historian seizes it and
says, 'This word has meaning.' Now it is he who persecutes the persecuted word, and makes of it what some call an intellectual object. Is this
the last snare of all? Perhaps it is one of the multiple avatars of the
historian, that hunter of the past and bearer of (ultimately poetic) illu-
sions: the word once evaded him, but this time he has painstakingly
extracted it from the archives, and will now restore to it that freedom
which the king took away so long ago.

That is, of course, a dream, but it is also a conviction. As one approaches the places where words were said concerning the events of
those days, or hearkens to street-corner opinions, one is creating a
sphere which may also form the plot of a story. The winged words will
remain dumb unless they are carefully gathered up, not to fill a museum
but to discover, in and through their very lightness, the weightiness of
revolt or consent coming from mouths which had never been asked, or
allowed, to speak any words at all.

Seldom can we rediscover the criticisms uttered by an anonymous
populace, and the historian knows how likely he is to stumble over that
ever-present absence of the word. Such words did not make history, and
they remain enigmatic despite the researcher's eager desire to find them
in his sources, as lively and tumultuous as they must have been when
the old days were new. Of that past eagerness, those appeals and interjections, those secretive or overt dialogues, nothing remains save the

opaque certainty that they once existed, and contributed just as much as actions – which are easier to trace – to innumerable important moments in past history. Sometimes a breach opens in the silence of the sources, and words come down to us – usually because they caused a scandal or boldly ventured into forbidden space. It may be gossip overheard in public places by zealous police inspectors, or conversations reported by chroniclers interested in the impetuous and subversive shifts of town life. Or it may be words reported by some informer who considered them suspect, in which case their author could find himself in trouble with the law; or again, graffiti on walls, or words written on scraps of paper dropped on the ground.

All through the eighteenth century, the authorities were goaded with words; they understood when those words seemed to express opposition, but were astonished when they appeared insignificant, or even an expression of loyalty. 'Speaking about' was as disconcerting as 'speaking against': it was a serious derogation of one of the profoundest ideas of the monarchy, that the populace, vulgar followers of instinct, had no business thinking about current events. All they had to do was to give their consent to the acts of authority, often canalized through ceremonial – ritual, festival, religious service or punishment.

The words which give opinions – this will do, that will not do – are a reality and show very clearly that the people of Paris did not blindly accept the conditions under which they lived. There is nothing extraordinary about that. What *is* extraordinary is that their view of events, and the words they spoke concerning what they had seen and heard, had no meaning for the monarchy, which actually feared the people more than anything else. This is the space which we must investigate; this is the speech whose meaning we must strive to discover. It will be no easy task, for the words are scattered through a vast number of sources. Once we have found them, we must then ask about their history, their reasons for existing, the motives which caused them to be uttered, the change in their inflexions as times and events went by. The eighteenth century, like so many others, was awash with rumour; was it unique, and can one talk of it in terms of public opinion or of an assumption of political attitudes? This is an audacious question which risks being anachronistic, since we know that at that time the men and women of town and countryside were subjects of the king, not political subjects. But it is nevertheless a real question, not because we are setting out yet again to seek the origins of the French Revolution which brought the century to an end in fundamental change, but because we wish to set those words in particular contexts and precise movements in the course of history. Words spoken and opinions pronounced could open up distances, cause displacements and organize something which was new to the spheres of saying and doing; and that is how we must take them, in the place where they were born, at the heart of the situations from which they sprang. That is how we can read 'the formation of newness, the emergence of what Foucault calls "topicality"'.[1]

The 'topicality' of the eighteenth century, as we see it, is made up of words (often punishable) spoken by people of no, or little, importance in the heated environment of the public sphere – or the public square. Novelists, of course, delight in the liveliness of such words and the buried dramas and tiny renunciations which they help to reveal; novelists, of course, aspire to communicate that 'living substance' through an art of dialogue which will in no way falsify it.[2] Theirs is a noble task; we shall leave them to it. Historians, meanwhile, have to cleave words so as to extract their meaning; their desire is above all to give a name to the thing of no importance, the ordinary everyday word which falls apart as soon as spoken, but pushes in between two morsels of time which were formerly indivisible. It is the space thus created which is 'topical'. It is those words which we are trying to speak. 'He claimed that he was pursued by vulgar words [*sordida verba*] and that he had to speak them . . .'[3]

Introduction

This book was inspired by the now-classic study by Jürgen Habermas, *The Structural Transformation of the Public Sphere*,[1] and by the interest recently shown in the subject by a number of historians.[2] Habermas has shown how, in the eighteenth century, a bourgeois 'public sphere' (or 'public space') was created; it was governed by reason, a reason which was capable of challenging those in power, meaning the king and the court. In this 'sphere' there arose an enlightened opinion, intensely rational and universal. This, of course, had nothing more to do with private opinion, and it could lay claim to a sort of 'truth' that challenged and opposed the public domain of the court, which was monopolized by the representation of royal power. It was in writing – journals and newspapers – that this new opinion was most at home: it was here that members of elite groups expressed themselves and constituted an educated critical 'sphere' with a precise historical outline. Here, says Habermas, public opinion related to 'a public sphere constituted by private people putting reason to use'. This is the model which his book is devoted to studying, and he makes it clear at the outset that his examination of this determined historical form (the bourgeois public sphere) 'leaves aside the *plebeian* public sphere as a variant that in a sense was suppressed in the historical process'.

'Suppressed'? The idea merits closer consideration. If that sphere was suppressed, then it must at least have existed, so there seems no reason why its outlines should not be sought. It was then that this book began – precisely as I read those words of Habermas's. He goes on to say that in the French Revolution 'there became active, for a moment, a public sphere which had shaken off its literary aspect. It was the uneducated

common people which was its subject, not the cultured classes.' Three
concepts here provoke a reaction: 'common people', 'uneducated', 'subject'. What was happening to these so-called uneducated common people
in the eighteenth century before the Revolution? Were they really quite
uneducated? Did they 'become active' before 14 July 1789? In what
way did they think of themselves as a 'subject', and whose 'subject'?
And how were they thought *of*, and by whom?

If we must express ourselves in more learned terms, then this book
is seeking to detect the political forms of popular acquiescence in, or
dissatisfaction with, events and the monarchy-as-spectacle; it is an inquiry into the existence of a 'popular' public opinion whose motives it
seeks to discover and articulate. Such questions cannot be asked without
some preliminary reflection. 'Public opinion' is not an object which is
easy to handle; when we are dealing with constituent societies of the
Ancien Régime we must be still more alert, and our methodology still
more cautious, lest we fall into facile anachronism, or even serious
errors of interpretation. For 'public opinion', as the expression is usually
used, 'is closely bound to parliamentary democracy'[3] – which was
obviously not the case in the eighteenth century. Moreover, at that time
politics was not the business of the people; there was far more concern
to keep the people out of it. Any 'opinion' issuing from among the
common herd was described as crazy, impulsive, inept – as when
Condorcet, in 1776, defined popular opinion as 'that of the stupidest
and most miserable section of the population'. Did this mean that I was
seeking an object which simply could not be found? I should certainly
have had to abandon it, had I not been convinced, for other reasons,
that a society always functions, in part, outside its own formal organization,[4] and that in this gap there is room to study the processes,
emergence and configurations of certain aspects of reality. The object of
history must be constructed with reference to the actors in society, their
strategies, words, deeds and under-the-counter dealings.

If this is the case, it becomes less hazardous to look for motifs emerging
from the contents of certain words spoken by an eighteenth century
which, by its very essence, forbade the common people to have any
well-developed opinions. We are dealing with a long tradition: in his *De
la sagesse* ('On Wisdom', 1601), Pierre Charron wrote:

> The people ... constantly grumbles and murmurs against the State, all
> swollen with slanders and insolent comments about those who govern
> and command ... In brief, the commoner is a wild beast, all that he
> thinks is but vanity, all that he says is false and erroneous, what he
> blames is good, what he approves of is bad, what he praises is infamous,
> what he does and undertakes is but pure folly.[5]

These ideas reappear, almost unaltered, in writings by scholarly free-thinkers such as Gabriel Naudé (*Considérations politiques sur les coups d'Etat*, Rome, 1639) and by many eighteenth-century philosophers and memorialists. However, in the age of the Enlightenment something different was happening. The lieutenant general of Paris police and his squad, created in 1667, devoted a large part of their efforts to placing informers in certain public places (promenades, cabarets, gardens, squares and crossroads) with orders to listen to what people were saying about the king and about current events. Police observers and spies (they were popularly known as *mouches*, flies on the wall) flitted about, listening to exclamations and comments and transcribing them in reports which they sent regularly to the lieutenant general of police, who then, in his weekly visit to the king, kept the monarch informed about the current climate.

This systematic reporting of opinions expressed among the common people was not a mere amusement: it was one of the grounding activities of a police system which was obsessed with the detail of what was said and articulated, and required to report the essence of it to the highest authorities of State.

It now becomes obvious that we are dealing with a flagrant contra-diction: the people of Paris had opinions on what was happening – visible, real, everyday events – opinions whose pertinence, and existence as a political element, were *denied* by a government which, at the same time, was observing them continually, and moreover, through its policing system of spies, inspectors and observers, was using them to help shape its policies of repression, or demonstration. The contradiction was particularly violent when some great social or political event took place: wars, peace treaties, revolts, or even parliamentary crises or stirrings of Jansenist resistance. But it was also very obvious from day to day, when prices rose or when executions became particularly frequent.

Such 'opinions', though officially kept out of the political field, be-came one of the main terrors of the monarchic government, one of the things to which it sometimes took up a distinct attitude. This inevitably created widespread after-effects and triggered an unavoidable process of action and reaction between the government, events and people's response to those events. It began a curious spiral effect, which in itself shaped fresh configurations of popular opinion, even if it meant (as of course it did) that that opinion was expressed in an unregulated way. What ordinary people said had no existence and no status: it was politically non-existent even while it was a commonplace of social action. Hounded by governmental power, it took on form and existence and developed in the heart of the very system which was both denying it and reckoning with it – and so, to a certain extent, creating it. Both existent and non-existent, popular speaking about current events dwelt in a kind of limbo: in politics it had no place, but its suspect nature was nothing if not a commonplace.

This non-existence of popular opinion, confirmed in high places, contradicted its persecuted real existence; the contradiction sparked off new and accentuated meanings. It was, surprisingly, this very contradiction that determined the way in which monarchy and people went through the century constantly changing the way they related to each other. Grumbles and criticisms existed in this state of exclusion from the political sphere, which simultaneously contained and repelled them. Unless we realize that, we cannot study them: anything else will lead to anachronism. While there was no public opinion, in the modern sense, in the eighteenth century, there were popular opinions, whose form, content and function developed within a monarchic system whose attitude gave them life even as it rejected them. It was amidst this curious tension that rumours arose, and perhaps at times gained a life of their own.

In the light of the foregoing reflections we might suggest that, if we assume that any individual is competent to criticize,[6] then by tracing the history of that competence we may be able to determine the sphere within which that criticism can be active. Indeed, grumbles and expressions of public discontent are of real interest only if we take care to connect them with the sphere which is allotted to them. That sphere itself is shifting and multiple, so that we will do well to 'hook' the complainings on to a multiplicity of different phenomena. What were the events and the sites which at certain moments allowed the unification of the words which were spoken? Were there certain facts around which themes of popular criticism were particularly inclined to crystallize and be verified? How did the reception – and repression was only one possible process of reception – of the word cut it short, or reactivate it?

If we are careful to relate all our considerations to a particular context we shall avoid two traps. The first, that of believing in a fixed and invariable expression of discontent ('men and women have always criticized their government and living conditions'). The second, that of setting out to find, in an eighteenth century which we know ended in revolution, a current of hostile opinion becoming continually stronger until it naturally reaches the upsurge of 1789. Let us turn our backs on these approaches, and work along the uneven line of public opinion with all its diverse orderings and mechanisms, its specific engagements with institutions, political facts, discourse and social practice.

Popular opinions are contained in several kinds of sources: chronicles, newspapers, memoirs, police reports and news-sheets supply a goodly number, as do the archives of the Bastille.

Every depository of this kind of opinions structures them in its own way and appropriates them to different ends: chroniclers and memorialists deride or worry about them; the police watch them and are ready to pounce; the news-sheets use them to inform; the underground press uses them as ammunition against the opposition; the king ponders them so as better to govern the realm (as he thinks); and so on. Scorn, interdiction, solicitation and appropriation are the poles among which these opinions move. The social and political functioning of the witnesses to this speaking is the subject of part I.

In part II we examine the forms and motifs of complaint: how does it arise? And what are the traditional, or exceptional, reasons which lie behind the attitudes assumed?

In the final part, which centres on a single source (the Bastille archives), I work on the dossiers of prisoners sent to the Bastille for their evil intentions towards the king (grumbles, insults, anonymous letters, plots or denouncing of plots). These words from the Bastille tell us the way to discover the complex and ambiguous relationships between the king and his subjects, and the moments when opinions are formed.

From first to last we shall have voluntarily hitched our wagon to the words of others. At the end of our journey it may be possible to read, or discern, a sustained discourse, a knowledge of everyday things which hitherto we had scarcely noticed because we believed them to be formless, or, worse, deformed from birth.

PART I

Journals, Newspapers and
Policemen: Scenes from
Street Life

No one could be indifferent to what ordinary people were saying: the street was an active member of society. It could be denied or rejected, but its noisy exuberance was ever present; rumours escaped it or entered it with equal speed. It was under constant observation from its social superiors, from the press and the police, and its echoes – reported inaccurately or with dread, with indignation or without it – fill their writings. Earlier on it was viewed with scorn and suspicion; later, as we shall see, it was seen as a mine of information. News stories and tavern gossip were enlightening to the chief of police, but they also delighted hack writers avid for news and anecdotes and spicy, saleable stories – not to mention the underground press whose impact depended in part on the weight of people's reactions to particular events.

Popular gossip, interpreted on these varying levels, could have a formidable influence. Scarcely had it been uttered than it was spreading, via carriers who all put it to their own use. As the century grew older its sphere was transformed: it invaded the street, the press, the royal court. Its real presence, even manipulated, distorted or hyped, could cause consternation in its hearers, who might fear it, but could not avoid it. So it took its place amidst a plethora of commentaries and attitudes, feelings and policies, all equally incapable of keeping it under control.

1

Words scorned and persecuted

I shall make use of two kinds of sources. The first is the printed documentation coming from the higher echelons of early eighteenth-century society. Between 1715 and 1726, three great observers wrote their *Journals* or *Memoirs*: Jean Buvat, Mathieu Marais and Edmond-Jean Bourbier, three men of widely differing social backgrounds and outlook.[1]

My second source is unpublished, and is neither literary nor journalistic. It consists of reports by police inspectors and observers who were paid by the lieutenant general of police to keep him informed about Paris gossip. These reports, now in the Bastille Archives in the Bibliothèque de l'Arsenal,[2] cover the years 1725 to 1740, and are of incomparable value, since it was at exactly that time that popular talk acquired a sudden importance.

Diaries and memoirs from the early eighteenth century

This was a political interlude, the regency during the minority of Louis XV. There was an outburst of exuberance after the sorry end of the Sun King's reign, but people were also waiting, with affectionate impatience, for the child-king to reach adulthood. History gives us a favourable image of those years, which seem to have been unaffected by the decay of royal prestige which (so historians tell us) did not begin until the mid-century.[3] Moreover, the *philosophes* and the Enlightenment outlook were not yet supreme, and it is a relief to be able to study the diarists' attitudes towards the common people, untroubled as yet by the horribly difficult question of how popular thinking influenced the Enlightenment and vice versa. This is not to say that the regency was uneventful. Some events were in fact to leave a lasting impression on men's minds and attract a good many reactions.

When Louis XIV died he left France in a sadly chaotic economic and financial situation, bled almost white. The attempted solution was the Law system, named after the Scottish expert called in by the regent to restore financial order. In 1718 a Royal Bank was set up to receive all state revenues, and the king became sole proprietor of all financial securities. To stimulate the economy, he began to issue banknotes guaranteed by the State. At the same time, Law set up a great trading company which was originally called the *Compagnie d'Occident*, the Company of the West. This referred to Louisiana. Louis XIV had granted the exploitation of that territory to a financier, Crozat, who later resigned. The Conseil des Finances then entrusted the task to Law, on condition that he borrowed two million *louis* to help colonize the territory. Law extended his economic power to many other countries, such as China, Mongolia and Japan, and renamed his company the *Compagnie des Indes*. It soon became popularly known as the *Compagnie du Mississippi*, for Law was particularly interested in implementing plans to move settlers to the Mississippi and Louisiana.

These new plans were to go through many vicissitudes. In January and March 1719, and again in 1720, the police took severe measures against begging and idleness: to clear up a floating population which they now saw as a nuisance, they began a rigorous policy of detention. Dubious characters and vagabonds were arrested on the streets, and in early 1720 transports of the poorest men and women were sent off to colonize and fill up the all-too-empty spaces of Louisiana. The lieutenant of police, d'Argenson, was particularly harsh: his habit of having people snatched in broad daylight, or forcing them to marry, caused a scandal. In 1720 there was a serious uprising.

As for Law's system, it turned out to be inflationary: the printing of notes outstripped the cash available, vast fortunes were made and lost and the whole system spun out of control. When it finally collapsed, there was panic. Fights broke out in the streets, Law had to flee for his life and wall-posters attacked the regent, while the ground was strewn with vicious pamphlets. The *parlement* did not stand aside. Using the right of protest granted it by the regent, it admonished him and quarrelled with him over the bull *Unigenitus*, of 1713, which had condemned certain forms of Jansenism. This was the first of a series of harsh criticisms by the *parlement* of the royal authority; it also led to the former's noisy exile to Pontoise in July 1720.

That was indeed an eventful year. Plague broke out in Marseilles,[4] and the Parisians, fearing an epidemic at home, grew more nervous of immorality. Their attention and imagination were soon to be focused on the famous arrest, in 1721, of the thief Cartouche and his execution a few months later. His trial, intended to serve as a warning to others, turned him into a hero, but he was to drag hundreds of accomplices after him in his fall.

The first quarter of the century ended in a riot. In 1725 bread was expensive and food short, and Paris erupted. D'Ombreval, the lieutenant general of police, was dismissed, and in 1726 the hated Duc de Bourbon was disgraced. It was then that Fleury began his long ministerial career.

During those eleven years, the mob had had more than one occasion to make its feelings known. We must now see how memorialists and diarists brought that mob into their writings, how they saw it and how they spoke of it. The intrusion of the mob into these journals and memoirs did not happen by chance.

With a few exceptions, diaries and memoirs have received little literary attention. For this very reason they are of interest, though we need not think that they always tell the truth. At the very least they belong to 'that intimate and confidential side of historical writing which, under the title "Memoirs", conveys day by day, with casual honesty, the thoughts of the moment, and records freely, inconsistently, diffusely, but with tolerable fidelity, the very making of history.'[5]

With fidelity? Let us examine the writing of three famous chroniclers of the early eighteenth century: Jean Buvat (1660–1729), Mathieu Marais (1665–1737) and Edmond-Jean Barbier (1689–1771).

Buvat began his journal in 1715 and finished it in 1723. He was a simple man, a copyist in the king's library. He was curious about events and jotted them down pell-mell, with no attempt at a coherent narrative. Aubertin was to call his work 'history in disorder';[6] no matter, for his viewpoint is valuable for its very naivety. His information, picked up in the streets or from various churchmen of his acquaintance, gave him a clear idea of the disturbances caused in 1713 by the bull *Unigenitus*.

Marais was of another sort: he was a lawyer, a born parliamentarian, and he wrote his memoirs between 1715 and 1737. He was very cultured and witty and combined a sense of style with an acute critical outlook, which he directed principally against the Jesuits. He lived among parliamentarians, most of whom were of the Jansenist persuasion, and was no friend to absolutism. He was not much interested in street life; his attention focused more on royalty, and especially the regent. He watched displays, took part in ceremonial, immersed himself in the celebratory atmosphere the better to describe it later on. He was looking into the same mirror as the common folk, but from a different angle.

Barbier must be the best known of the three. His chronicle is very long, for he went on writing from 1718 to 1763, and historians have always regarded him as a major source, especially for the parliamentary disputes of Louis XV's reign. His detailed descriptions of the quarrels between *parlement* and king show a certain foreboding of the future. Reading him, we immediately sense his moderate outlook and his nervousness. A lawyer who became head of the council of d'Argenson (keeper of the seals), then of the councils of the Princesse de Conti and the Duc d'Orléans, he was never at ease with the common people, whom he feared even when they were in celebratory mood. He was mildly anticlerical, no Jansenist, a lover of order who avoided enthusiasm, hating impetuosity and passion, but observing each successive crisis with scrupulous care.

These three sharply contrasting witnesses all lived in a somewhat turbulent intellectual and moral climate. In spite of their differing styles and personal outlooks, they all three speak in almost identical fashion concerning the 'people'. First, they all give the people a prominent role. They do not, of course, get as much space as news of the court, the prince, the dukes and duchesses, or as treaties, church affairs and the *parlement*; but in comparison with memoirs from the reign of Louis XIV, their presence is felt much more clearly. There was a reason for this: the court had left Versailles, for the regent was living in the Palais-Royal, in the heart of Paris. Observers of Paris, the regent's city, who were anxious to keep track of the court and its master, could not but be aware of the crowd. In the capital, feasts and entertainments were provided for public consumption and drew their importance from this immersion in the urban sphere. The court was no longer, as in the seventeenth century, a décor meaningless without the king's presence, but a collection of varied, unlocalized scenes exhibited to an audience whose multiplicity determined the nature of the play itself. Thus, any chronicler observing the court was forced to see those before whom it preened and pranked. In a word, the news was made by the court in its favourite resorts – the Comédie Française, the Opéra, Saint-Sulpice or the church of Saint-Roch – which were thronged with an audience invited not to participate in, but to assent to, the brilliant demonstrations organized before their eyes. The observer could not get away from the audience.

The common people may have been unavoidable, but they were not allowed into every cranny of a chronicler's meticulous account of the times. Buvat, Marais and Barbier all bring them on in two ways, and two only: in anecdotes concerning a single individual who has had some extraordinary experience (unpleasant scandal, weird accident, wonderful dream, astonishing cure); or collectively – not to say generically – when a visible and solidly constituted crowd assembles to complain, jeer or applaud.

The anecdotes are entertaining, and sometimes amazing. On 15 January 1716, Buvat noted that 'on the night of the 21st, a girl was found on the rampart, tied to a tree stark naked and dead of cold.' June 1719: 'A marriage took place in the church of Saint-Eustace: the husband was aged 108, the bride, ninety-five.' Apart from such unusual occurrences, the people appear as an undifferentiated mass, responding *en bloc* to all kinds of events which concern them, such as a rise in the price of bread, an abortive revolt or some incidental rejoicing. Nothing can be made out save an aggregate of anonymous figures which, when gathered together, are always more or less frightening. To this hovering fear we must add scorn, condescension and a certain irony. There is no need for numerous examples: it is always the same story.

Buvat, May 1719: 'In Paris bread was being sold for 2 *sous* 6 *deniers* or 3 *sous* the *livre*, at which the populace protested.'

Buvat, 4 May 1720, after the king's order not to annoy the archers who had been sent to arrest vagabonds and poor beggars whether crippled or sound in body: 'The populace and shopkeepers had revolted several times against the untrustworthiness of these archers.'

Barbier again, in 1723: 'Despite the poverty of the times, there was good cheer this carnival.'

March 1722: 'As the people of Paris must always be kept amused to console them for their lack of money, ceremonies of astonishing magnificence are being prepared for the arrival of the Infanta of Spain, who will be here by Sunday or Monday, and we expect the very streets to be hung with tapestries, which is quite out of the ordinary.'

Thus the people appear episodically, via a collection of more or less exotic but minor events; or in a general way, when the size of the crowd itself constitutes an event. There is no half-way house, where there might be some consideration of their varying ways of life and behaviour, some analysis of their social stratification and their aspirations. Not until the *Tableau de Paris* by Louis-Sébastien Mercier (1782) do we find some close observation of strategies within a diverse population. Individual members of the populace can be chronicled only when they have strange and unusual adventures (not unlike some curious animal which we observe without understanding), or merged into an aggregate of impulsive and simple-minded men and women whose behaviour is hard to channel or to control – again, much like animals.

Having presented the 'people' in this way, between curiosity about the oddities of some of its members and an obsession with its collective stirrings, which of its actions were most often recorded by memorialists?

That is easy to answer. The people appear in three different kinds of situation: to express their joy or sorrow at royal ceremonies (marriages or funerals, Te Deums for a victory or the birth of a prince); when the criminal element among the people of Paris plunges the whole place into cut-throat insecurity; and when there are ugly rumours of popular discontent in the city.

It is fairly obvious that the chroniclers are interested only in collective retorts and reactions: fidelity to the monarchy, revolt and criminality are responses to an order imposed from above. There is no trace of other aspects: leisure, social custom, everyday and home life, buying and selling, or the struggle to keep alive at all; what, for example, might we have learned from a description of popular migrations?

The people are generally described from the outside. We hear their acclamations, 'Long live the king!', and see them fighting on street corners, an unending round of violence, quarrels, crimes and emotions, unvarying noisy gestures and gross physical appearances. It is bodies which we are shown: there are very few notes on the mental or intellectual capabilities of the crowd. The people are *there*. We hear both their noisy agreements and their equally noisy, and threatening, denials.

As for scandalous stories, the chroniclers' somewhat dubious tastes introduce the reader to some macabre scenes: dismembered bodies, severed limbs scattered broadcast, women cut in two – as if the authors' imagination were fixated on butchery. On 6 February 1716 Buvat recounted this horrid anecdote:

> Some ice came away [he is referring to the frozen Seine] and smashed up several boats, so that several washerwomen perished and were cut in two; the heads of some of them showed above the ice, but their bodies were trapped underneath, so that they could not be saved; which was a sad sight.

In 1717 he gives a variation on the theme: 'There were found in the church of Notre Dame, the church of the Carmelites in the Place Maubert, and in that of Saint-Germain-l'Auxerrois, bundles of linen containing pieces of human bodies.' And again: 'In a street in the Faubourg Saint-Marceau, they found the body of a girl roasted on a spit, the spit being stuck through her head.'

This state of the imagination could be connected with the contemporary medical obsession with dissection; or it could be viewed symbolically: the body of the people exists either *en masse* or in pieces, it cannot be perceived otherwise – especially as the most familiar sight for everyone was the executions in the Place de Grève. Several times a week the crowd gathered to see executions, as bodies were torn to tatters, cut in pieces, quartered. In 1721 Cartouche was caught, and he denounced a great number of accomplices who were then torn to pieces week by week. The chroniclers never tire of describing these executions with their almost immutable rituals. Cartouche's henchmen would come up to the Hôtel de Ville, confess all, and then, after their last, sleepless night on earth, would climb the fatal ladder.[7] The crowd was always there, the court was sometimes represented (let us not forget the regent's taste for rotting bodies, witnessed by his morbid celebrations). Even before this execution-rich period, Buvat had shown no reluctance to describe spectacular punishments. In June 1716 he recorded the execution of two forgers, a pair of lovers who afforded their judges some amusement before going to the gallows, and who obviously fascinated Buvat: 'His concubine had dressed her hair very elegantly and with very handsome ornaments, as if she intended to charm Death. She was still only twenty-two, very handsome and well made.' This made the ensuing execution all the more deplorable.

Marais, usually more intrigued by court life than by that of the people, sometimes yielded to the attraction of scandal and executions. In March 1724, he recorded his astonishment at two odd stories.

A few days ago a donkeyman of Montmartre was burned alive. He used his she-asses for a quite different purpose than providing milk, and was guilty of all kinds of blasphemies. His tongue was cut out and his hand cut off. His uncle went with him to the end, on the hangman's cart, and exhorted him to offer his tongue, to hold out his hand, to submit to the burning.

Later it emerged that there had never been any affair with a she-ass – but this discovery came too late to save the victim.

On the same day Marais told the story of La Perelle, a *valet de chambre* of M. Puysegur.

He used to neatly cut off his friends' heads and arms, then robbed them and got rid of the bodies as best he could, throwing them either into the latrines or into a river. A head found on a boat led to the investigation of this crime . . . So he was broken on the wheel after making a detailed confession of his technique of dismemberment.

The people always appear in an explosion of joy or anger; excess is as native to them as a bee to the hive. Or, if the chroniclers give this impression, it is because they are quite unable to imagine the lower orders having any sort of intelligent understanding of, or interaction with, events.

As the controversy over the Jansenists developed, things changed: the people discussed it at such length that the chroniclers had to modify their attitudes. Those committed to either the parliamentary or the Jansenist cause found out how to make the most of this ready-made audience and this new atmosphere, seeking to win over or appropriate both. No longer could they lament the public indifference which was sadly noted by President Hénault in his *Memoirs* of the exile of the *parlement* to Pontoise in 1720:

> The people, who by our absence were deprived of their only remaining protection, nonetheless regarded our departure with indifference. The yoke which had been imposed on them eighty years since had accustomed them to suffer many things in silence, and the excess of their misery had dulled their reactions.[8]

Was that really true? In any case, by about 1723 things had changed a good deal.

The real subject of these journals and memoirs was not the people but the life of the court, the petty doings and scandals of the regency. Chroniclers opened their pages to scenes of court life, while the princes solicited the public eye by public celebration. Their status, too, was confirmed by the spectacles they offered to a public greedy for festivals and novelties. Marais had a great appetite for such anecdotes and told them with verve. Insatiable, voluble, he peppered his pages with princely personages in whose activities he delighted. Between 1717 and 1720 he told, without passing value judgements, a great number of spicy anecdotes, obscene puns and saucy little stories which circulated among the princes: all without apology, without any comment and with jesting amusement. The princes' unembarrassed conduct, and Marais' unembarrassed reporting of it, make striking reading: one is surprised by the nonchalance of the court whose cynical amusements could sometimes be dangerous, if they came under the public gaze.

From 1720 onwards his tone changes from the descriptive to the accusatory. A strain of indignation mixed with anxiety runs through his prose. In 1722 he is even talking about 'abominations' in the court, feeling himself submerged under the regent's too-frequent changes of mistress, the number of 'ruined' ladies at court, the contamination of debauchery. 'Dreadful games are afoot here,' he writes. 'This is how the court indulges in debauchery . . . there is love-making everywhere' – and homosexuality is becoming a commonplace of these spurious joys . . .

Court aesthetics are crumbling: day by day this blatant self-indulgence causes fresh cracks in the edifice. No secret is safe amidst these dissolute lives, and the court, living in 'open debauchery', is becoming unworthy of itself. It is falling apart, with no vigilant kingly eye to restore it, and in the very midst of this public disintegration, the regent is even exposed to public insult. In July 1721 'there was talk of a night-time misadventure in the Tuileries, where the regent was strolling with those ladies. He was insulted by three men, who handled him roughly, and his mistress also.' Marais misses the gaze of the Great King, Louis XIV, who by his mere presence could sustain all needful propriety and civility. Even if Marais never concerns himself with the real effect of this 'debauchery' on public opinion, what he recounts shows obvious alterations in the relationship between people, court and king. The social (public) gaze is incessantly attracted to the court; in this new and public sphere, between the court and Paris, there is evidently room and to spare for criticism and judgement.

Police records, 1725–1740: secret policing and the persecution of words

The *gazetins*, police records from between 1724 and 1781, are a source of exceptional value.[9] They are complete only for the years 1725 to 1740, doubtless because of the vagaries of preservation. They originated in an urgent request from the lieutenant general of police. He had a number of informers stationed in particularly public places: the Palais Royal, the Tuileries gardens, the forecourt of the Palais de Justice, and also a variety of more or less notorious taverns and, more rarely, a few tollbooths and barriers at the edge of the suburban 'liberties'. These observers, who were paid to listen to city gossip and were little inclined to penetrate really deep into the heart of a 'populace' which invariably found them out quite quickly, were supposed to write a report once a week. The lieutenant general awaited these reports anxiously and informed the king about them at regular intervals; Louis XV heard them with particular eagerness and used to have them read out at length by his personal lieutenant. Eager he may have been, but he was also quick to punish any among all the thousands of remarks which had overstepped the bounds of propriety or expressed forbidden opinions.

The observers reported their labours in letters or loose sheets which they sent to the lieutenant general. Later they were bound in leather and included in the Bastille archives, which are now in the Bibliothèque de l'Arsenal. They were handwritten by observers who were all very different from one another, which explains the variety of handwriting and of style, and the abundance of different viewpoints on Paris. Some seem passionately interested in their task and describe vividly what they have seen. Others, more hasty or less interested, are satisfied with a rapid list of the remarks they have overhead. In either case, it is clear how strictly they were subjected to the authority of the lieutenant general of police: it was no good irritating him if you wanted to be properly paid. Any lapse or carelessness was notified to the organizer, and reprimands were communicated directly or indirectly to a lazy or inattentive observer. The lieutenant expected a certain originality in every report; he was not at all pleased if he found only commonplace gossip, and expressed himself forcibly on the subject, as is shown by this reply of 18 February 1726 from an observer:

> My lord: I have sent no report to Your Eminence this week because I could only have sent one full of the news which is circulating in public places, as I customarily do. And as Your Eminence has told Monsieur Bazin [first secretary of police] that you wished it to be full of more important things and that I ought to insinuate myself more cunningly for this purpose, I hereby take the liberty of repeating my request [for an advance], and then within a month my reports will have so changed that you will be pleased with me.[10]

The informers defended themselves: if they were to 'insinuate themselves more cunningly', they also had to be better paid, and there follows a tough game of protest, demands for subsidies and hard bargaining. One informer offered a lengthy self-justification, not without criticism and irony, on 11 December 1726:

> I have worked for Your Eminence under your orders; I have not done anything outstanding for lack of opportunity; however, truth has always governed me, but that too depended on chance and on better emoluments: the task is a very delicate one, it incessantly threatens my life and honour; the better paid an honest man is, the better he can enlighten you, but I was not in that case, I cannot do my duties promptly on less than 300 livres a month. Journeys and meals at 30, 40 or 50 sous apiece from the best-known suppliers, where important people go, together with expenditure on clothes, are making my life a perfect misery.[11]

The observer had a strange job; it was risky, and he felt entitled at least to make a profit. He had to eavesdrop on the discontented lower orders, but he also had to be seen amongst their betters in places where one was expected to keep up appearances, which meant good clothes and expensive meals ... The observer was not always very good at disguises, and might easily be recognized on any street corner. To be good at the job one had to cover one's tracks skilfully, be immune to embarrassment and be extremely loyal to the lieutenant general of police.

The last skill was not easy to come by, for informers were often recruited from among petty criminals or old lags. The lieutenant general was demanding: he needed firsthand information, which some lazy observers did not bother to seek out, preferring to feed on news-sheets.

The style of the reports is in fact similar to that of news-sheets or handbills: raw information presented without comment. Besides the desire to please the lieutenant general and satisfy the known bent of his curiosity, we find a confusion of information delivered in gobbets, with no attempt to rank events in order of importance. We pass abruptly from the discovery of an outrageous hermaphrodite to a grumble against the war, or some acerbic street-corner remark concerning the king's hunting. What mattered, it seems, was to catch the news, not to waste time on discovering links between events or even making sense of them – far less to distil any moral from all those randomly overheard remarks. A good many things are simply taken for granted, so that a twentieth-century reader can have difficulty in understanding what event is being talked about.[12]

However, if we persist in reading through these hundreds of reports, we gain a somewhat unexpected impression: though the writers themselves were unaware of it, a certain critical outlook does float gently to the collective surface. The unfavourable reflections, acerbic remarks and sometimes radical questionings, heard at random, create an overall effect of dry vigour. Not that the authors ever set out to be critical: they were not there to criticize, but to overhear and record, and they make no attempt to justify themselves. But their notes, raw and unpolished by any attempt at contextualization, actually throw the intrusive criticism into relief. The informers make no excuses; perhaps they took a covert pleasure in transmitting so many black remarks, laced with some humour. 'It is said that His Eminence gives the king the title Louis the Pacific, which makes people say that he might better be entitled Louis the Hunter' (September 1728).[13]

The list of criticisms is long and lively; it swamps the news itself and eventually conveys a real harshness which is never mitigated by the style. This harshness comes from the conditions of writing: be quick, lose no detail, note what seems most dangerous, transmit exactly what you have heard – which means concentrating on the oral expression of the eighteenth century, swift, succinct, with a feeling for the telling word or turn of phrase. The informers absorbed everything, indiscriminately, and delivered it unaltered to the lieutenant. But there was more. Words were being denounced and persecuted (those who spoke ill of affairs were arrested), and this made the work ever harder: the streets were so full of criticism and discontent that the reports became a faithful

mirror of those streets in their entirety. The harshness was not necessarily a result of the format. It was part of the social fabric.

In fact, the status of popular speech was to change, little by little,
overflowing from the sphere of amusing gossip into the atmosphere as
a whole, to become not simply a possible source of information, a way
of getting news and guiding government – at a time when popular
opinion was notoriously considered to be formless and vulgar – but also
a mainstay of an underground press with a thoroughly worked-out
strategy of opposition: such newspapers, for instance, as the Jansenist
Nouvelles ecclésiastiques, which undoubtedly had considerable influence.

2

Words caught in flight: government, information and resistance

The early eighteenth-century chroniclers and diarists had their own attitude to popular reactions and only paid attention to them at a few defined moments, without using them to support their social or political comments. The police reports were there to observe and denounce. But popular speech was becoming so intrusive that the treatment of it had to change. Three sources go to prove this. We shall look once again at the police reports and the gradual change in them: popular remarks were still persecuted, but they were so pervasive that they became a source of information for those in power; as for news-sheets, they disseminated a quantity of diverse information which was eagerly read by the upper echelons, but they plunged their readers into a unique atmosphere in which truth and fiction alternated with dizzying speed. One newspaper in particular is worth examining separately: the clandestine, but much sought-after *Nouvelles ecclésiastiques*, which kept the population informed of the events succeeding the bull *Unigenitus*. Its innovative wooing of popular interest led to a restructuring of speech even among the lowliest inhabitants; its way of appealing to public opinion was to have a discernible effect on the relationship between the monarchy and its subjects.

Popular gossip invades the police reports

In 1728 the king's minister, Fleury, launched a great offensive against the Jansenists and those priests and bishops who had protested against the bull *Unigenitus*. Three hundred clergymen were put under interdict in 1730; almost as many were dismissed and expelled from their parishes. At the same time, in the cemetery of the parish of Saint-Médard, miracles were occurring in ever-increasing numbers at the tomb of the deacon Pâris, who had died in 1727, aged thirty-seven, after a life spent in exemplary poverty in a tumbledown house in the Faubourg Saint-Marcel.[1] He had died in stubborn opposition to *Unigenitus*, and became a kind of archetype of the eighteenth-century Jansenist ecclesiastic, determined to stay among his poor parishioners and casting off his priesthood for that purpose.

The first recorded happenings at the deacon's tomb were a few timid cures and quasi-miracles. But events picked up speed, crowds were drawn to the cemetery and convulsionaries were seen there in unexpected numbers. Two hundred and fifty of them were to be arrested between 1732 and 1760, and imprisoned in the Bastille or the Châtelet. The police undertook to keep a constant watch on the cemetery and to note down, day by day, the conversations and prophecies of the sufferers and their attendants. Eventually the situation got out of hand, and the authorities decided to close the cemetery by royal decree on 27 January 1732; there were no more burials at Saint-Médard until 1807, when the cemetery was reopened.

From 1730 onwards the police reports are entirely dominated by these events and by the popular comments which they sparked off in all directions. The observers were hard put to it to do their duty, so deafening were the echoes from the streets: in every place, at every opportunity, everyone had something to say about kidnapped priests or unbelievable miracles in the cemetery, about the king and his bishops, or about the attitudes assumed by members of the *parlement*.

It is natural enough that the police reports for this time should show a general disturbance of the public mind, and doubtless this was happening; but what is most interesting is the way the observers react to the outburst of talk. The informers were taken aback: their reports express their surprise and anxiety at the thoughts everyone was expressing, and the entirely novel way in which these thoughts were being put. The surprise was twofold: it seemed odd to hear some of 'the simplest folk' continually and boldly taking sides, and they were disconcerted by the stubbornness and detail of the convictions expressed. They were paid to hunt down rash words and critical comments, and now they were being washed away by a tide of words that did not fear to speak their names and clearly expressed the themes and arguments – even theological arguments – over which they disagreed.

This changed the tone of the reports. The new talk was so invasive and so variegated that the observers tried to show its new countenance to the lieutenant of police; they were the first to realize that public opinion, usually left out of the political account, was turning into a perceptibly political discourse. They remained faithful to their work and carefully reported what they had heard, but they found themselves immersed, more deeply than before, in a popular environment which sent them from the Jansenist parishes of Saint-Roch, Saint-Germain-l'Auxerrois and Saint-Jacques-du-Haut-Pas to the Saint-Médard cemetery in the Faubourg Saint-Marcel. They wrote and reported without any condescension, and were sometimes so astounded at what they were hearing that they even lapsed into the first person. On 1 July 1733 one of them wrote, 'It does not surprise me that everything is going badly.'[2] And indeed, nothing was quite as it had been: the habitual mutterings against the princes and the court had become a persistent murmuring which obeyed its own complex logic. Faced with this, the informers were not sure whether they were suffering from delusions or if they were in the midst of a mass of organized reactions, the existence of which had been unsuspected one or two years previously. Everything had changed in those two years: it was no longer a matter of bread riots or insulting sallies during a royal procession, but of being surrounded by new words and attitudes which were changing the very face of the people.

These half-astonished, half-anxious reports are an attempt, if not to warn against such fundamental upsets, at least to convey the sudden amazing new vigour of popular thinking. Words were recorded so as to show authority how they were shifting, how they were put together, what strong certainties they expressed. The very style of the reports conveys surprise, and betrays a timid inclination to challenge the authorities.

The first surprise was the way individuals expressed their opinions and resentments quite openly, as if it were natural to do so: 'People are saying quite directly . . . people are speaking openly about it . . . people are crying out loud.' Comments were being made unambiguously, perhaps even fearlessly, impelled by total conviction and considerable ardour. Thus we find observers penning phrases like these:

Paris is flooded with words, people are speaking loudly and openly; leaflets are scattered in the shops, people are stubborn in their opinions.

Everyone, great and small, has his opinion, and all pay close attention to everything that is said and done every day.

One hears nothing but opinions from the least educated, the water-carriers and housebreakers, all clamouring and speaking in the most unsuitable way.

Everyone wants to know the whys and wherefores.

It was amazing how simple men could argue: the observers' pens almost froze to their hands, and they thought it boded ill. 'No good will come of this,' they wrote, or 'We shall have a revolt or a cruel civil war.'

Their way of reporting bears witness to an awareness (clear in some, vague in others) that discontent was rapidly and uncontrollably becoming more solid and more organized, and had a firmness and tenacity quite contrary to the stereotyped idea that the people's moods were changeable and inconstant.

The disquiet passed up the line to ministers and leading police authorities. In 1733, Fleury wrote to Hérault, the lieutenant general of police, concerning the interrogation of Bastille prisoners, usually on 'crimes of Jansenist opinion': 'It is scarcely likely that you will gain any enlightenment from the prisoners, for there is something *supernatural* about the invincible obstinacy of all their kind, even down to the very dregs of the people, from whom one cannot extract the smallest admission or the least enlightenment.'[3] The monarchy, in the person of its minister, was so taken aback that it could find only supernatural explanations for the vigorous thinking of 'the dregs of the people'. That the people should be thinking at all was veritably against Nature.

As well as retailing comments and rumours, the reports transcribe placards and notices, stray leaflets and pamphlets, so sometimes revealing a link between rumour and seditious literature. These 'oral after-shocks of events' (to use Pierre Rétat's words)[4] eventually add up to a continuous narrative which takes on meaning and becomes something quite different from the mere enumeration of insults which we find in the 1720s. The massive invasion of popular speech had transformed their habitual transmission of news, for now opinions were being forged under their very noses. Most observers still thought, however, that no 'truth' could really come from these unworthy lower levels. They sought support for their accounts in other sources which they considered more authoritative, especially when dealing with very grave, or even sacred, matters. One, working on rumours of the king's death, took great care to ensure that they should come from the houses of people of quality: '30 January 1732: they say that the king does not look as if he will live long, it is a punishment which will come on him because of the Abbé

Pâris affair; one says with confidence that this is not street-corner gossip, but from the best public places, and even private houses.'[5] It was rather risky for an informer to report on the life expectancy of the king, but the evidence of upper-class conversation evidently made the thing seem credible.

Thus the reports reveal, almost unconsciously, the radical changes in the Paris scene, and pass them on to the lieutenant general of police, replacing the persecution of words by a process of informing on the whole people; in the long run this modified the tone and style of the reporters themselves. They became more active: initially they had merely narrated and denounced, now they gaped in astonishment at the new surge of words, and collected popular comments as proof of a sudden and unexpected change in individual social practice. A new sphere was opening up before their eyes, though it was not – yet – a sphere of power. But we can already sense that a trial of strength was looming.

News-sheets

News-sheets seldom speak of the lower orders, but they do occasionally mention them. They were emphatically not aimed at informing the lower orders, and yet contemporaries complained of their influence on them; chroniclers and police authorities spilt much ink in pursuit of their insatiable curiosity about these productions.

They were, in fact, loose, handwritten, undercover productions which competed with official journals, for everyone at the time knew that the latter dispensed 'truths' so thoroughly censored in advance by the monarchy that they had little contact with real events. News-sheets provided a sort of hasty counter-information about domestic and for-eign affairs. They were sent out to subscribers or discreetly passed on; they passed the walls of houses and the boundaries of provinces, giving news of the court, of spectacles and books, along with satires, anecdotes and amazing incidents. They often drew on news from abroad, where censorship was less savage, and they were eagerly sought after, even by the police, whose reports drew on them at times. News-sheets scurried hither and thither with ferret-like cunning, going to ground when they scented danger. Needless to say, they answered a deep-felt need, and no one worried about their obvious unreliability, since 'Paris is the place where one can learn more than anywhere else in the world, and where what one learns is less reliable than anywhere else in the world.'[6] Louis-Sébastien Mercier often points out, in his *Tableau de Paris*, the thirst which was so energetically nourished by news, newsmongers and readers:

'There they are, sitting on a bench at the Tuileries, the Palais-Royal, the Arsenal, the Quai des Augustins or elsewhere. Three times a week they avidly read these sheets, and eagerness for political news has seized people of all ages and conditions.'[7] Insatiable readers called for indefatigable newsmongers; Mercier again gives a description: 'A group of newsmongers discussing the political interests of Europe make up a curious tableau in the shady purlieus of the Luxembourg. They dictate to kings, arrange the finances of potentates, and send armies hotfoot from north to south.'[8] The worst thing that could happen to a newsmonger was to have no news: 'I am suffering a frightful famine of news, and without a ridiculous event in a house opposite Saint-Médard, I would have nothing to tell you. A glazier, who . . .'[9]

Organization, content and repression

The organization, content and repression of the news-sheets were inseparable; at some periods they were more leniently treated than at others, and this always meant a change in the atmosphere in which they were produced. When the police authorities were more or less shutting their eyes to this trade, the newsmongers' offices were openly displayed and easy to find. Ordinary people knew them all and unhesitatingly went there for information whenever they felt like it. When repression pounced, the sheets were produced by secret – and sometimes extraordinary – means, and this could give rise to notorious trials, or just to a rain of *lettres de cachet* and orders of imprisonment intended to kill off whatever trade or traffic was considered suspicious.

There were authorized offices whose procedures were relatively straightforward. A police note of 1724 prescribes their conduct:

> Private individuals wishing to give news to the public are obliged to bring two copies to the lieutenant general of police, who will read them and remove what he considers necessary; after which he will deliver to the individual one copy approved by himself and keep the other to compare with the copies delivered to the public.[10]

An 'authorized office' was one which was under the eye of the police, who would censor, withhold, cut and scissor away at the product. But once this had been done, the office could register[11] and settle as best it could at some precarious address – in an attic, or below a workshop or tavern. It would have an editor, the 'news chief'; an editorial secretary; and, most important, informers. There would also be scribes and copyists to copy the news as it came in; these copyists were watched particularly closely, for they were notoriously inclined to fabricate the news themselves, inventing it or adding zest to the stories they received. Then there would be a handful of carriers or casual workers to distribute the handwritten sheets to customers, or to take them out to faithful and impatient subscribers in the provinces.

It is easy to see that the most important people in these newsmongers' offices were the informers. Since the news-sheet had to 'focus public curiosity',[12] informers had to dig everywhere for news, and were recruited from all over the city. Some specialized in literature or the theatre; others patrolled fashionable meeting places, going from the Tuileries to the Palais via the Luxembourg, gathering gossip on the way; these were the word-of-mouth newsmongers. In the suburbs, with their fights and scandalous incidents, some tavern-keepers doubled as informers. Most highly esteemed were domestics in the great households, lackeys and liveried servants, porters and grooms, who for a consideration would regularly provide what was called 'small news', daily echoes from the loves and liaisons of the great. Not forgetting, of course, the agents abroad who transmitted news from journals in Holland and elsewhere, together with rumours and overheard comments on French foreign policy.

The readers of these hastily, and usually roughly, written sheets were mostly from the upper classes, in Paris or the provinces. Subscriptions were expensive: in 1728 it cost six *livres* a month to receive a twice-weekly news-sheet from one's selected authors. Provincial châteaux were usually well supplied, and it was not uncommon for certain customers to subscribe to several offices and so ensure a relative objectivity. To get information from Paris was a sign of distinction, and it was naturally preferable for the information to be accurate. In a Bastille dossier from 1750 a subscriber complains to a friend: 'Please write to the man who gives you news-sheets, and ask him to give us only true, or at least believable, news.'

Some offices had more prestige than others; some were chronically precarious, run undercover by unscrupulous individuals scribbling away at a tavern table and changing their address more often than they changed their shirts. Such was the demand for news that the various offices were in fierce competition. At some times it was more savage than at others, but it was always intense and overt. Counter-advertising was possible when the atmosphere was more permissive; otherwise it was better to slip a few comments about dishonest competitors into the news-sheets themselves. But the greatest anxiety was caused by thriving foreign journals with an established clientele. They were more permanent than the cobweb fraternity of newsmongers, they were penetrating

France in strength and they annoyed those whose position was less secure.[13]

The news-sheets had an agreeable habit of copying from one another. This necessitated extra informers and a certain unscrupulousness, as is shown by a Bastille dossier of 20 October 1730 concerning Lamy (nicknamed Jourdan) and his accomplices:

> Master Corset, major-domo to Mme Doublet[14] at the Filles Saint-Thomas in the Rue Vivienne, was the head of a distribution agency working from the aforesaid lady's house but without her knowledge, since it is positively said that he steals this news from his mistress and abuses her trust in him; that this chief is currently employing six people to conduct his correspondence with both Paris and the provinces . . . that Master Corset, who can scarcely write his own name, was obliged to call upon his brother Paul, *valet de chambre* to the Comte d'Argental, who arranged all services for him; that, Master Corset being very slack about visiting his own office, the six scribes had each found a means of setting up his own distribution office hidden to all other eyes; and that each had taken on as many subscribers as he could find.
>
> That each of these scribes, having finished his work in the general office, went with a stolen sheet to his own hidden office to work on his correspondence. That these sheets, fabricated by these faithless copyists, contained nothing of interest; that they radically abridged the articles so as to include more of them, and then gave them away very cheap, since the coachman's son would sell them for 3 *livres* and even 40 *sous* a month; we have seen several shopkeepers and workmen in the Rue Montmartre who are receiving them at that price.[15]

Let us note in passing that ordinary lower-class readers were not forgotten: the shop and small factory had their place, although handwritten news-sheets were not officially aimed in their direction.

In times of repression, or of greater or lesser social tension, producing the news-sheets was not such a simple matter. After the Fronde and the trauma suffered by the monarchy over the *mazarinades*,[16] the news-sheets were considered a public danger. Louis XIV had loathed them and treated them with merciless severity, forbidding them by royal decree in 1662 and persecuting writers and hawkers, who were imprisoned or exiled. This repression was useless, for every sheet that disappeared was replaced by a fresh one, and the hordes of distributors turned out to be uncontrollable. From the regency to 1743 the atmosphere was different: it was the golden age of the newsmongers, and only the 'calumnious' were prosecuted. Authorized offices flourished, restricted only by the obligation to show their works to the police. A very fallacious procedure developed. It was mentioned earlier that the lieutenant of police reserved the right to make corrections, and this was no light matter; it became graver still in 1738, when the new lieutenant, Marville, decided to make himself master of public opinion. In 1745 some very rigorous penalties were instituted. From then onwards the police used the news-sheets for a dual purpose. First, their own informers and spies were sent prowling round the offices so as to appropriate the news for police purposes (police reports often mention this rivalry between newsmongers and observers). More pernicious was the way in which the police fabricated their own news and introduced it into the news-sheets which came to them for inspection. They inserted favourable rumours to cancel out unfavourable ones; between police and newsmongers there flowed a strange current which poured an inextricable mixture of truth and falsehood into the end product. This was not without consequence for the atmosphere in Paris and among the population at large.

Secrecy and repression stimulated the imagination of the newsmongers. There is a Bastille dossier[17] which tells of the infinitely cunning ways in which news-sheets were produced and distributed even in the most difficult circumstances. The dossier concerns the arrest of what was called a 'blackbird', meaning a newsmonger who favoured the Austrian cause. The police, who had been hunting him since 1742, finally caught up with him and discovered his multiple stratagems and his networks of accomplices. This Tollot was an editor-in-chief who had fifty copyists and 280 subscribers. His news-sheets were scarcely first-hand. They were not, like other surreptitious journals, derived from letters written from abroad, but were based on 'things said by Austrians in Paris', which limited the objectivity of the information that was transmitted. The copyists were a lowly lot, mostly draft-dodgers or unemployed domestics, who had no other means of sustenance and did not look far for their news. They had an ingenious way of avoiding accusations of falsehood: 'They send news into foreign countries to be printed in the journals there, then bring these products back from abroad, hawk them round Paris and spread them through the provinces.'[18] It was not easy to keep hidden, but Paris had room for a good many cunning ploys. Some called themselves musicians and lived in chambers where the fire was always lit, to destroy all copies at the first sign of danger. They were always on their guard, keeping only one copy of the news-sheet at home, with another perhaps hidden in their mistress's stocking or even between her thighs – a risky procedure, for the police were well aware of women's role in this fleeting and shifting underworld. They went from man to man, with news-sheets next to the skin and an air of utter nonchalance.

Yet more extraordinary was the activity of copyists *after* they were imprisoned. Poussot, inspector of police, gives the evidence:[19] 'When copyists, and even authors, find themselves in prison [in this case it was the prison of For-l'Evêque], they reconstitute their newsmongers' offices within the walls and go on working, safe from any procedures which may be taken against them.' The same thing was going on, to Poussot's indignation, in the Conciergerie: 'The Conciergerie is not the only prison infected with these rogues; for several months the prisons in the Petit Châtelet have been on the same footing. Some have had themselves put in there by virtue of sentences for non-existent debts, and yesterday we saw four busily writing, of whom some were not even prisoners' – merely visitors!

The news-sheets were a sort of underground resistance movement, as elusive to contemporaries as to historians. Anonymous, inconsistent and ephemeral, seldom preserved with care, most of them are gone with the wind, not to be found in any archive. A product of the twilight, written and distributed in haste, they flooded every household, great or small, and are impossible to pin down. The police, fearful and angry, persecuted and manipulated them: they were necessary sources of up-to-date information, and it was still more necessary to fill them with rumours and tittle-tattle to neutralize other, supposedly dangerous rumours from other quarters. Intended principally for the greater folk, they were, it must be admitted, little interested in popular opinion, giving precedence to court news and diplomacy; but in the last instance it was, by virtue of their way of circulating information, the common people that they addressed. The police would not have made so much effort without good reason.

The tangle of truth and falsehood

The news-sheets were the foam on the stream of time. Bruised and pillaged, they tantalized Parisian opinion by a jumble of scattered stories which brought much joy in the morning, but much indignation in the evening as people realized that today's stories quite contradicted those of yesterday. Essentially they were rumour-mongers, never still, ever transformed and contradicted. For even the most level-headed Parisian, news-sheets were an enjoyable but insoluble riddle. He could never know if they carried lies or errors, proven facts or extravagant imaginings; but what mattered was the sum total of rumours which assured him that he was missing nothing of what went on. His eagerness to know more and more was inseparable from his fear of being deceived, and this mixed reaction, far from discouraging him, only increased his fervent devotion to the sheets which were furtively thrust into his hand by this or that street-corner author responding to an avid public. Louis-Sébastien Mercier foresaw the difficulties later historians would have: 'The historian will be in difficulties when he tries to depict the state of mind of Parisians amidst these great upheavals ... he will look elsewhere for records which have not been contaminated by pusillanimity, passion and ignorance.'[20] People found it difficult at the time, but they preferred such confusion to the public prints issued on government orders – a fact that astonished the lieutenant general of police and many others who were reluctant to believe that over-rigorous censorship created its own escape routes: 'Parisians were more inclined to give credence to clandestine pamphlets than to facts printed and published with government permission.'[21] But the king feigned ignorance of the way the police reinforced the impossible entanglement of truth and falsehood in those pamphlets, of how they 'tore up the page of truth, disguised, suppressed, and shamefully mutilated, accentuating the element of lies and deceit'.[22]

The news was a war in which everyone was involved, and the newsmongers were not too particular about their strategy, which was disconcertingly fierce: 'Each one is shouting out the item he is anxious to perpetuate, when the latest comer brusquely dismisses everything said hitherto, the morning's victor is beaten hollow at seven o'clock in the evening; but the next day, as soon as the newsmongers are up and about, yesterday's news restores its hero to complete victory.'[23]

Almost nobody believed that the news was accurate, especially among the greater folk. From Marivaux to the Princesse Palatine, from Mercier to Commissioner Dubuisson, everyone complained about the thousands of complete lies, or embroiderings on truth. But who could really sift the pile, or tell who really knew the truth? You could only say that you knew; which was a good start. 'In Paris, news is like a collection of toads emerging in stormy weather: they grow up in one instant and disappear in another.'[24]

Paris was fond of stormy weather and emerging toads; the thirst for knowledge was supreme, and the first to read and reread the news were the first to rend it with criticism. Authors and readers, great and small, all shared the impression that they were caught between truth and falsehood, and moreover that the 'probable-improbable' they relished so much was being manipulated by the complex strategies of the court, the police and the petty hordes of the evil-minded. We cannot understand the curiosity of the Parisian public without realizing that they did at least know one thing: the extent they were being made fools of. Which knowledge did not in the least discourage their constant, breathless search for more information, even if only to verify something, grasp some hidden reality or to forge their own identity as men or women who thought about events of public concern – who even saw such thinking as a duty.

Are they polluting the people?

The news-sheets travelled the streets with disquieting speed; behind the mistrust this aroused lurked the idea that affairs of state must be secret. Nothing was more alarming than to find that secrecy was unattainable. Very early in the century there were complaints from high up that information was escaping. In 1717, for example, Dubois, the prime minister, reacted with panic to the repercussions of *Unigenitus*. He wrote to the regent from London: 'News-sheets are being read in houses, published in the streets, and an affair of this importance is being *chattered* about by everybody.'

It was unthinkable that the affairs of Rome and of the monarch should be *chattered* about by the man in the street, especially when it was forced upon one's notice that unworthy servants of the realm were encouraging the chatter. And what if the news came from the court itself, trickling down into the market-place and then returning to the court in the guise of new information?

> Some lily-livered courtier makes up some infamous verses, and passes them on via a set of flunkeys to the markets and herb-sellers. From the markets they are conveyed to the artisan, who in his turn brings them back to the great folk who forged them, who immediately start to whisper in one another's ears, in a tone of the most consummate hypocrisy, 'Have you read about that? I'll tell you. All the people of Paris are talking about it.'[25]

The court came to the people, the people went back to the great lord who went back to the court, and the latter believed the news simply because it was echoing through the streets. This senseless circulation of rumours so frightened the authorities that they encouraged the process by introducing their own subterfuges and manipulating the image of the people in their own, contradictory way. The people ought not to be informed in the first place, but if they were being, then they should get the right sort of information. They were credulous enough to believe it, and, following the old paradox, the greater folk themselves would give credence to the resulting rumours just because the people believed in them. Popular speech was first disqualified, then refabricated for political ends; those who wished to negate it ended by inciting it.

However, the great majority of contemporaries were still convinced that the ordinary public had to be taught ('There must', wrote Mercier, 'be [books] for those of all conditions, for all have an equal right to emerge from ignorance'),[26] but they disliked the idea of their having a right to information, or a personal opinion about it. The spiral continued, sending the people back to their credulity and reformulating the old cliché that knowing what was going on could not possibly enlighten them.

Historians, news-sheets and public opinion

Contemporaries were lost in the news-sheets as in a thick and worrying fog; historians find them, and their impact on opinion, equally baffling. The most recent studies of the subject take up the most divided attitudes.[27] Some (probably including Daniel Mornet and Robert Darnton), while not sharing identical views, think that the repeated harping on one theme by the multitude of pamphlets, placards and handwritten sheets in circulation helped to desacralize the image of the monarch and destroy the links which bound him to his subjects. Others, such as Myoncheol Jou, think that pamphleteers 'took advantage of social discontent so as to launch their gross and ill-intentioned products'. Some time ago Funck-Brentano said, in his study of *Figaro*, that 'The newsmongers transmitted opinions. They might be hostile to the head of state, his court, his family, his ministers. Everywhere, journalists appeared to reflect the general feeling.'[28] These antinomical interpretations are opposed by Chartier, who disputes the direct link between 'reading and believing' and focuses on popular political practices which were already conveying discontent and desacralization: 'Disaffection from the sovereign was not necessarily the result of an intellectual process. It could have emerged from the immediacy of everyday activities, unthinking gestures, words which had become commonplaces.'[29]

Let us shift our position slightly and consider another phenomenon, copiously described by Mercier and taken up again in part by Chartier: Paris was always a-whisper with rumours both true and false, and the result might be saturation. To put it another way, people's reactions, though intense, might be rapid and ephemeral, while at other times they might remain – again temporarily – indifferent. People passed continually and unrepentantly from the one to the other. As one placard was pasted over another people might be agitated, but they would soon forget. 'If they were not soon torn down by the same hand that had posted them, the streets would eventually have been blocked by a sort of papier mâché of the sacred and the profane: mandates, advertisements from charlatans, decrees of the Cour du Parlement; decrees from the council annulling the decrees of the *parlement*; ... lost dogs, disquisitions on the Sacrament, treatises on the soul'[30] – not to mention placards, libels and contradictory news-sheets written one evening to be eliminated next morning.

Thus the atmosphere was agitated, and often impassioned: it did not much matter if what went around was true or false, for people lived in a half-way house where both were constantly to be found. It made people rather edgy, and the air was full of squalls. They were quite capable of detaching their opinions from the news, and there is no need to believe that either was the immediate cause of the other. Moreover, as we shall see later in our chapter on slanders, popular opinion did not emerge from the cumulative reading of pamphlets and placards; it was not unilinear and did not base arguments on the sum total of what it read. There was a distance between the reader and his reading matter; he might read with a smile and then promptly forget, as Mercier, once again, clearly conveys: 'Very well rendered details, read so eagerly to-day, will be a matter of absolute indifference a fortnight hence ... these daily chronicles will fall into the profoundest oblivion ... we pass by, we look, we smile, we shrug our shoulders and forget all about it.'[31]

Indeed, it is abundantly clear that there were many other ways of viewing politics than through the newspapers. People's day-to-day acts and habits took account of events in the worlds of politics and royalty; support or resentment of the king were based on judgements nourished by the ever-changing theatre of royalty. It was highly visible, and equally visible were the enthusiastic, grumbling or aggressive responses it prompted.

People's opinions related to a plurality of phenomena which invited participation and encouraged reflection: phenomena on many different levels. The king might solicit opinion by a royal ceremony or a public execution; it might be guided by reading, of notices or newspapers; but it was guided still more by doings: strikes threatened when money was short, public emotions coagulated around what were thought of as illegal acts. 'What-people-think-about' certain hard facts would display distinguishable motifs and develop according to an internal dynamic influenced not only by the event itself, but by the form and anatomy it had this time assumed, and even the place where it had happened. It was not that events which gave rise to shared opinions tended to pile up in such a way as to produce a progressively more massive, measurable and effective body of opinion. That would be too simple a view: the actual mechanisms were quite different, in fact the reverse. Opinions assumed the form appropriate to the way the events had happened; thoughts attached themselves to certain definite points and were expressed on that basis; discussion flowed from something seen or read about. From this emerged an ever-growing conviction that people had a *right* to know and to judge. This, in the eighteenth century, was something new: thinking about things might be forbidden, but it was also, and triumphantly, legitimate. This transgression was effective; in the cultural and political circumstances of the time it engendered a bold assurance which was itself one of the major features of contemporary politics. That the sphere of thought was still limited did not matter: public opinion was not a swelling wave, breaking on an untrodden shore, but a series of organized judgements prompted by individual circumstances, which, elsewhere, later on and for different reasons, was to permit other ways of thinking, not necessarily connected with the earlier ones. The criticism or approval accorded to this multitude of events was to give birth to other convictions, far removed from the initial ones; what was essential was the novel idea that it was legitimate to claim the right to demand, think otherwise, detach oneself, think oneself away from the State. This fundamental change in attitude changed the way events were read, and the attitude of the upper classes who were thereby forced to acknowledge that lesser folk had their own views on society. We can now see that the news-sheets were one encouragement to this swift and voluble alteration, but were not central to it.

The *Nouvelles ecclésiastiques*

Journals, memoirs, police reports and news-sheets gave a varying status to popular speech: some took little account of it; some were amazed at its occasional weirdness; some forbade it to articulate at all; some were surprised when it did so. It was observed, repressed and used as a source of information; the police learned how to manipulate it and where to strike at it. Now rejected, now gathered, now put to use, it became stronger and more articulate by virtue of this varied reception, crystallizing around precise events which could temporarily alter its contours.

The *Nouvelles ecclésiastiques*, the lynchpin of Jansenist propaganda, is of major interest: as far as I know it was the only newspaper to give much space to popular speech or to appeal to public opinion, and it based its strategy on the idea that the people were one of the best and most active justifications of Jansenist endeavours. The people were, to an extent, the repository of that truth on which Rome, the Church and the monarchy were forever seeking to trample.

The *Nouvelles ecclésiastiques* first appeared in 1728,[32] with the principal aim of telling its supposedly impartial readers all about *Unigenitus* and its multitudinous after-effects. Although the first wave of Jansenism seemed to have been annihilated – Port-Royal-des-Champs had been razed to the ground in 1711 – the redoubling of attacks on Jansenism that came with *Unigenitus* only encouraged the spread of Jansenist thinking among the lowest orders of society. When, in 1713, *Unigenitus* condemned Quesnel's *Réflexions morales*, this produced an impressively strong reaction. It sparked off a political battle in which the *parlement* took an active part, indignant that two of Quesnel's propositions had been singled out for attack. They concerned excommunication. Quesnel admitted that the Church had authority to perform it, but added that 'The fear of unjust excommunication must never prevent us from doing our duty. We can never quit the Church, even when it seems that we have been banished thence by the ill-well of men, if we are attached to God, to Jesus Christ, and to the Church itself, through charity (John 9:23).'

The *parlement* rejected this condemnation, fearing that the excommunication sent from Rome would encroach on the power of the king or his subjects. Priests and people passionately seconded this attitude, and began a widely supported resistance movement against the pope's authority, denying him the role of intermediary between God and the king. Things were to go further yet, as the Jansenist search for purity and for absolutes led to a demand that priests and laymen should oppose anyone's idea of compromise – including the sovereign's.

The *Nouvelles ecclésiastiques* gives a blow-by-blow account of that battle. Like contemporary literary journals, it appeared irregularly but frequently, every three or four weeks. It generally had four or eight pages (sometimes fewer), and belonged somewhere between the newspaper and the book. It offered bishops' pastoral decrees, reviews of works by Jansenists and Jesuits, summaries of theses presented at the Sorbonne and also long and detailed accounts of the multifarious happenings among Jansenist parishioners, convulsionary minorities and those who refused the sacraments – not forgetting the parliamentary disputes and secessions, the *lits de justice* and remonstrances and royal decrees which punctuated the mid-century. The governing principle of the *Nouvelles ecclésiastiques* was to 'put before the public' all the persecutions visited on the Jansenists since 1713, the date of *Unigenitus*, the cause of so much ill. Here are the first sentences of the first issue:

When the bull *Unigenitus* appeared in 1713, there were already great evils within the Church, which had been growing steadily for several centuries.

Pious persons, who were seriously concerned at this, thought that that fatal Decree was the final straw, and was going to be the most general, the most absorbing, and the most unhappy affair that had ever affected the Church. The outcome has justified those views all too well, and the issue will put them beyond dispute ... a large number of churchmen persist in believing that it was only an academic opinion which ought to be left to theologians to discuss ... that the faithful had no need to take part in it or be informed ... We have realized that the affair was more serious ... We universally desired to be informed of what was happening ... What better could we do than to find a means whereby the facts might be brought before the public? This is what we are doing in this little missive entitled *Nouvelles ecclésiastiques*.

News came from all over France, though that from Paris was the most abundant and detailed. Needless to say, from the time of its first appearance the *Nouvelles ecclésiastiques* was a terror to the authorities, which persecuted its authors uselessly and unremittingly; they continued to publish, and the authors and editors were never arrested, although printers and distributors were pitilessly hunted down and often imprisoned within the harsh walls of the Bastille.

If the police, and in particular the lieutenant general, Hérault, were obsessed with the *Nouvelles ecclésiastiques*, the chroniclers treated it with malicious admiration. Marias, Buvat and Barbier all quote it frequently and with deference, pleased by its continual defiance, its unfailing subversiveness and its successful game of hide-and-seek with the authorities. Ever-present, but eluding every grasp, the *Nouvelles ecclésiastiques* had all the more impact on the chroniclers in that it was at the same time fantastic and real: an obsessive fantasy from whom nothing, even the person of king or pope, was immune, and an astonishing reality, since its distribution network became well known, but its authors never did. Barbier describes, with unfeigned astonishment and admiration, the almost magical way that it travelled around:

When the author of these *Nouvelles* has composed his issue, he throws his notes into the fire; then he gives his draft to another, who also throws it into the fire after copying it. A third person takes this copy to a printer and comes back for the issue, which he distributes around Paris. There are some twenty offices in different parts of the city, that is twenty individuals who each take, I suppose, 100; it is not the same person who takes the copies to these twenty offices, it is twenty different people. The man who keeps the offices pays the person who brings him the 100 copies and gets one free, as happens with everything that is printed on the affairs of the day; he then knows to whom to give his copies so as to get his money back. If one of these private office-owners is arrested one morning, all the others hear of it immediately, and the copies are taken to another place. So that, whatever person may be arrested, the handle goes on turning.[33]

It was evidently a well-handled affair!

Although this was a very particular kind of publication, it can be treated as we earlier treated the writings of chroniclers and memorialists: we shall see at what point it brings in the lowest classes, what its attitude was to the words and actions of ordinary people in moments of enthusiasm or affliction. We shall also try to understand how words performed in a narrative strategy which was intended to supply readers with a record, and to judge severely wherever such a judgement was called for.

The stories in the *Nouvelles ecclésiastiques* were the only ones of their kind at that time. Amidst all the reviews of theological books and theses there were moments of dramatic narrative, covering events which affected the daily lives of ordinary people. The stories themselves were studded with dialogues, from remarks by parishioners after Mass to conversations on current affairs between priests and congregations or lively arguments between police exempts (officers in temporary command, exempted from ordinary duties) and parishioners. As an example we can give the case of a priest whose bishop announced his 'displacement'. A last Mass was said for him before he left the parish, and in his sermon he said what he thought of the decision which had so greatly affected him and had confirmed his Jansenist convictions. The police, fearing a riot, were waiting outside as the Mass ended, with archers of the watch and exempts ready to contain any threat of trouble. The *Nouvelles ecclésiastiques* described the words and gestures of the parishioners as they said farewell to their priest and denounced the intrusiveness of the police. Nothing was left out: the names of the protagonists, what they said, how they wept, knelt and attempted to convince the police that it was all an injustice.

The *Nouvelles* always gave minute attention to the behaviour of ordinary people, every aspect of which was valuable, significant and communicated meaning. As a way of describing events, this differed sharply from the tone of a Buvat, a Marais or a Barbier, who saw the sentiments of ordinary people as typically oscillating between scorn, negligence and surprise. The *Nouvelles* trusted what the people felt and said, and encouraged each one of them to participate in events. The 'appeal to public opinion' went hand in hand with the 'encouragement of lay participation'.[34] This meant, first, that the *Nouvelles* believed in public opinion, and secondly, that it had no doubt about the capacity of laymen to make their own decisions. This was quite new at the time (we are still in 1728), and the consequences were to be major. No other chronicle or newspaper had any intention of cultivating either aspect. The *Nouvelles*' attitude to popular expression was the opposite of all the others': popular expression was its foundation and support, and it was not hard to see that later it would enable ordinary men and women to follow routes other than those laid down by this Jansenist pioneer.

All narrative is strategy, and the strategy of the *Nouvelles ecclésiastiques* was one of popularization: there was war to be waged against the bull *Unigenitus*, and the most humble of the faithful must wage it. This was a strategy, but also a conviction. Barbier spoke of the handle which went on turning; much more recently, Catherine Maire called it 'a machinery addressed to an imagined public'.[35]

At no time was the *Nouvelles ecclésiastiques* 'inventing' the authority which confronted it; indeed, it took particular care to gather from that authority the way that certain events had affected it. But it was far from including every event which affected the people: it only recorded the peripateia of the bull, and there is no point in seeking, through all those thousands of pages, for echoes of other situations. There are no interesting scandals, none of the singular or extraordinary anecdotes so beloved of the chroniclers; nothing about the great trials which so stirred public interest, or about uprisings; no mention of the kidnapped children of 1750, or the bread shortage of 1775. There is scarcely anything about Damiens' attempt on the life of Louis XV, which filled pages in newspapers both official and clandestine. It was 30 March 1757 before the *Nouvelles* alluded even indirectly to this event, which had taken place on 7 January. As for the coronation of Louis XVI in 1775 – not a word. But every page is black with news to stir the Jansenist mind, and on that point the people are featured to an extent which no other newspaper could match. It must be emphasized that the heart of the *Nouvelles* did not beat to the world's rhythm, or even that of the people, but to that of the threatened Jansenist movement in its encounter with the people. Here, surely, is a paradox: while the prolix columns of the *Nouvelles ecclésiastiques* were stuffed with unmatchable detail about a social class normally avoided by the press, and described its words and actions at great length, it ignored most of the scenes which brought those ordinary people on stage. One cannot but believe that the space offered, for the first time, by the *Nouvelles* was of extreme importance: once one had admitted that individuals were capable of thinking about the Church and about Jansenism, one realized perforce that they could have opinions on *any* aspect of public life. Moreover, readers of the *Nouvelles ecclésiastiques* were called upon to witness to truths which they themselves had spoken: this made them, as individuals, far more capable of speaking for themselves against the State.

Tales of repression

The *Nouvelles ecclésiastiques* recorded every repressive act of the police authorities against priests, congregations or isolated individuals suspected of Jansenism, showing clearly how these acts fitted into an everyday reality which included the thousand and one difficulties of individual existence. The year 1728 is typical. Everyone in Paris had supposed that its archbishop, the Cardinal de Noailles, would oppose *Unigenitus*. When, on 28 October, his pastoral of acceptance was published everyone, police as well as people, took fright. From that day onwards, the *Nouvelles* filled its pages with petitions and *lettres de cachet* issued against priests and parishioners, police raids on suspect priests, house searches and churchmen frogmarched before Hérault, the lieutenant general of police. 'In Paris all the talk is of threats, kidnappings, imprisonments and even something worse. A sinister mob called the "Flies" [informers] has taken over the Montagne Sainte-Geneviève ... a deacon called Monsieur Gallard has been taken to the Bastille.' Other tales followed, like these police raids on the priests of Saint-Etienne-du-Mont:

> Hearing about this expedition, all the district had come running: these gentlemen, emerging, found more than 200 persons assembled, men, women and religious, who showed them, each in his own way, how much they sympathized with their predicament. A large number of girls and women assiduous in the exercises of the parish recognized them; they wept and moaned to see so flagrant an injustice; several went down on their knees ... Even the archers were moved by this.[36]

The situation had scarcely changed by December 1728, and the *Nouvelles* gives a litany of vexations. Vanneroux, an exempt, and Renard, a commissary, who had to perform the unpleasant task were followed on every incursion; everywhere they were pointed at and berated for their errors, as when they happened to suspect a hatter in the Rue Galande, in the Maubert district. This man, Choisi by name, had made the error of including among his admiring clientele a large number of churchmen. The street informers thought they had found a nest of Jansenists; Vanneroux and Renard performed a daylight raid on the shop. Scarcely was he through the door than Renard recognized Choisi as a friend of his and apologized for being there on the king's orders, mumbling that he had to check shops for smuggled goods. 'Nevertheless he had to go away, with his shame, to report to M. Hérault.'

One might doubt the veracity of such tales, but not for long: the police reports for the same year, 1728, recount the same incidents and emphasize the indignant reaction of the populace. Under the date 16 October 1728 we read:

> People are saying that the imprisonment of three priests from the parish of Saint-Etienne-du-Mont has turned the whole clergy bitterly against the government; people are saying that what occasioned their imprisonment was that they had been suspected of being authors of the ecclesiastical newspaper . . . however that may be, everywhere they are saying that it is worse than the inquisition, and everyone regards the Comte de Fleury as a tyrant.
>
> All minds have been in turmoil since the pastoral of M. de Noailles, and people vie with one another to vomit invectives against His Eminence . . . all Paris is in turmoil . . . everywhere people cry that Fleury and Noailles are imbeciles and heretics.

The informers, overhearing such violent language, were amazed at the intensity of the disturbances.

> People speak with astonishment of the uprising which was preparing here in Paris for this cause, and it is even said that archers were needed to contain the women who went to draw water from the well of Les Innocents, and who smeared mud over three copies of the pastoral posted on church doors.[37]

Here and there it was whispered that the lieutenant general of police himself was getting tired of all the rigorous orders he had to carry out, and 'even that he is asking for some to be withdrawn, seeing that (they say) it is not his job to persecute the public without foundation.' This observation agrees with an odd little note by Barbier, who seems to have doubted Hérault's inner convictions:

> There is no way of knowing what is really in the heart of M. Hérault concerning Jansenism; on the outside, he does what he can and must do by reason of his office; but three-quarters of these officers, commissaries and exempts are of the Jansenist party and it is not surprising that not all has yet been discovered which could be. [Is this also what was meant by the 'combustion' of Paris, i.e. of police officers whose hearts inclined to Jansenism?] It is only the commissary Régnard [sic] and the exempt Vanneroux who are whole-hearted in their work and make their incursions unflinchingly. Hence they are called the commissary and exempt of the constitution.[38]

What more need be said of this outbreak of popular speaking, which fascinated and occasionally frightened informers?

What is certain is that one hears nothing but speeches by all the most unlettered folk against the constitution: even the women drawing water, or crocheting before their doors, speak out openly against it and speak disrespectfully of the court of Rome.[39]

Thus the *Nouvelles ecclésiastiques* was deceiving neither itself nor others, for what it relates is firmly recorded in the austerity of the police reports. The two sources echo each other unawares. Naturally, they do not use the same narrative method. The *Nouvelles* puts the actions of the police into a particular kind of context, pigeon-holing each incident as one more unworthy oppression or unjust humiliation. Each case comes with a ritual lamentation and an appeal against passivity. 'No one can remain neutral in this' was the watchword and strategy of the *Nouvelles*. Naming and denouncing the perpetrators must have its due effect: the facts were established, but the intention was also to stir the reader by a narrative system which would sweep him into conviction.

Maire has remarked on the immense task of documentation accomplished by the *Nouvelles*. To this we might add that its narrative style was creating a cement for the words of the man in the street. Or, better than a cement, a pedestal, which could later become a launching pad as the words, once read, diffused, even into domains other than those of Jansenist polemic – and that was something new. No other chronicle gives such status to popular speech; the *Nouvelles*, as it popularized, communicated and denounced, was inaugurating a system which would go beyond its own remit. News-sheets scattered opinions and broke down their coherence; newspapers took them for granted once spoken; the *Nouvelles*, by concentrating on a few strong points in the popular mind, gave them a new impact. In addition, its open criticism of the exempts, the police and the authorities made such criticism possible and legitimate – in a word, autonomous.

The *Nouvelles*' inspiration was religious, but the change it brought about was spectacular: it gave validity to the speeches of even the humblest.

A place for the individual

The history of *Unigenitus* is one of war, a war of crowds. As the historian of this war, the *Nouvelles* focused its attention on the humble, ordinary individual: what happened to him, how he reacted, his singular, personal and atypical experiences – which were, however, common to many others.

The man and woman in the street had ceased to be, as in the

chronicles, an anonymous unit in a crowd or the nub of some unusual, criminal or adventurous happening: they were individuals in their own right, in all their singularity, enmeshed in their own adventures. This care for the individual, albeit anonymous, is one of the mainsprings of the stories in the *Nouvelles*, whether they concern Paris or the provinces. However, it offers a very wide spectrum of information, on publications, on books, on the attitudes of bishops in every diocese, on the activities of the *parlement*, both of these latter in great detail. The place given to the people is not constant, and only becomes fully precise when it emerges, in a very original way, to show an individual's personal experience of the history going on around him.

The *Nouvelles* takes charge of the individual, but also trusts him: trusts the sayings and judgements of the poor, the humble, the sick, as much as those of an archbishop. Here, as never before, individuals are detached, one by one, from the nameless crowd as if their concerns were worth serious attention. This is a new intellectual posture which makes the conscious individual into a capable and competent subject. It inverts the normal attitude to which we have been accustomed by the diaries and memoirs of the early eighteenth century. Ordinary people are no longer singular because they are monstrous (thieves or murderers) credulous or naive, but because they are part of a story which shows them forming themselves by reacting to what they see. Their view of things and people gives them dignity and – perhaps more important – a way of realizing that they have the power to influence.

The normalizing of doubt and criticism

Ordinary people are not only noticed, named and individualized, they are also brought into a community. The *Nouvelles* often says 'we' when referring to its readers, allowing them to join a collectivity rather than wasting themselves in ineffectual solitude at every exciting juncture. 'Whether those who imprison us, who drag us before the tribunals, priests and laymen alike, who interrogate us, believe it or not, we shall still answer on our faith and for our faith.'[40] After describing people's lives and the strength of their feelings, restoring their individuality, the *Nouvelles* uses 'we' to bring them all back into a thinking, resisting whole. When it criticizes the power of king or pope, the 'we' makes it easier for readers to follow suit. This is operative rhetoric: by alternating descriptions of individual cases with addresses to readers as members of one body, the *Nouvelles* offers to each a new sphere, in which he can identify with the common cause without ever losing the uniqueness of his own story. Stories of police repression, for example, suggest a good many criticisms of police authority. It was not particularly difficult to make the people of Paris hostile to the police; the two were always opposed, and it certainly was not the Jansenist affair which first set them at odds. It was not so easy, however, to set up a muted and subtle opposition to the king. The *Nouvelles'* strategy was exemplary, and it was easy for the reader to go along with it, especially as he had already been named as an active subject and part of a community afflicted with injustice. He was now capable of following the subtle arguments against the king, and becoming an active element in this new attempt to reconcile due respect to the prince with disobedience.

> We cannot think ill of so good a prince, but we can believe that he will not take it amiss if he is not obeyed, when we cannot obey him without disobeying God ... We say to him ... that a prince has no power to make the law of a universal Church into the law of his State, and that he has been deceived in his religion by being given the bull as the law of the universal Church ... Where faith is involved, no power has the right to impose silence.

There are many other examples of this cunning way of involving the reader in a critical attitude which is given to him as his own and that of his companions, with an assurance that it will not even anger the prince. It dissociates the king from the faith, which is, admittedly, a radical position; but the radicality is mitigated by the assurance that the prince himself could only agree with it. Disobedience to the king becomes a natural attitude, which does not challenge his goodness or detract from the respect which is his due. The rhetoric takes the drama out of disobedience – for nothing could be graver, in the early eighteenth century, than to refuse the king's orders. And without the drama, the reader had room for criticism and opposition, happy in the conviction that he could still love his king and be loved by him.

The word as competence[41]

The editors of the *Nouvelles* were convinced that men and women were competent to enter the theological debate, if only to influence it. This competence was recognized as natural, an intellectual capacity which could be served by words. The logic of this recognition further implied the rejection of anything that stood in its way. At two decisive moments in the history of Jansenism, the *Nouvelles* paid particular attention to the demands of its humblest followers: during the debate on access to information and Christian culture, and during the scandal of the 'notes of confession' and the refusal of the sacraments.

The *Nouvelles*, knowing the difficulty of getting information about current events, gave its readers an abundance of detail. Realizing (as police observers did) how eager people were to understand, it always said when it thought knowledge was being kept from 'simple folk'. The tone was set after the publication of the Cardinal de Noailles' pastoral signifying acceptance of the bull, by the authorities' way of communicating the news and the people's distrustful reception of it. Notices announcing it were deliberately placed very high up, guarded by sentinels to prevent the crowd from tearing them down. Archers of the watch were posted at every square and crossroads. Nevertheless, 'Despite the vigilance of the sentinels who guard the notices, here they are covered with mud, there they are torn down without them realizing it, and even before the end of the day they have almost all been removed.' Putting the notices too high up was an ineffective trick that caused general derision, but there was more. The cardinal's pastoral had been accompanied by the text of the bull, but the authorities had taken care to give this text, 'which the Pope addresses – which is addressed – to all the faithful', only in Latin, 'so much do they fear that the condemnation of the [Jansenist] propositions will cause revolt and scandal.' The *Nouvelles* chatted fluently about public reactions.

> You will doubtless be curious to know the impression made on people by this strange proceeding, and the reception given to this notice. It was good to see, at every corner and crossroads of this great city, how each according to his estate, way of living and of speaking, expressed from his heart the witness of a naturally Christian soul concerning this event. First, there was general astonishment at the appearance of the new notice ... People read without understanding.[42]

All the evidence was considered, whether from rich or poor; the thoughts of all those people, so different in their ways, were equally interesting. An indignant woman:

> She expresses her surprise that a thing they want her to regard as a rule of faith and conduct has been given to her in a language that she does not understand. Others go further and use terms and expressions which we dare not repeat.[43]

Imaginations were hard at work to increase understanding; in the long run the Latin was no obstacle, for the readers of the notices helped one another. Those who could read and understand a little Latin strove to 'retain its substance so as to convey it to all those who could not read'. This led to some curious scenes in the squares and at the cross-roads: up above, the notice; down below, looking up, those who could decipher it, surrounded by those with a smattering of Latin; all round, anxious listeners, repeating what was read to those behind, who could not hear or see anything much. Further off would be indignant commentators, surrounding the group and staring at the archers, embarrassed but still doing their duty. Everybody knew how unjust it was to give information in a way which gave unequal access to knowledge; the trick was both clumsy and dubious. While the people grumbled on the brink of revolt, the editors of the *Nouvelles* espoused their cause, lending its columns to a lively debate about access to education, especially education in Christian doctrine. The Jesuits were harshly accused of trying to prevent the faithful from reading the Holy Scriptures, and especially the traditional reading of the catechism; the Jansenists declared in favour of an informed congregation. 'It would be a waste of time to repeat how ridiculous and false it is to conclude that the people must also be deprived of their catechism because they are not able to understand every theological treatise.'[44]

Point, counterpoint: now the *Nouvelles* was discussing the people's obvious eagerness to know; now it was publishing complete dialogues between men and women who had that eagerness. An example is the story of Martin Baudrier, a driver who was put in shackles for distributing prohibited works, then refused all contact with the *parlements* of Paris and Rouen. He was first imprisoned in the Châtelet, then transferred to the Bastille, where a Jesuit came and harangued him.

> The Jesuit basely taunted him with his former status as a servant, thinking he would be greatly humiliated to be told with disdain that a lackey should not turn theologian. The word 'lackey' was repeated several times, but the prisoner, who was less dishonoured by such a reproach than was he who made it, answered that, without necessarily being a theologian, one ought not to be ignorant of one's religion, and that one had only to know one's catechism in order to realize that the bull was opposed to the faith of the Church.[45]

The twin themes of knowledge and social hierarchy colour all the *Nouvelles'* columns; no reader could remain indifferent, even if he noticed the strategic aspect and remembered that in the early Church the lowliest of the faithful had always had an important place. Between 1728 and 1730 the *Nouvelles* opened up a territory which offered room to many other affairs as well as the Jansenist cause. To grant competence to popular speech, thus early in the eighteenth century, was inevitably to communicate a message so powerful, so original, that is hearers would appropriate it on the spot. The *Nouvelles* had its own politics, but it was the assurance that this publication reached even the most humble that offered every man and woman a place at the heart of public affairs.

1748–1750: the affair of the Paris hospitals

The campaign of repression against the Jansenists was harsh and insidious, but one wonders if the official Church and the monarchy were always aiming at the right targets, and if some of their strategies did not backfire. Alarmed by the growing influence of Jansenism over the people, the authorities decided to take over the places where they thought that influence was most potent. After having turned out the parish priests, the ecclesiastical authorities in Paris decided to 'purge' the great hospitals run by priests and laymen suspected of Jansenism. In the Hôtel-Dieu, the Hôpital Bicêtre and the Salpêtrière were many benevolent persons who offered assistance to the sick and poor. These 'pious laymen', who were much beloved, were removed without warning.

> 10 April 1749. For fifty years, pious laymen had been visiting the sick in the Hôtel-Dieu. Acting independently at first, and gathering from every quarter of the city, they did not know one another; but, as they often met, the spirit of charity soon created a close sympathy among them . . . In the eyes of the archbishop, M. de Beaumont, this work became a work of iniquity. It was assumed that these pious laymen must be Jansenists. On the mere suspicion of Jansenism, it has been decided that these gentlemen must be removed from the Hôtel-Dieu.[46]

This decision provoked a tumult of bitterness. The hospital was a very sensitive place, one of the most familiar, and most feared, horizons of the poor.[47] All the lesser folk knew that they might find themselves there one day, as deserving or undeserving paupers, patients, beggars or, worst of all, prisoners. Any attack on the charitable framework of such a place, which to the popular imagination was a stronghold of both succour and terror, could not fail to cause resentment.

The affair of the hospitals did not stop there. The archbishop, Christophe de Beaumont,[48] expelled (though not without misgivings) some of the choirmasters, restricted the activities of certain priests, and, to soothe anxiety, spoke of the intrusion of ill-regulated persons into the houses of restraint, of deism and Calvinism . . . He never used the word 'Jansenism' and merely said that the Hôtel-Dieu was in danger of becoming a 'new Geneva'. One detail caused particular disquiet: in the libraries, 'all the French books have been taken away, and to replace them the archbishop has sent little Offices of the Virgin in Latin and rosaries . . .'[49] To this were added other, less credible rumours, of priests who dressed up as laymen to serve the poor in the hospital. Naturally, the archbishop and the ministers were deluged with complaints about these new decisions, which had brusquely changed the atmosphere of the three principal hospitals.

In one incident, a book for children was found to contain a prayer by Deacon Pâris. This led to the rector visiting the Hôpital Bicêtre and its little library, where he ignored the children's wails of protest and confiscated everything he could find. One of the children rebelled: 'Is this what you used to tell us, that in you we would find a kind father and confessor? You are tearing from our hands the word of God. You want us to make our first communion, and you are taking away the books which serve to prepare us for it.' The rector continued his visitation by interrogating the priests one by one, in search of Jansenism rampant. The rector revived the old accusation of saying prayers in French: 'You are suspected of making the poor pray in French,' he said. 'I do,' replied the priest so accused, 'for then they understand what they are saying.' It was a telling reply which showed how much was at stake.

The narrative strategy of the *Nouvelles* in all these stories was clear and effective: each event was related through its implications for some individual – a woman in the street, a child in the hospital – whose personal involvement was then followed through. Moreover, the *Nouvelles* accepted as 'reason' things which others despised or affected to ignore: the ensemble of cultural reactions to some divulging of information or religious questions; ordinary people's ability to learn; the importance of reading; the dignity of the servant, equal to that of his master; the possibility of influencing the event that one has lived through, known and seen.

It was an out-and-out combat, for the 'orthodox' archbishop, his staff and the clergy took things very seriously. The authorities' invasion of the poor folk's hospitals, the harassment, the expulsions, the reprimanding of little children, show the virulence of the confrontation. By 'naming' acts of repression and giving ample space to the cultural debate, the *Nouvelles ecclésiastiques* allowed popular speech to gain in self-confidence and to make a greater use of its ability to resist and defy.

1750–1756: the refusal of the sacraments

In 1750 a scandal erupted over the 'notes of confession' and the refusal of the sacraments. (Dying persons were refused confession until they had shown a note from a priest signifying their approval of the bull.) The scandal threatened to become serious. Here again the *Nouvelles* played a major role, giving detailed descriptions of the consequences both to layfolk and to monks and nuns. From Paris and the provinces came emotionally charged stories of people on the point of death being brutally refused the sacraments for lack of the note which proved that they had no truck with Jansenist priests. At the Salpêtrière, notes of confession were demanded from all forty of the nuns, which was seen as unparalleled harassment.

> Here they do not await the hour of death to make use of them. These poor girls are hounded until they either give a note of confession or name their confessors and so deliver them to certain interdict . . . They threaten them with *lettres de cachet*, for they never proceed otherwise when they are seeking subjects for the bull. They talk of doing nothing less than to imprison, strictly and for life, the superior and several of the sisters.[50]

Christophe de Beaumont, now nicknamed *boutefeu* or 'fire-raiser', continued the campaign with vigour, and some curious sermons were heard in churches round about the city: 'People heard with horror a preacher in the pulpit saying that it would be better to give the bread of life to the dogs than to give any part of it to rebellious persons.'[51]

Then came a spanner in the works. In order to change the rules of the General Hospital, a royal declaration was required. Such a declaration, containing a new set of regulations for the hospital, was presented to both chambers of the *parlement* on 23 March 1751. After much serious discussion, the *parlement* assembled on 20 July to examine the declaration, debating whether to register it with modifications to be agreed, or to petition the king to withdraw a declaration so contrary to all the ancient rules. The first suggestion was approved by a majority of seventy to forty-five, and the declaration was registered, with a clause containing modifications without which it could not be put into practice. A printed leaflet was hastily distributed around Paris, telling the public what the changes were and why they had been decided: the 'Précis of the reasons for the modifications contained in the act of registration of 20 July 1751 of the Declaration of the 24 March preceding'.

There followed a serious quarrel between the king and the *parlement*. On 3 August 1751 the first president and the procurator general were summoned to the king at Compiègne. The atmosphere was not conciliatory: the king made them wait for more than a day before he would receive them, then kept them waiting for another hour and a half after the time eventually appointed. Scarcely had they entered his study than the king addressed them as follows: 'I sent for you to tell you that I am very displeased with the decisions given by my parliament concerning my declaration of the 24 March last. I forbid them to be executed and wish my declaration to be executed pure and simple.'[52]

The president and procurator conveyed this reply to the *parlement*, which refused to give way: on 30 August it presented its remonstrances to the king, while the publication of the 'Précis' was forbidden. Butard and his wife, Villeneuve, who had done no more than to print and distribute the leaflet, were sent to the Bastille by royal order and without police formalities; they remained there for a long time under conditions reported to be exceedingly unpleasant.

On 5 September the king replied to the remonstrances and renewed his order to put the declaration into practice. Meanwhile, refusal of the sacraments was becoming more and more frequent, accompanied by pointless harassment which caused public indignation. To obtain a note of confession you had not only to accept the bull and declare that Deacon Pâris was damned – which was already bad enough – but also bring out all the books you owned. Forbidden ones were burned: these often included the *Imitation of Christ* and the *Instruction on the Sacraments of Penitence and the Eucharist*, both very popular and owned by almost every family, sometimes in pocket editions. 'All the city murmured,' reported the *Nouvelles ecclésiastiques*, and a good many people were saying out loud that nobody should listen to sermons or even go to confession. This, again, was something new, emphasized and encouraged by the *Nouvelles*: in 1730 it had merely reported the repression of Jansenists, but now it was stressing the purity of each person's conscience, which in certain cases, such as the notes of confession, could oppose the king's orders. This was an enormous leap forward in attitudes to the individual. Each was granted his own personal sphere, the rational possession of his soul. There he was face to face with God, and no other could enter – not even the ecclesiastical authorities, not even the king. The more the *parlement* stood up to the king, the more fervently the people rallied to it; a breach was opened, and the deputies, with their political power, helped to defend it. Resisting the king was not a crime but a duty, for there was no room for unjust orders between a dying man and his God. His encounter with death and confession must not be tainted by repressive practices contrary to the faith: here again the *Nouvelles* pleaded for the wisdom of the poor and demanded respect for their innermost convictions, which must not be violated, even for the king. The territory between the self and God was 'officially' occupied, and the monarchy had now to vacate it. The combination of religion and politics in the sacraments affair made it potentially subversive to an extent which no one, perhaps, fully realized at the time.

In the midst of this fierce contest, so essential to our understanding of this genesis of the individual, the Sieur de Prades defended, on 27 February 1752, a thesis at the Sorbonne. This would scarcely have been a major event if certain propositions in his weighty tome had not been condemned as 'pernicious to society and public tranquillity'. The archbishop of Paris took fire again, and issued a pastoral insisting that it was truly scandalous to declare 'a pretended right to equality in conformity with reason, with which, so the Sieur de Prades claims, all men come into the world'. The *Nouvelles* assigned considerable importance to this affair, entwining comments on de Prades' thesis with stories of denials of the sacrament so as to throw emphasis on the idea that all men were equal in reason. Daily happenings well illustrated the arguments in the thesis, while de Prades' ideas nourished those who fought against the notes of confession. Descriptions of prominent individuals who resisted the orders of king and Church combined very effectively with the idea that every rational person could reasonably claim freedom of conscience. The *Nouvelles'* style gained further in vigour, combining events and thoughts in such a way as to widen still further the space for individual convictions.

The long dispute over refusal of the sacraments became a political matter,[53] pursued with such venom that it finally led to the *parlement* being exiled for several months in 1753–4. The king had decreed the exile, but it was the monarchy which was weakened: Louis XV sought a reconciliation with the *parlement* and paid heed to their opinions, which were keenly focused on the ensuing host of remonstrances and *lits de justice*. In 1755 Louis summoned twenty-six bishops to Paris and asked them to suspend the notes of confession (he had already tried to do so in 1752, but had changed his mind). However, this was not the end of the affair, for on 16 October 1756 the pope issued an encyclical which, while appearing to agree with the decision, actually renewed the attack by affirming that it was imperative to refuse the sacraments to all declared Jansenists.

From religion to politics

Briefly to conclude our discussion of this clandestine, but widely known and highly influential publication, we must remind ourselves that its view of ordinary people and their world, however effective it may have been, concerned only the occasions on which that world intersected with the story of *Unigenitus*. This may seem little in comparison with the long sequence of events which made up the eighteenth century. But while the events concerned were restricted, they unfolded new spaces of freedom where every man was his own arbitrator. The refusal of the sacraments, so eagerly recorded, recounted and distributed by the *Nouvelles ecclésiastiques*, created a particular juncture at which the relationship between the king and his subjects shifted on to a terrain of possible disobedience. The further shift which connected the religious and political fields gave individual attitudes an unprecedented effectiveness, with the hallmark of novelty.

The *Nouvelles'* readers had every reason to apply their capacity for decision to many other domains than Jansenism alone. The Jansenist press monopolized popular speech to help it resist the monarchy and the Church. One undercover publication, by accepting that speech as reasonable, had given it something which no other newspaper or history had ever offered. The gift was not to remain unused.

PART II

Speeches of Discontent:
Forms and Motifs

Paris was all ears and eyes and speaking and cursing: the people of the city were always said to be avid for curiosities to look at and discuss.[1] Paris gobbled rumours and spectacles with a voracious greed which was only stimulated by the difficulty of procuring firsthand information. Parisians were interested in everything: that has become one of the most commonplace elements in any historian's analysis of Parisian society. Let us spare a few minutes to look at examples. Any dozen pages from the chronicle of Hardy, a bookseller and observer of Paris in the later eighteenth century, brings back to life that atmosphere in which everything was turned into news or spectacle:

8 June 1769. A rumour is running through Paris that the new pope has died unexpectedly; this rumour has persisted for several days, and it was even being said that the nuncio was receiving no news from Rome. We were assured that what had given rise to this rumour was the king's announcement of the death of a certain Lepape [le pape 'the pope'], a soldier who died at the Invalides at the age of 100.

4 September 1769. Today five offices are being opened at the approaches to the Pont-Neuf, at which the public are furnished with parasols to shelter them from the sun as they pass over the bridge. For each parasol one gave six deniers, which one paid as one took it; one gave it back at the other end of the bridge. This drew a considerable crowd.

9 December 1769. Today there is a rumour among the public that there are ghosts in a room in the house occupied by Monsieur Louvet, master lute-maker, in the Rue de la Croix-des-Petits-Champs near the passage into the cloister of Saint-Honoré. Several persons of standing made their way there out of curiosity, and there is even a crowd of people so numerous – not a surprising thing considering that the Parisian is always particularly eager for novelties – that M. the lieutenant of police getting to hear of it, gave orders for the affair to be closely examined, and for guards to be posted at the door of the house.

27 September 1771. There was an enormous crowd to see the arrival of a stone weighing 62,875 pounds, 10 feet long, 9 wide and 5 thick, intended as one of the two cornerstones of the façade of the church of Sainte-Geneviève. They had taken since last Thursday, walking day and night, to bring it there from the wharf at the Invalides where it had been disembarked, coming from the quarries at Conflans. They had come via the Barrière d'Enfer and the Faubourg Saint-Jacques and the stone had been dragged along on a sledge by soldiers of the Swiss Regiment.[2]

A building stone, a dead pope, a haunted house, a parasol for crossing the Pont-Neuf: anything could serve to astonish, amuse and tell to others. But Paris was equally interested in the functioning of Church and State, justice, prices and taxes; it passed judgement on princes and magistrates, administrators and tax-farmers; it knew the police and all their devious ways. Parisian opinions on society and political affairs took established forms and were based on motifs which gave them force and logic. Let us now examine them, combining information from various sources: police documents, diaries and memoirs.

3

Mobility and fragmentation

Judgements issuing from diverse mouths, and public criticism, did not drop from heaven in any anarchic or repetitive way, but arose out of particular situations. Their intensity varied, for sometimes they might enter a space which would amplify and favour them; they could be expressed directly or obliquely; they were often supplemented by tales passed from mouth to mouth, or by emblematic stories which stimulated the imaginative content of rumours in circulation.

Comment on affairs of state was based on a gathering of circumstances which meant that its status and organization were constantly changing. Grafted onto an ever-changing situation, opinions would be affirmed and reaffirmed, then disappear, attach themselves to other incidents and be transformed by new perspectives and means of expression. There was no method for measuring opinion, but devices were occasionally put to work to crystallize 'public' judgements. These devices had a life of their own – pictures, writings, words, sometimes a great deal of violence; they were born and died quickly, or on the contrary became frozen into an infinite series of leitmotifs. Opinion cannot be weighed up by adding individual opinions, one by one, to the pile; it is more like a plastic mass in perpetual agitation, whose outline changes constantly, and whose tenor and thickness can be altered by pressure. It was rarely spontaneous, always interactive, and to an extent regulated; some of its products were nourished by a favourable reception, while others withered rapidly on the stony ground of collective rejection.

What is initially most striking about this opinion is its mobility. New items and criticisms constantly appeared in response to the lively social life of the streets, which made events and gossip about them accessible to, and manipulable by, anybody and everybody. The inhabitants of a building, district, market or parish easily absorbed anything that was said: the (as it were) fluidity between indoor and outdoor life allowed the immediate diffusion of thoughts and feelings, some extravagant, others serious. It was the echo of such impressions which did – or sometimes did not – form the nucleus of an incipient *opinion about* . . . Opinion, like those who made it, was nomadic through time and space, a fact which led people on a higher level – diarists and monarchic authorities – to conclude that it was capricious and changeable. At the very least it was hard to pin down, always coming to birth in one place as it perished in another from the ageing of its forms and motifs. In Paris, indeed, it could enter a thousand homes, for a thousand reasons, and assume a thousand different forms: there was no one 'public opinion'. It was multiform and fragmented in proportion to the diverse interests which produced it: while in one place they are discussing work regulations, two leagues away the talk is all of strikes. There has been a battle between beggars and archers, and the police are blamed; today, a public execution is considered unjust; tomorrow the queen is to be churched and we shall see how the monarchy is 'doing'; yesterday there were posters on the walls which caricatured the regent, but nobody took much interest.

Such fragmentation corresponded to the mobility within society; information, unrestrained by class or hierarchy, gusted through the city scattering gossip and rumours as readily as important news. People learned from what they saw or heard, perhaps without order, but certainly without disorder; opinions were modulated by news, and although the news might soon be forgotten, the will to know and to have some grip on affairs remained. It was hard to steer a course between the true and the false, and it was best to stay as close as might be to the possible.

Opinions, personal and public, would latch on to minor incidents as readily as those of collective importance. There was particular interest in individual people and individual news, so that (for example) the public eye was never turned on the court without neatly detaching the king from the queen, the princess from the mistress or the mistress from the dauphine. This individualization of motifs matched the theatricality of state affairs, which were also diversified, with many scenes being played by individual actors, all of whom would be judged individually, and the judgement spread abroad. Political life under the Ancien Régime attached as much importance to individuals as to policies. The political architecture of the court itself depended on distancing and separating the persons surrounding the king. Indeed, in court society every individual was placed by his rank, and so affirmed his difference from others.[1] An order was carefully maintained in which everyone had his place, so that 'the social being of the individual was totally identified with the representation given of it by himself or others. The "reality" of a social position was only what opinion held it to be.'[2] At court every individual was visibly part of a system of representations largely conditioned by what was *said* about the place each person occupied; thus it was not surprising if the public at large followed, as closely as it could, the daily manoeuvrings on the courtly chessboard. Moreover, giving information was not, in the eighteenth century, a method of government, so that the affairs both of the State and of the great appeared segmented, passed on to the public gaze through a filter of alternate opacity and ostentation. Secrecy was the norm, with only the odd gesture being intentionally revealed to the public, and the public eye was sharpened by this lack of access to the complete picture. It made the best of available detail, deducing what it could from every element and looking for meaning in the fragmentary information placed at its disposal, or captured in defiance of the general obfuscation. This explains not only the fragmentation of opinions, but also the taste for singular and unique items which could prove instructive in the absence of abundant overall information. It also explains the difficulty of ranking certain facts with any accuracy, for the more rigorous the secrecy maintained in political affairs, the greater the importance given to the smallest incident, with no means of telling if it were really important or not. Popular opinion, fastening eagerly on anything it could drag from under the veil of secrecy, was made all the more virulent by its awareness of being excluded from active politics.

Placards and satire: the dangers of laughter

The empty space on walls was constantly being invaded by 'abominable and seditious' placards. They frightened the authorities, but it was a hard job to get rid of them, given the zeal of the bill-posters.

9 November 1768. This morning a new, abominable and seditious placard was found in the market-place. They had taken the precaution to apply it with strong glue to a board which had then been stuck to the wall. It was so frightful that the commissary who removed it felt obliged to have it covered with a cloth while it was being detached from the board, so that it could not be read any longer.[3]

We recognize the habit of hiding things from people and refusing to inform them, but Barbier and Hardy both tell us that placards sprouted everywhere like daisies in the springtime. Some, like Hardy, were sorry, thinking that it would only 'stir up people's minds' and make them revolt. Others, like Mercier, claimed that so many placards were competing for attention that people read them with a smile and soon forgot them. Whether they caused indifference or amusement, placards were a recognized technique of opposition from the regency onwards. Anonymous, ill-written and usually misspelt, they punctuated the city with denunciation and anathema. They commented on one another, repeated one another, adding grist to the voracious mill of public curiosity. They also shared in the biting irony so characteristic of popular comment. When people criticized, they usually mocked and satirized, and we shall never know whether the placards suggested the irony or themselves borrowed the habitual modes of denunciation. Certainly the raw and unfinished style of the placard was faithful to the forms of traditional spoken intercourse.

Popular judgements were conveyed through laughter, mischief and mockery. Hardy said that satire was 'an ordinary product of the judgement of Parisians, a weapon of the mind', used when it was hard to take any direct action.[4] Gossip was indeed a redoubtable weapon, especially the much-feared feminine variety. Violent, voluble, inflammatory and hard-hitting, it left the police authorities standing.

These satirical and defamatory public judgements were a natural way of reacting orally to permanently truncated information. Against the violence of fact they set the power of mockery, the devastation of words, knowing that this put the speaker in a position of power. 'Admiration', wrote Chevrier in his *Almanach*, 'is the style of the stupid,'[5] and he went on to emphasize how satiric intelligence could crush its adversary. Satire was also a travesty of reality – and that suited everybody, since the reality was sometimes unsayable and, if political, never revealed to the public save in incomplete dribs and drabs. These they seized on, making a travesty of the words in an attempt to grasp a situation whose mechanisms were never fully explained. An author with a satirical style had a right of expression which would otherwise have been inhibited, or worse still forbidden, or even subject to what Jean-Claude Lavie, in his preface to a reissue of Freud's *Jokes and their Relation to the Unconscious*, called an 'interdictory inhibition'.[6] Satire put words in the very place where nothing was supposed to be said, and 'the insatiable greed [of Parisians] for anything which breathed criticism, satire or derision'[7] was rooted in that nothingness. Defamation and mocking incredulity were a means of public access to what was supposed to be secret. It was the converse of the flattery which ruled the society of court and princes. They set up 'favour' as a principle of government and distinction; against it, the people, who were not subject to that rigid architecture, set up a violence of mockery which could find the parts that flattery could not reach.[8]

Between archaism and modernity

The people not only judged events as they happened, but also interpreted royal acts and deeds in accordance with the public mood. At times of discontent, the personal histories of king and queen were read in the light of that discontent. King and princes were ensnared in a criticism which left their failures and inadequacies mercilessly exposed. Their bodies, their attitudes, were the grammar of a critical language used (among others) to express social and political dissatisfaction. Social discontent was used to break the code of royal living, and any royal action, however trivial, which was open to criticism was cited in proof of judgements on the whole political system.

This 'extraordinary' perusal of the body royal shows just how important the latter was considered to be. The criticism is original in that it is often contradictory, veering between a need for archaism and an enthusiasm for change. It leaves small space for innocence.

A moment in history may serve as an example. In 1728, much criticism was being voiced over the bull *Unigenitus*, and especially the inconstancy of Cardinal de Noailles, who, after some initial support for Jansenism, had published a pastoral, execrated by the people, in which he declared his acquiescence in the bull and demanded its implementation. The tension in the streets could almost be felt, as the people lamented their abandonment by their own archbishop. They denounced the pastoral; far more important, they began for the first time to read every gesture from the king as another betrayal. He was seen in a new and comprehensively disappointing light: disappointing *vis-à-vis* the traditional functions of royalty, which he was suspected of neglecting; disappointing to those in search of new expressions of religious and political feeling, which the king refused to employ. This antinomically disappointing monarch was actually in a cleft stick, expected to continue with outmoded gestures in the name of tradition, but blamed for not understanding the political shifts which had already taken place among his subjects. The two-way pull created enormous tension.

In 1728, then, the king was perceived to be neglecting his accustomed functions. The memory of Louis XIV became the foundation for an altered vision of Louis XV. The Sun King was an unchanging image which shone all the brighter as political difficulties clouded the skies. During the regency people very quickly forgot the sorry end of Louis XIV's reign, and remembered only its power and grandeur. In the shadow of Louis XIV, Louis XV was scarcely visible at all. Through the years of the Jansenist controversy, every royal act had reverberations. The king loved hunting, a traditional and manly pursuit in which every king should engage, but it turned against Louis XV. He loved hunting but did not love war, that high aspiration so energetically pursued by Louis XIV (until his subjects were too exhausted to pursue it further). Everywhere people muttered that the king was idle and could only make war on the deer: if he loved hunting, he *must* love war, and not neglect the one for the other.

By a strange turn of logic he was then accused of cruelty. Of course, if he had loved war, no one would have detected an ounce of cruelty in him. But his immoderate appetite for hunting, and nothing but hunting, made his ferocity seem both more tasteless and more conspicuous in its apparent gratuity. Proof was ready to hand in the story of a girl who had been raped by a member of the Swiss guard in the royal apartments. The girl's outraged father petitioned the king to have the criminal severely punished. Louis XV paid little attention and had the man unceremoniously ejected. The story raced around Paris, heightened by the death of the girl (she was under nine and did not survive the trauma); everywhere it was whispered that the king was turning savage, and in that case, it would be better if he went off to the wars.

Savage the king may have been, but also physically weak: he was often ill, another bad sign for those who preferred a conquering hero. When he was ill, however, the people worried, and they rejoiced at his successive recoveries. But even that he could not get right. In November 1728 the women from the markets came, according to custom, to congratulate him on his recovery. Unlike Louis XIV, the king did not allow them in and refused to receive their good wishes. They returned indignantly to Paris and solemnly swore never to follow that custom again – a radical change in women who were deeply imbued with ritual. Since the king would have none of them, they bitterly withdrew from him, convinced that Louis XV, like the Church, had declared war on ordinary people.

On the other hand, Louis XV refused to listen to his subjects' demands for change: at times he was too traditional altogether. The kingly ceremonials of 1728 were intensely watched and discussed by a people rendered distrustful by the *Unigenitus* affair and the persecution of their parish priests. Thus, on one of the king's and queen's visits to Paris, police observers noted the Parisians' general disapproval of Louis's (very traditional) distribution of alms to the populace. There was bitter criticism and talk of abuses. In some café or other somebody said that if the king wanted to fool people, he might at least do it a bit more generously – in fact, a lot more. Somebody else retorted, 'It would have been better to give that money to the parishes and ask the priests to share it out.'[9] These remarks had a twofold significance: first, you should not give manna to the people like a farmer giving fodder to his cattle; second, there should be trust in parish priests and their well-judged charity, instead of this degrading atmosphere in which the best priests were arrested after the Sunday sermon. There was a logic to all this discontent.

Another incident came to disturb the convictions and beliefs of a scandalized populace. In October 1728, the queen, who to her sorrow still had no male child, decided to come to Notre-Dame and make a novena to Saint Geneviève. This was considered 'extravagant', and a violent argument broke out among the population.

> Some say that it is within the power of God to give male children to France, but that Providence should be left to take its course; others, who apparently prefer to leave God out of account, say that it would be unworthy of his immensity to stoop as far as to preside over the intercourse of mankind, and that it is only the action of animal nature ... others say that all religion is full of mummeries, that novenas, pilgrimages, indulgences and other devotions are mere human inventions, and that God is offended at them; people also say that it would be enough for the queen to stay at Versailles and pray, and that that would have been a better idea than to come to Paris in such state – which is paganism.[10]

The opinions differed, but all were critical: the king and queen were somehow in the wrong. Either they were suspected of refusing to submit to the divine will, which was a serious thing in a monarch; or they were very arrogantly trying to transcend their own nature by asking God to stoop to take care of it (which was a very odd thing to say: if king and queen were seen as an integral part of animal nature there was small danger of paying them superstitious reverence!). Impasse – especially as the queen came (or so it was said) without humility, and without setting foot to ground as Louis XIV and his consort had always done.

The police observers, mingling with the crowds, heard them criticize the public prayers (which lasted several days), and people even said that 'it matters little what the queen conceives, for even if the king cannot get male children, we shall not lack for a master in France.' This was the shaft of ultimate defiance; and a few days later, an individual added that 'if God gave kings to the people, He gave them in His wrath, and they should be regarded as tyrants.'

If we connect these reflections on the king and queen with the surge of protest against the king's anti-Jansenist policies, we can see a shift in public attitudes. A tension was created between conflicting demands which the king was unable to satisfy: he disappointed the people by breaking with rituals which they still thought efficacious, while adhering to others which had lost all meaning. The discourse of opposition to the king, cemented by the *Unigenitus* affair and the effective resistance of humble parishes to papal and monarchic high-handedness, now set hard. Everything he did, or failed to do, was perceived through a haze of 'police kidnappings' and imprisonments; every detail of kingly ceremonial was reinterpreted unfavourably in tune with the prevailing discontent. Public opinion read royal actions as a footnote to contemporary affairs.

The function of anecdotes

Whenever an (at least mildly) exciting political episode engaged public attention, it was accompanied around Paris by a trail of anecdotes and disturbing scandals. Street commentaries on the ups and downs of political life were interspersed with curious tales. These tales did, however, have some connection with reality, as if to organize facts into easily comprehensible and plausible narrative; as if society found it easier to appropriate information which overawed and outstripped individual understanding if it was presented in the form of allegories and legends. There was a close link between the social and political happenings which attracted public attention and the appearance of semi-fictional (and wholly unverifiable) narratives which circulated freely from mouth to mouth. One of their functions was to bring distant events into a nearer focus; to unravel meaning from a context wholly opaque; to subject areas far removed from politics to the accustomed forms of folk stories and 'popular tales'; to get hold of State secrets. Three episodes – the regent's death in 1723, the convulsionaries of Saint-Médard and the closing of that parish in 1732 – were very productive of stories of this half-real, half-imaginary type; they helped carry the populace over some difficult junctures which the authorities had shrouded in mystery. Stories, rumours and scandals helped to lift the veil and voice the unsayable: they were reassuring metaphors for a menacing reality.

The death of the regent, on 3 December 1723, was recorded by three annalists, Buvat, Marais and Barbier. Although they each give a different account of the circumstances surrounding his decease, they all suggest a strange atmosphere in which the truth was hard to discern. Moreover, their anecdotes reflect the way in which the populace reacted to the drama.

Jean Buvat recounts that the regent, on the point of death, asked for the company of certain ladies so that their 'conversation' could entertain him; then he lamented his 'unhappy life'. Marais approaches the event more circumspectly and begins every sentence with a prudent 'They say that . . .'. They say that the regent was with his mistress when he died and that it proved very hard to find a surgeon to bleed him, at which one of his lady friends, Mme Sabran, reportedly said, 'Don't bleed him, he's just come out from under his whore.' Further on, Marais recounts that once the regent was dead his body was taken through Paris to the accompaniment of 'ribald jokes' from the large crowd. As for Barbier, who considers himself the sole repository of truth, he tells how something awful happened, something which was 'as far as possible kept hidden, but absolutely true'. Since the regent's heart was to be buried at Val-de-Grâce, they opened up his body; at that very moment, one of the Great Danes which had belonged to him sprang up, grabbed the heart and ate three-quarters of it on the spot. This, adds Barbier, must show that the regent was accursed, since that kind of dog is never, by repute, particularly greedy. The craziest stories ran through Paris: here a heart, there a dog, here a half-eaten body, there a mocking crowd. Here society shows a violent side to its collective imagination, its vision of crime and punishment. A lackey was asked if he had seen the heart go by; he answered, 'No, but I saw his soul going along the Rue d'Enfer' – which means the Street of Hell. The body once opened, the soul escaped, and its choice of street was not coincidental. Whether the people grumbled as the regent's body went past, or whether a dog devoured his heart, came to much the same thing. The anecdotes amount to an analysis of popular sentiment: the regent's death was greeted with contempt, it exposed the hatred which had overshadowed his last days. This guilty and monstrous hatred could not be expressed openly, only through images; the dog devouring the heart is surely one of the most harshly vivid. It cleared the people of an implied desire for cruelty: subjects could not devour their king, but a prince's hound could devour his heart. Since the prince had died ignominiously in mid-intercourse, the people insulted his body and the dog ate his heart. The field was now clear for contemplating the future career of the boy king Louis XV. That strange and terrible allegory was a euphemism for a break with the past.

In another episode women, in particular lower-class women, had a leading role. After the death of Deacon Pâris, many people came to pray and meditate at his tomb. Then, very quietly here and there, there began to be whispers of miraculous cures. Soon the cemetery was crowded with men and women writhing in convulsions, calling for help or prophesying at inordinate length. Such spiritual and physical phenomena, inexplicable in terms of contemporary logic, seemed to manifest themselves more readily in the female than the male body. The women's prophecies expressed a veiled but vehement threat against the threatened pollution of both religion and society as a whole. They hurled anathemas at those who stained religion and persecuted the church of the poor; they were fond of proclaiming that the end was nigh, that apocalypse would overtake the world before it could return to God. This upset everybody, and the police authorities, on Fleury's orders, made sure that their inspectors, informers and observers were constantly present in the cemetery to report each convulsionary utterance verbatim, and to infiltrate the crowds of spectators and overhear their murmured comments.[11] Few people spoke aloud, but numerous anecdotes circulated which cast doubt on the purity of the women, who had allegedly fallen victim to lustful priests. 'Even the common people utterly condemn the court of Rome and speak of it with the utmost contempt, some saying that the pope has as much religion as a dog, or as those who protect his constitution.'[12] Men of the church behaving like dogs? Women their victims? The crowds were pulling no punches! They often contrasted this debauched clergy, point for point, with the Jansenist church – poor, rigorous and respectful of women. Here and there people zestfully recounted the shameful lives of certain monks, or the atmosphere of debauchery in the archbishop's palace. On 12 August 1773 'there is a rumour which revolts all decent people: a priest of Saint-Paul has abused the young blind daughter of a counsellor of the *parlement*, and made her pregnant'.[13] Then the diatribe passes to the king's officers: 'Officers are raping women on the riverboat to Auxerre'; 'A very young girl has been raped in the Rue Saint-André-des-Arts'; and a marquis accused of raping a chambermaid, who died from her injuries, has escaped unpunished! Everywhere people were saying, 'There is no justice.'

When the lieutenant of police himself was involved, the scandal was enormous.

I feel obliged to report that people are talking about an amorous affair involving a *valet de chambre* or lackey of the lieutenant general's wife, and in his very house: it is said that she is making a set of embroidered furnishings for summer, and for this she has hired nine girls from the Community of One Hundred Girls in the Faubourg Saint-Marcel; that the man in charge of these furnishings is a domestic, who (so they say) has made each of the said nine girls pregnant ... this story has been openly recounted these last few days in every public place.[14]

Examples are too many to quote. A parish priest visits women every night; a Carmelite from the Place Maubert has kidnapped and run off with a girl whom he is now keeping as a slave. On the other hand, there are stories of a different kind, in which impeccably virtuous women go to the king and entreat him to change his policies.

> It is being said in public that there is a lady of good standing, or at least dressed in a way that suggests she is, who wormed her way into the king's chapel at Versailles while His Majesty was hearing Mass and said these words: 'Your Majesty, you have a *sou* under your tongue which is stopping you from speaking, and if you do not have it removed it will shortly kill you, along with the whole royal family.'[15]

And all the time the miracles and convulsions were going on at Saint-Médard.

When some event made a tear in the social fabric, there were always emblematic stories to serve it as proof and counter-proof, an effective support grafted onto an insupportable reality. The convulsionaries disturbed the social order; their proclamations and prophecies were a threat to public tranquillity and often carried conviction among a populace already deeply impressed by the Jansenist persecution. This magnified certain scandalous tales and made them easier to remember. Whether true or imaginary, they came at the right time to fill a void and so make reality endurable. If society's problem was impurity, it was natural that women should be the protagonists. The burden of purity rested chiefly on them, and they were chiefly responsible for the loss of it; thus it is only natural to find stories of women being raped, or conversely, of pure and virginal women destined to save the world. While young women went into convulsions and called upon innocence threatened by a tainted Church, people at large told each other ugly stories about actual monks and bishops who were scandalously violating the purity of women by the most reprehensible acts of rape.

Events which occurred in certain types of place lent themselves particularly well to amplification, for some places had power to dramatize events. Translated into words, this effect produced long, and more or less alarming, anecdotes designed to mitigate, or reinforce, the effects of a social or political situation. A cemetery was one such highly symbolical place: being situated in the middle of town, it was a significant link between the living and the dead, and within its walls it enclosed all the mysteries of religion and of life. Nothing that happened there could fail to draw the imagination into unknown regions, more of shadow than of light. It was a sacred place, where strange and sinister things happened. It was said that noisome vapours issued from it, making people faint or even causing explosions during the night; often you could hear inexplicable noises which might well be the anguished cries of people who had been buried alive;[16] and, also by night, furtive shadows (really students of medicine) came to drag out still-warm corpses for anatomical dissections through which they hoped to make a decisive contribution to science. The cemetery, at once familiar and phantasmagorical, was a social space riddled with rites and taboos. Since 1728, the cemetery of Saint-Médard had been saturated with happenings. There, Deacon Pâris had been buried in holy humility; there, the sick had found hope of healing; there, convulsionaries had shrieked their curses and supplications, and been savagely beaten in what was commonly called 'succour'.

Crowds came to Saint-Médard to see the marks of God, but the police had to spoil it by coming to make arrests. 'This', people murmured, 'is beyond the pale, for them to interfere even in the mysteries of God,' and everyone knew what was written on the famous notice-board set up for all to see: 'From King to God, a message clear: Miracles are forbidden here.'

For the king to attack the people in a place where God performed his miracles was verging on the criminal. The public was further scandalized to hear that 'police officers swear and say b— and f—; they really should (so people say) respect the cemetery, which is a holy place.'[17] It was equally intolerable that God's house should be guarded by armed archers: 'such procedures dishonour both the king and religion.' Criticism was backed by assurance: the king could not set himself above God without drawing fire from heaven upon his head, and all and sundry predicted that 'staggering punishments will descend on the king and Fleury.'

But who among the people could punish the king? Rumours and stories started to spread, repeating the accusation of monarchic impiety and describing exaggerated examples of the curse coming home to roost.

People are saying that two archers have dropped dead in the cemetery because they did some irreverent act; they were buried immediately and on the quiet.

People are saying that the lieutenant general of police went along to Saint-Médard at about midnight, accompanied by two masons, to exhume the Abbé Pâris; that one of the masons dropped dead in the cemetery as he was about to strike the first blow with his pickaxe, and that the other, called Serviat, died suddenly a few days later.

Later, in 1732, they said that 'some prelates will die suddenly as a punishment for their wickednesses.'

It was not by chance that the commonest stories were about people dropping dead. Sudden death was much feared in the eighteenth century,[18] because its victim could not receive the sacraments and so had no chance of redemption. Here it shows the reprobation of God; moreover, it opens the eyes of onlookers, for each instantly reads the punishment he has dealt out.

Most of the anecdotes accompanying public events are clearly contrapuntal, and their themes do not recur by chance. This recurrence is a reminder that the populace preferred to retain details which they could use for or against some event which was affecting them. The anecdote which was passed on was selected from hundreds of others which could equally well have been told, and it functioned as a determiner: popular discourse seized on it because people were constantly striving to live in the midst of meaning, and to find in the most immediate circumstances of daily life some nourishment and foundation for their assurances.

Differentiated opinions

The people were seldom unanimous. Although police observers did note different opinions from differing social groups, they do not seem to have taken much real account of them, preferring to stud their reports with generalized remarks about discontent or satisfaction. That suited the mental outlook of the authorities, for whom, in the last analysis, popular opinion resided in a sort of social and political void. If observers occasionally detected variations, this did not make them revise their judgements, or even think of categorizing the opinions which they spent most of their time pursuing and were paid to pursue.

The people never expressed its judgement *en bloc* and with a single voice, without any nuance or possibility of modification. Those who believed otherwise had a traditional mental picture of a 'populace' whose reactions were instinctive, emotional and invariable, and who were incapable of seeing the finer points and minute shifts which politicians were able to manipulate. In fact, the people's relationship with the king was continually changing and ramifying into contrasting positions, all different from one another, each shaped by a quite distinct set of interests.

Here is an example: quite a trifling one, but it gives us a glimpse into the heart of the people. On 4 September 1729, a dauphin was born. A police report for that date begins as follows:

> The coming of the dauphin has caused general satisfaction to all, but particularly to the common people; one can say that they are beginning to manifest their joy and flatter themselves that this prince will complete their happiness, in that they think that it will ensure the tranquillity of the State, that this same tranquillity will procure them some relief through the diminution of taxes, and that this will make life easier.[19]

Up to this point the popular sky was blue and the horizon cloudless: the 'populace' wished only for a tranquil public atmosphere to banish the spectre of the Jansenist troubles. They were all the more pleased in that they expected a reduction in taxes – all that was needed for complete happiness. This stereotype of a populace bathed in bliss at the announcement of a royal birth is only to be expected, although the police observer goes on to make a whole series of remarks indicative of a climate of disagreement and anxiety among the people, which completely contradict his opening sentences. Some people were already speculating anxiously on a change in the relationship between the king and queen. Now that she was at last mother to a male child, the queen would certainly acquire more and more influence over her husband, which was not a bad thing, but there were fears that she would bring over her father, the king of Poland, either to Saint-Germain-en-Laye or to Vincennes, to help the king in his labours. This idea was frightening, though it delighted those who firmly believed it would lead to the downfall of Fleury. Such forecasting illustrates the people's greatest fears: a weak king who neglected his wife; a minister (Fleury) who abused his authority and was trying to take the king's place. The birth of the dauphin was a chance to throw away the old, insoluble puzzle of Louis XV's early years (generally held to be catastrophic) and to start work on some alternative scenarios.

An influential group among the people of Paris were the artisans, though racked with internal conflict and shaken by the demands of the *compagnons*, a kind of early trade union.[20] Times were never easy for the artisans, and they were very vulnerable to economic difficulties, so much so that when the dauphin was born they 'complained because they had been ordered to shut up shop'. The losses thereby incurred seemed to them out of all proportion to the importance of the event, and they said they 'would be delighted to do it, if they were given something to live and make merry on during the celebrations'.[21] Told that the festival *Te Deum* would be accompanied by a suspension of the poll-tax, their suspicions overcame their jubilation and, to curb the latter, they complained in advance that the proposed measure might never be carried out: 'If it doesn't happen, they say, then we have nothing to hope for.'

A gloomy atmosphere, then, contradicting the first enthusiastic paragraph of the report. Here again, however, the contradictory details are strung along without the slightest attempt at comment.

Worse was to come. There was an ominous incident which annoyed everybody and convinced them that the birth of the dauphin would bring them no relief. Some inhabitants (*manants*) of Versailles had celebrated the festive occasion by presenting the king with a memoir asking to have 'certain privileges restored which had been taken from them'; but a decree was immediately posted in several places 'forbidding any person to ask anything of the king on penalty of being put in a dungeon'. This measure was ill received: such a harsh punishment for making requests to the king did not exactly encourage the festive mood. The news got around, the people received it sourly, blamed Fleury and were sorry that they had thought that the queen would at last have some beneficent influence. The streets were invaded with placards, and in the cabarets there was talk of the king's 'barbarity'.

The king proved doubly disappointing when, on 12 September, he decided to send Fleury to represent him at the festivities announced by the Hôtel de Ville, where there was to be 'a splendid supper and fireworks'. This news pleased nobody and nourished opinions of the king's barbarity. A sulky placard appeared at a crossroads giving the dauphin the title 'the Pacific' and his father 'the Melancholic'.

All this was brought to an abrupt halt on the king's personal initiative: he was so annoyed by what he saw and heard, or rather was told, that he had all the rejoicing stopped. Thus 1729 brought the man in the street a short respite, a glimmer of hope, and then sent him back to his old preoccupations. Everywhere 'there is talk of sedition in the kingdom if Fleury continues to persecute the Jansenists.'[22] On 26 September some satirical placards were posted on the door of the little church of Sainte-Madeleine, with some very ill-natured remarks about the king and the archbishop of Paris. Elsewhere, the king having refused to lower taxes, his royal barbarity was freely placarded and everyone wished yet again 'that His Majesty could have one quarter of the perfections that his mighty grandfather had'.

The dauphin 'affair' showed a people divided in its initial reactions to a situation which might have been very promising. Above all, it witnesses to the continual adjustments by Parisian social groups to what they saw. They interpreted the gestures and signs which they detected amidst the monarchic ceremonial, using them as grounds for giving, refusing or trading their consent. Attitudes were varied, changes of attitude were radical; and if we read the police reports and the street gossip carefully, we can detect a good many lines of thought at work.

We are struck again by the rapid modifications in popular thought, which were pegged to the slightest shifts in the monarchy's own position. People changed their opinions and positions on the basis of limited and almost imperceptible facts. This incessant revision shows the extreme changeability of the population – writers at the time called them 'instinctive' – and also their determination to react very closely to public events, never to neglect anything and not to become fixed in one invariable attitude.

There were circumstances which people found disturbing because they could not discover the truth about them. That gave rise to diverging opinions and widely differing versions of the facts, whose sole common feature was a certain respect for logic and for the bounds of plausibility. In 1762 there was an incident which led to a great trial and a public execution. La Chaux, a royal guard, gave himself some nasty cuts with a knife and then claimed that he had fought against two men with evil designs on the king.[23] Everything conspired to blow this incident up to enormous proportions: Damiens' assault on Louis XV, in 1757, was still vividly remembered, and the Jesuits had just been expelled. Moreover, any incident which involved a (real or supposed) threat to the king's life was bound to provoke great emotion. This theme of the death of kings always had repercussions; it was a spectre which might be desired or detested, but a spectre nonetheless. Merely to mention it was to stimulate the imagination and arouse all kinds of talk, bringing out the difference between those who used it to harmful effect and those who were 'criminally' indifferent. Such an incident could never be greeted with indifference, and the La Chaux affair was no exception; the news spread through Paris like wildfire. The lieutenant general of police was not pleased, knowing very well that the truth would be hard to find, all the more so because of the public's anxiety to find it, and their eagerness to give their own versions of the facts. Saint-Florentin, secretary of state, confessed in a letter to Lieutenant General de Sartine that 'I am persuaded that if it [the incident] had been known only to us two, we should soon find out the truth, but there are too many people taking an interest in it.'

Faced with such a plethora of rumours and quests for the truth, the police sent their observers, as usual, out into the capital to get a better idea of 'what troubles people's minds and impresses them with different ways of thinking'. From the moment when it could be hinted that the king's life was in danger, it became urgent to know people's reactions, and if necessary to influence them. The police took their task seriously. First, an informer was dispatched to a café on the corner of the Rue du Jour and the Rue Saint-Honoré, a habitual resort of 'a quantity of merchants dealing in cloth, fine stuffs and silks'; then he was to go to a cabaret where surgeons met, and in the afternoon to a café in the Rue de la Verrerie frequented by men of law. Meanwhile Inspector Framboisier went off to listen to conversations in the gardens and promenades, and Damotte stalked the suburbs. They all found the same thing: 'Everyone tells the story as he knows it, and everything remains perplexing, amidst a silence interspersed with "buts" and "Oh my Gods" ... "they are being very rash" ... "it's a great pity that those people have not been arrested" – words which, in the way they are spoken, show grief and anxiety.' There was a wealth of evidence that the populace was really upset. On the other hand, the inspectors and informers were surprised to find such a variety of discourse, so that every individual had his own idea of what had happened and immediately broadcast it: 'Everyone reports the adventure in many different ways'; 'Many of the versions are so different from one another that it is impossible to establish how the affair happened'; 'This story has already gone through more than a hundred editions.' Inspector Delahaye, watching some very well-attended cafés, summed up the situation well in his report to the lieutenant general: 'Everyone tells the story as he thinks fit, following the first notions he has heard; nobody knows how the affair came about, or rather it is told in so many ways that one does not know what to believe.'

This multiplicity of accounts irritated the police authorities because it made the people insecure. The widespread rumours impelled the judges to act with extreme severity: by a parliamentary decree of 1 February 1762, La Chaux was condemned to death by hanging. The poor royal guard had merely sought to draw attention to himself, hoping that his subterfuge (a fictional fight with other guards whom he accused, equally falsely, of intending to kill the king) would bring him some favours and improvements in his pension which he had not managed to obtain hitherto. A few months earlier this had given him the idea of wounding himself with a knife and putting it about that he had received the blows from the king's would-be assassins. If it was a grave crime to spread the idea that the king's death was a possibility (an eventuality which should not even have arisen in anyone's mind), one reason was the fear that the populace would think themselves into an attitude threatening their devotion to the king. In fact, the parliamentary decree used this argument when pronouncing sentence: 'All these facts, capable of giving the king some alarm over the love of his subjects, and his subjects over the safety of his sacred person, have given rise to the gravest of rumours and have disturbed public tranquillity.'[24]

What did people really think of this singular occurrence? From the police dossiers, taken together, there emerge three more or less distinct attitudes. Some people made an immediate connection with Damiens and his assault. The link was all the clearer in that the accident had happened on the festival of the Three Kings, 'recalling the awful memory of the execrable and abominable assault committed on the sacred person of the king'; and they told that the bodyguard was in fact the man who had first 'laid hands on the unhappy Damiens, for which His Majesty granted him a pension'.[25] This experience, they said, had encouraged La Chaux to invent some further way of drawing attention to himself and increasing his pension.

A second group preferred to believe that there had merely been a quarrel between the royal guards and two private persons in a tavern. The two private persons wanted to see the king 'at his dinner', and the guard, tipsy and quarrelsome, had fought both at the same time.

A third view was also current in street and cabaret: 'The two strangers are probably envoys of some sect which should be cut off root and branch' – meaning that well-known 'sect' of Jesuits with whom the Church was in violent conflict.

Each version followed its own logic. The first fed on the memory of Damiens and his assault, without believing for a minute that the king had really been threatened. The second put all the blame on tavern quarrels in the town of Versailles, and here again nobody felt the slightest anxiety for the king. Only the more politically-minded thought it opportune to arouse passions by accusing the two private persons of being Jesuits 'seeking the death of the king'.

Some informers reported hearing that Jesuits were traitors who could not be trusted; here we are back in a Jansenist atmosphere. Supporters of the Jesuits, unhappy with this rumour, feared for the future of the Society of Jesus, especially when people heard that one of the private persons, as he struck the guard, had cried 'We must strike the guard of the oppressor of religion and the people!'

Opinions, then, followed a logical schema: all were plausible, or at least they contained some morsels of reality. As the truth remained obscure, people ordered their thoughts according to what they knew: it might be a memory (Damiens), everyday events in society (a tavern brawl) or a political situation (the combat between the monarchy and the Jesuits). The authorities did not like such competing interpretations, whose ramifications they found hard to trace. Despite the numbers of informers at work, it was hard to establish just how widespread the rumours were, and the authorities took fright at the variety of tales being told. They thought that a trifling adjustment would make them downright dangerous, and that public order was threatened when politics was stirred into the brew. Now that the story had 'gone through one hundred editions' it was time to make an end: La Chaux was executed because he had, in a way, 'touched the king', but more because his act had drawn the populace into hazardous conjectures which threatened the stability of the monarchy.

4

Motifs

Popular opinion – mobile, fragmented, readily adjusting to circumstances as shifting as itself – was never short of a motif on which to graft its more vivid imaginings. Some of these motifs are very easy to detect; their themes can be isolated from written or manuscript sources. Some perennial preoccupations would always feed or duplicate a conversation: the price of bread, the filth in the streets, the more or less amiable looks of king or queen when they visited Paris. There were also lesser anxieties which could retain attention, or occasions for astonishment which excited chatter, the thousand and one curiosities which offered themselves daily to a Parisian eye. Opinion veered now towards the probable, now towards the fabulous, unveiling one mystery, believing the next wholesale. There were exciting moments which broke through the day-to-day monotony and diverted the course of discussion and thought, rending the fabric of ordinary news and inserting unexpected distortions into the rents. Riots, for example, knocked the times off balance, and there were many in the eighteenth century. No one riot was like the next, though it might recall the last; each one had its own face, its own motifs, expressions, modes of improvisation which gave rise to new gestures, new discourse, new stories. Riots were fleeting events, holes in time; sometimes the hole closed up quickly and it was possible to believe that everybody was going on as before – which was both true and false.

The motifs which set people talking were linked to the twists and turns of the event. They existed alongside one another, or one without the other, reducing into varied structures whose logic could be mutually contradictory, or mutually supportive. The circulation of gossip did not follow a long, progressive and linear chain of 'reasons' leading up to a cut-off point in 1789; those 'reasons' were themselves fault lines, discontinuities whose every sequence could produce some instant in which people could plant the insistence of their speaking, and glimpse the future course of a discourse which would deviate from what they were currently hearing. Nor was there any necessary logical order in the enumeration of those motifs; they are better described singly, in the disorder they wittingly or unwittingly created, and in all the contradictions which opened on possible shifts, however minimal, in the patterns of discourse. It was these microscopic variants that could produce a moment of autonomous judgement or analysis. We must not be reluctant to pay attention to short, apparently unimportant sequences. From them came reorganization, new practices, new thoughts.

The traditional objects of popular concern

Parisians divided their thoughts between two antagonistic universes. These could conveniently be called their own, and that of the Other. Their own was the world of everyday, the sphere they walked in and tried to live in: the street, their daily bread, the law's delays. Opposite, and just as absorbing though inaccessible, was the brilliant, yet opaque, sphere of the monarch, that spectacular universe which was supposed to regulate their own.

The universe of the everyday

Before examining the social problems which occupied the population, we must say a word about the mysteries and prodigies which solicited their attention, and then describe that contradictory eighteenth-century atmosphere of belief and superstition mingling with Enlightenment.

Prodigies, catastrophes and singularities No journal, chronicle, police report or even news-sheet could omit those thousand facets of reality which would surprise a populace with an appetite for unexplained mysteries, for unusual and improbable happenings on which to base their reasonings and their dreams. This remained true throughout the century: mysterious lights in the sky, the passage of comets, monstrous births, the king's sons disguised in rags, were eagerly discussed. People marvelled, then trembled; rationalization was mingled with belief in a disquieting cosmology. At every opportunity they contemplated the amazing works of nature – and then went on to explain them from a multiplicity of causes among which God rubbed shoulders with science and Satan. Sometimes the explanation was political, as when a monster was glimpsed in a Venetian canal, bellowing horribly. Buvat, writing in April 1716, attributed its presence 'to the armament of the Turks, which is said to be of 800,000 men, with a fleet of 200 sail intended to attack Venice, Corfu and Hungary'.[1] If the explanation of the mystery seemed unsatisfactory, people would wait for something else. On 20 October 1726, Barbier tells us that:

> Yesterday there appeared, at about 9 o'clock in the evening, a phenomenon which lasted until two hours after midnight. This was a considerable area of the heavens all of white fire, which seemed to open into two arcs, and from it came very bright and agitated rays. The gentlemen of the Observatory have furnished an explanation, but it greatly astonished the people of Paris, who are consequently awaiting some great event.[2]

Science was not always convincing. In 1771 there were meteors, which were found no more reassuring than those mysterious lights seen earlier in the century, and the thunder of their passing left people trembling: 'This phenomenon', says Hardy, 'alarms and disquiets a great number of people.'[3] A year later people were looking to religion (rather than to science or politics) for help when the rumour spread in Paris that two comets had met and that this collision would have fearful repercussions.

> Everyone was saying that, in consequence of these rumours, the confessionals had been much fuller at Saint-Sulpice and Saint-Germain-l'Auxerrois than during the fortnight of Easter [it was now 15 May 1773], and (they said) it had been noticed, especially at Saint-Sulpice, that a very large number of persons had gone up to the Lord's Table.

Hardy, the narrator, grumbles at these acts of piety, which seem to him quite uncalled-for: 'a dubious motive which, alone and of itself, will produce scarcely more than a few ephemeral confessions and illusory repentances which are almost always fruitless, because they are not, as one might say, embraced except by force and in spite of oneself.'[4]

There were other strange pieces of news which were not commented on, but accepted as true without further question: 'A young girl at the Hôtel-Dieu gave birth to a daughter who had a turban on her head, without eyes and without a nose, the body well proportioned, but she lived only two days.'[5] This abbreviated lifespan reduced the event to normality: a newborn baby with a turban was not a long-lasting stimulus to laughter.

It was hard to know what to say about the exemplary stories which embellished the news-sheets and invited the reader to identify with the adventures of unfortunates unexpectedly succoured by Providence.

> All the public prints have spoken of a young man aged between ten and twelve, deaf, dumb and a foundling; this unfortunate lad, having experienced all the miseries incidental to indigence and his own unhappy situation, was brought down to the Hôtel-Dieu, where he was employed in the vilest of tasks; and by chance, guided by Providence and seconded by the edifying charity of Monsieur the Abbé de l'Epée, has been recognized as the son of the Marquis de Solar who is in the service of France; this child was abandoned about four years ago on the highway by the order of his dead mother; since when, unable to make himself understood and pressed by the most urgent need, one cannot express all the sufferings of this young man; thanks to the talent which Monsieur the Abbé de l'Epée has for making the dumb speak, we shall discover through him what treachery was used against him to cause his ruin.[6]

If an abbé could make the dumb speak, it might be that every Cinderella was really a beautiful princess ...

Beliefs and superstitions   Under this heading I shall merely indicate, with a few examples, how the public reacted to situations which evoked belief in the supernatural, or when they were surrounded by individuals anxious to offer the 'help' of magic and sorcery.

'Beliefs' may be quite remote from 'superstitions', or alternatively the two may exhibit some striking convergences. The eighteenth century offers some intriguing examples, mingling the power of reason with a lingering climate of superstition.[7] According to Paul Ricoeur, the action of believing 'is a mental attitude of acceptance or assent'; but he adds that 'the word "belief" has been uncomfortably spreadeagled between opinion, appreciated negatively in an epistemological and ontological system which puts it on the bottom rung of values; and faith, appreciated positively in a basically religious value system.'[8] 'Spreadeagled' is certainly the right word; and in the eighteenth century the best-educated often tried to clarify the differences between faith, belief and superstition. Unless even the best-educated found the question embarrassing, and took up a critical or malicious attitude towards it ...

A cult unique to Paris, which is often referred to in the archives, shows the subtle interplay within this idea of belief, especially when it was favoured by Church and State: this is the regularly maintained cult of Saint Geneviève.[9]

Geneviève[10] died in the early sixth century and was buried on the hill of Lutetia, which was later renamed the Mont Sainte-Geneviève. On the same spot, Clovis founded a basilica dedicated to Saints Peter and Paul.

It soon became a centre of pilgrimage; miraculous cures took place and drew the crowds. But in 857 the canons fled with the saint's relics for fear of marauding Vikings. They returned in 873 and restored the basilica. In 1130 there was a fearful epidemic which went down in history as the 'burning evil' (mal des ardents). The bishop of Paris solemnly invoked Saint Geneviève's help against the scourge, and the epidemic miraculously ceased. The event was celebrated in Paris every 26 November. In the eighteenth century, the canons built a new basilica; during the French Revolution it was to become the Panthéon. Amid the fever of revolution, the saint's relics were to be burned.

As well as the annual commemoration on 26 November, there were some special occasions, appointed by the monarchy at times of public calamity, on which the reliquary of Saint Geneviève was carried in procession. Official publications are quite clear about this, especially Delamare's Traité de la police.

> It is a custom almost as ancient as the monarchy itself to have recourse to Saint Geneviève in all public calamities . . . the first of these processions was arranged in 857 to induce God to raise the siege which the Northmen had laid to Paris.
> In all the public calamities which have afflicted France since that day, that powerful protection has been invoked, and the effects have always been prompt, perceptible and miraculous. They had been felt mostly in time of war, famine, crop failure, flood and collective or contagious malady. It is for the parlement to judge when it is necessary to make the appeal. The archbishop of Paris then gives the orders for everything pertaining to the spiritual side, and the magistrate of police immediately adds his contribution, making sure that everything which takes place outdoors and in public is done with the decency and calm suited to so great an action.[11]

The solemn procession was initiated by the monarch; the parlement decided whether or not it was necessary in disquieting circumstances which seemed to pose a threat to the people and to public safety. Only later did the archbishop of Paris make his contribution, organizing the liturgical and spiritual aspects of the event. The lieutenant of police was left with the stern task of ensuring that the public celebrations went off well. The ordering of the procession was exceedingly complex and gave rise to an abundant literature.[12] The procession was held twice in the eighteenth century: in 1725, by decree of the Cardinal de Noailles during a period of continuous and catastrophic rain, and in 1765, when the dauphin, already very ill, developed an abscess on the lung.[13] Did it work? In 1725, if we are to believe Barbier, the rain stopped.

> Nothing more fell save a few drops of water, and as the wind was blowing very strongly, the road was dry . . . One must acknowledge that

the weather has changed entirely since the procession. There was a new moon, it is true; but it had gone on raining through all the previous new moons.[14]

In 1765, a few days after the procession – the dauphin died.

Besides the general processions decreed when the monarch felt that the peace might be disturbed by some external event, Saint Geneviève was in great demand for many other purposes. On such occasions it was not necessary to parade the reliquary, but only (for example) to 'discover' it and call for public prayers; thus, in 1721, when Louis XV had recovered from an illness, Buvat recounted (with an abundance of detail) what happened on 3 August when the reliquary was 'discovered' in the church.

In 1775 things were not so simple: discovering the reliquary did not prevent Louis XV from dying. And Bachaumont tells the following story:

They say that Monsieur the Abbé of Sainte-Geneviève being at dinner in a house where there was a large company, some young men met with him and badgered him about the saint, whose power seemed wholly vain that day ... He let them talk, and when they had finished their reproaches, 'Well, Sirs!' he answered, 'What is your complaint against heaven? Is he not dead?'[15]

One could refer to other occasions on which the monarch decided to refer matters to the saint, maintaining a very ancient tradition while at the same time securing an effective means of control over a population which could be dangerous if it erupted. But this popular veneration for Geneviève, normally under the due control of the monarchy, could sometimes turn against it. In 1740, France, including Paris, was hit by a severe famine; people gathered in diverse places and murmured against the king. On 30 May the situation got worse, and things took an awkward turn which was duly reported by police observers.

It is said that Saint Geneviève has appeared in the form of a young girl in the church dedicated to her at Nanterre; that this appearance took place during Mass and after the consecration; that the priest who was saying Mass asked some questions of the supposed Saint Geneviève to which she answered that God was infinitely angry ... People are also reporting an appearance of the saint before the vicar such that the said saint supplemented the speech she made to the general by adding that God is angry with the king, with Monsieur the Cardinal de Fleury and in general with almost all bishops and other churchmen because they are infringing the law; as for the minister, unless he ceases to persecute the elect of God, his wrath will not be appeased ... You may be assured that although those who present such strange notions are described as mad-men, this does not stop them being discussed in all public places.[16]

Here, Geneviève, normally subservient to the royal will, obeys the will of the people and rebels against the monarch who is usually the one to invoke her. The world is upside down; in their anger, the people of Paris take over Saint Geneviève and hurl her in the face of the king. Normally it was the other way round.

This made little difference as far as the saint's cult was concerned; it could get along without the king. Paris lived with Saint Geneviève and appealed to her on any number of occasions. People came to her asking to be cured of all kinds of fever, and the church was seldom empty. It offered a strange spectacle, men and women rubbing the shirt of a dear one against the reliquary so that the owner should be cured. While Barbier, though with a touch of scepticism, seems to believe in the saint's beneficence, Mercier rails with mordant irony against such practices, and especially against the rebuilding of the basilica.

> God forbid that I should mock at Saint Geneviève! Poor people come to rub sheets and shirts against the saint's reliquary ... the *échevins* [magistrates], the *parlement* and the other sovereign courts do indeed ask her for rain in times of drought and for the healing of princes! ... I have seen tears shed there. I have heard sobbing and sighing and at such moments I have respected this cult so suited to the vulgar and those of limited intelligence, and even better suited, perhaps, to their poverty ... They are building a magnificent church, to place this reliquary under a superb dome which will soon be costing 12 to 15 million or even more. What an enormous, unnecessary expenditure of money which could have been used to allay the poverty of our people! ... The curious will go and see the architecture, and the populace the saint ... The bones of Descartes rest in the old Temple; will they now be lodged not far from the miracle-working reliquary? What a combination, Saint Geneviève and Descartes side by side! They may be conversing in the other world; what will they be saying of this one? But the humble Descartes has no reliquary![17]

Descartes and Saint Geneviève side by side: it was one of the problems being faced by the men of the Enlightenment. Bachaumont, for example, writing in 1770 in his secret *Memoirs*, expressed astonishment at the way in which persons possessed by demons were healed, year after year, in the Sainte-Chapelle, and wondered anxiously whether the cures were 'true' or 'false', without reaching any satisfactory answer.

> Unbelievers claim that these obstreperous individuals are beggars who have been paid to play the part, and are being used as cat's-paws. But one can scarcely believe that ministers of religion would lend themselves to so

unfitting a charade. At the very most, perhaps, faced with a shortage of genuinely possessed persons, they may have had recourse to such a pious stratagem so as not to disturb the credulity of the faithful, as would happen if a miracle which has endured for so many centuries and is so well suited to confirm them in their faith – now being shaken in so many ways – [were to cease]. Happily, possessed persons are so common that it is probably not necessary to concoct bogus ones.[18]

Bachaumont cannot believe, believes a little, doubts, cannot doubt. The frontier between beliefs and superstitions was not very visible, and the distinction was hard to make in practice. Indeed, the new practice of scientific advance only made it more difficult: was it outlining the truth or delineating an area of probability in which error might grow? If superstition is indeed 'a collection of practices and beliefs . . . incompatible with an achieved level of theological and scientific knowledge',[19] then in the eighteenth century it was very hard to fence it off from the fields of religion and truth. In any case, neither Church nor monarchy found it in their interests to make the distinction over-clear. However, they took measures against the excessively credulous and fought against the large numbers of tricksters who were always ready to take advantage of naivety on either side.

An edict of July 1682, signed at Versailles by Louis XIV, Colbert and Le Tellier, had solved (after a fashion) the problem of identifying witchcraft, denying the existence of diabolical pacts and witches' sabbaths. The only things that counted were sacrilegious acts and the use of poisons. As Robert Mandrou says,

> Thus, diviners, magicians and enchanters were all one and the same family of illusionists who lead astray the credulous. The edict set up a clear gradation among them: as exploiters of ignorance, they deserved neither the rope nor the whip but, at worst, banishment; if they were duly convicted of sacrilege or poisoning, they were subject to the death penalty.[20]

In fact, the archives of the Bastille, of the police and of other prisons contain a goodly number of trials of poisoners, treasure-seekers, fortunetellers and bogus magicians. The trials are long and ramifying, with lengthy and repetitive interrogations by commissionaries who specialized in such difficult cases – Commissioner Rochebrune, for example. Often the trial records are preceded by expressions of indignation: the dossiers contain numerous notes by police or *intendants* trying to work out why so much trickery was so easily accepted and even sought after by the populace. Treasure-seekers, for example, remained wildly popular throughout the century. For a long time the people of Paris had believed that large amounts of treasure were buried underneath royal mansions such as the Louvre, the Tuileries and their outbuildings.[21] Many individuals put their trust in people who promised – for a consideration – to help them find those long-buried secrets, and poured their faith and fortune into curious practices which combined prayers, nocturnal excavations and summoning of spirits with straightforwardly fraudulent transactions. Some wrote learned tomes allowing speedier access to the undiscoverable treasures; others engaged in evil dealings, swearing over a woman's womb that the child-to-be would know all secrets. 'Dinot had made her drunk after making her pregnant and having hoisted up her petticoats had put a large stone on her womb, telling her that it was a spirit taking possession of the child she was carrying ...'[22]

In these dossiers, the trial records and the interrogations, the answers and comments by the police bring us into a world of contrasts. The police, while apparently sure of themselves, do not seem to be totally immune from the fascination of all these practices; their questions and investigations betray how they were drawn into the mysterious twilight zone between the diabolical and the merely crafty. Even if the devilish practices they detected were set down as 'follies' ('It can be seen from her papers that she had diverse secret remedies of which some belong to the folly which is called witchcraft'),[23] they seem taken aback to find secret remedies being used which apothecaries, summoned as expert witnesses, did not necessarily seem to reject, and concerning which they conclude, with excess of prudence, 'Thus all drugs can be good or bad, depending on the good or evil genius of the artist.' We are in a divided world: the police want to root out trickery but do not always know whether the devil is or is not really lurking on its fringes; some in the higher echelons of society are not too happy to see the devil sent packing, in case God goes with him; the tricksters have no scruples, and some individuals are conquered by their own credulity, victims swayed between plain silliness and a willingness to accept supernatural explanations which compensate for their lack of grip on a difficult world. The dossiers of pretended sorcerers provide material for some interesting reflections on systems of popular thought in the eighteenth century. Despite their apparently simple structure (investigation, trial, punishment), they do not really give the impression of a dual universe, with the learned – police and philosophers – working towards the eradication of credulity among the poor. On the contrary, they delineate an ambiguous universe with no inherent certainties, in which each person uses the nebulous opacity of deception to give meaning to his own world vision. All in all, 'superstitious people' were perhaps not quite as superstitious as is sometimes believed; the 'wise and prudent' nursed strange fears of the

Evil One, striving to drive him out of reasoning minds which were still imbued with his presence.

Of course, there were cases which everyone had a clear opinion about: cases such as the priest Gobart de Mainville and his sister, denounced as fortune-tellers in November 1705. The informer left no doubt as to the situation on both sides.

> Sir,
> Your efforts to purge the city of Paris of persons exercising themselves in ways prejudicial to the public weal, and in particular abusing religion and the sacraments to entrap the weak-minded by feigned devoutness and magic, oblige zealous persons to give you due warning about certain people of that character.
> There is, Sir, at the Montagne Sainte-Geneviève, a young person named Mainville who claims to be related to the king of England, who for more than twenty years has had dealings with spirits, and when the emissaries have found someone curious to know readers of horoscopes, they take him to her; first she judges the fate of people by their physiognomy and then by drawing numbers, and she gives answers using one key striking against another, and her brother, a priest, does it with a ring tied to a piece of string, which he calls a talisman.[24]

There was a plethora of 'simple' stories of that type, and an equal number of people who assumed disguises the better to deceive their clientele. Here is another abbé (there were a good many abbés skipping nimbly over the boundaries between piety and impiety), accused of illegal salt-making and spell-working. His appearance was rather disquieting: 'He has a reversible coat: on one side it is of leather with copper buttons, and on the other side of black stuff with black buttons, so that he can disguise himself as he feels inclined, and brown breeches in which he hides a good many things.'[25]

It was relatively simple to detect such ruses, and when the deception became visible, it effaced all possibility of believing what the trickster said. But there were cunning folk whose discourse slid imperceptibly from piety into magic, leaving people in a state of uncertainty, unable to detect the exact moment when the slippage took place. Getting hold of a few morsels of truth was a lengthy process. Jack Cochon, who led a hand-to-mouth existence at Châtillon, gave proof of uncommon powers of persuasion when, in 1754, he passed himself off as a wizard. The police had difficulty with this clever man and his extensive clientele, as is shown by a marginal note:

> This man is all the more dangerous in that he does not lack wits and is capable of deceiving simple folk who are not secure in the principles of

religion. He orders prayers and Masses before working his spells so that his operations appear at first under a cloak of piety and do not frighten timid souls, and he induces them by imperceptible degrees to agree to consult the spirit.[26]

Demonic possession presented other problems. In this case, talk of trickery meant relegating God to a distance which was unacceptable to many people. Stories and trials concerning possession betray an element of doubt, and belief, religious faith and suspicion of imposture rode side by side with no clear division between them. Between 1730 and 1738, again in the diocese of Bayeux, at Landes, there was a case of possession in which well-born young girls all exhibited extraordinary symptoms. An anonymous document in the Bibliothèque de l'Arsenal[27] gives a critical account:

> We have seen learned men of the first order be as credulous as children ... There is a conviction, shared by many people, that to disbelieve in possessions and spells is to make an attack on religion ... People have insisted that the devil must be the author of all things envisaged as marvellous which could not be attributed to God.

Having thus made things quite clear, the account bends round a little and refuses to stand foursquare with the Enlightenment:

> If the sciences were an obstacle to superstition, and a certain resource against fanaticism, would we have seen (as we have seen), in an enlightened century, possessed monsters appear with such audacity and find such a great number of defenders?

After several detours, the author asks himself if this may be a case of imposture, then ends his account by inveighing against both the devout and the unbelieving.

In this climate of conflict between faith and reason, supernatural happenings assumed a major importance, and Parisians were constantly brushing with charlatans and cheats all willing to deal with their problems, their lovesicknesses and their desire to live in prosperity to the age of 500 years.[28] The monarchy and the Church strove to stem the tide of popular error.[29] Too much blind enthusiasm for charlatans might make the population dangerous; the processions and festivals of Saint Geneviève were an outlet for the flood of popular fervour among those seeking relief from their anxieties. Witchhunting was an important element in the policy of repression. It had a double aim: dishonest rogues had to be punished, and public credulity must be channelled and religion safeguarded. It was hard to keep the balance, and the evidence given by victims of charlatans clearly shows the reasons for believing in sorcery: the philosopher's stone offered money; there were remedies for any illness anyone might have; there were elixirs for a quick abortion. Moreover, the evidence shows how neighbours collaborated by giving or asking for addresses. We can also make out how rural beliefs penetrated into Paris through migration. It was quite common for someone to fall victim to a deception when returning to his own village in search of remedies he had heard of in his childhood.

The eighteenth century made great efforts to reduce to a minimum belief in these unreliable inventions, which left room for the grossest of prejudices. The persecution of treasure-seekers, rascally pedlars of the philosopher's stone, summoners-up of devils, is an echo of the mental outlook of the educated elite who saw credulity as one of the most characteristic traits of the lower classes. The fight against error, against the undiscerning credulity of ordinary people, was based on a well-established conviction: that the populace, ignorant and uneducated, always latched on to anything that was put in front of them, and could never tell truth from falsehood. This disposition induced them to adopt attitudes which could be dangerous for the city. If magical practices and sorcery could be combated, the populace might be obliged to believe essentially in what the Church and the king presented to them as being worthy of faith and truth.

Poverty, insecurity, police and punishment

The populace complained regularly about rising prices and the shortage of bread, to which they had become extremely sensitive; everyone was constantly debating the 'poverty of the times' (an expression which comes again and again from the pens of policemen, defendants and writers), deploring it, crying out against it, pillorying whomever they held responsible. Some years were harsher than others, but the police reports show that even outside periods of crisis the theme was obsessively present: 'The discourse of the people turns only on the poverty of the times';[30] 'It seems to me that poverty is growing from day to day according to the continual complaints which are heard in every café, and all conversations turn on it';[31] 'They say that the countryside is in ruins, there is talk of poverty and bankruptcy';[32] 'They say that the flour is bad.'

The authorities were worried by such inflammatory rumours, and tried to warn the king of the dangers attendant on poverty. In 1739, the chief overseer of the Cour des Aides communicated to the king his anxiety about the grumbling against the rise in the price of bread and the man held responsible for it: Hérault, lieutenant general of police, who was thought to have put prices up so as to pay his daughter's dowry.

> Sire, the sound of the trumpet has just spoken to us of peace, but mean-while Your Majesty's subjects are languishing without bread and without money, reduced in many provinces to sharing or disputing their food with the beasts of the field. The luxury enjoyed by military suppliers is an insult to public poverty and anxiety.[33]

Time made little real difference to this state of affairs; one of the best witnesses from the second half of the century, Hardy, often spoke of penury and the Parisians' indignant reactions to it. In 1768, for example, the district commissioners were enjoined to distribute alms to those who were too hard hit by poverty, whole seditious and anonymous placards covered the walls of central Paris with calls to revolt; there were even threats to set fire to the whole city, and the king was accused of being solely responsible for the scourge: 'At the present time the dearness of bread cannot be attributed either to war or to a real shortage of corn, but [to the fact that] there was no king, because the king had turned corn merchant.'[34]

The placard war continued in this vein for more than a year; every time they were 'relieved' with care by guards and archers, they were stuck up again, elsewhere and in a different form, in the same night. Take for example the night of 11/12 September 1770, after which Paris awoke to these words, exhibited in several places: 'If the price of bread is not diminished and the affairs of the state are not set in order, we shall know *very well* what course to take.'[35] Worse still, a tree outside the Palais-Royal was found to be decorated by a portrait of Mme du Barry 'over which they had placed a bundle of rods and the letter V'.

Such restlessness and such throat-catching poverty were ever-present, for the poverty was endemic; the smallest upset in the weather, in politics or in economics could inflame and increase it, embittering peo-ple's minds so that they were constantly on the look-out for those responsible.[36]

This 'evil of the times' gave rise to a good number of consequences. Beggars were becoming intolerable, and police regulations intended to get rid of them sometimes led to decisions so repressive that they fomented yet more disorder. Not only did the populace rebel against arrests of beggars, but the prisons were crammed to bursting point and turned into breeding grounds for the gravest sedition. In 1720, after the infla-tionary effects of Law's economic policy and the repressive decision to export prisoners to populate the Mississippi, the prison of the priory at

Saint-Martin-des-Champs went up in flames, along with other places of detention in the city. Similarly, in 1740, a famine year, the prisoners in Bicêtre revolted against the reduction in the bread ration, which had brought hunger and serious diseases upon them.[37] Thirty years later, Hardy evoked some sinister festivities in the prison of the Conciergerie:

> In the prisons of the Conciergerie of the Palace, at about ten o'clock in the morning, there took place a kind of revolt that could only be calmed with the aid of a strong force of guards; two wardens and a soldier of the watch were dangerously injured. The lack of good bread and impatience to be brought to trial, together with ill-treatment by some of the wardens, were (so it is said) the principal causes of this revolt. It seems it was a sort of sinister festivity . . .[38]

The populace generally took a lenient view of such revolts; prison, like the hospital, was a familiar place to Parisians, who knew well enough that some day or other they might easily find a 'welcome' there. They were immediately and profoundly sympathetic, as always in cases of suspected injustice. Rebellion against excessively severe punishment was common, even at the beginning of the century, as two examples will show. In 1720, one of the lackeys of M. d'Erlach, captain of the Swiss guard, was paraded in public before being sent to the galleys. He had been insolent to his mistress. A sizeable crowd, estimated at some 5000 or 6000 persons, wrested him from the stake to which he had been attached, and the upheaval lasted all day. In the evening it was found that five or six people had been killed during skirmishes which had brought out more than 200 archers of the watch.

In 1723, the populace made a threatening demonstration before the prison of For-l'Evêque, where the authorities, wishing to transfer a prisoner from one room to another, met with total and fierce resistance. The prisoner threatened the archers of the watch sent to remove him by force. The king's procurator and the *lieutenant criminel* decided to have him killed, then put his corpse on trial. Paris was astonished but also angry, and Marais commented in his journal:

> The *lieutenant criminel* and the king's procurator are much censured . . . he could have been tried as a rebel, but he ought not to have been killed, and no one has the power of life and death over the king's subjects. But the officers and archers, accustomed to blood, had no respect for a man's life, and they ought to pay dearly for it.[39]

The populace, always faced with insecurity, a prey to thieves, cheats and pickpurses of every kind, reacted ambivalently. Of course they disliked being robbed, and they complained about the traffic in Paris and the noisy crowds among which ear-rings, handkerchiefs and tobacco-pouches could so easily disappear; and churches afforded no respite. But their reactions were muted if it meant going along with forms of police repression, punishments and public exhibiting of malefactors. There were many nuances to these attitudes, and not seldom was there a subtle interplay between forms of repression, stories about thieves' exploits which spread throughout the city and the lower orders' more or less confirmed habit of being sympathetic and admiring towards heroes who took on the powers-that-were in single combat – especially when it came to punishments and executions.[40]

The story of Cartouche shows how, between 1721 and 1728, police and populace played on the meaning of his criminal acts, and those of his innumerable accomplices.[41] There was much talk about Cartouche and his friends between 1715 and 1728: about their incessant evildoing, their gift of ubiquity and the impossibility of catching them. The dream came to an end in 1721, when Cartouche was arrested. Between 1721 and 1728 the populace was treated to a good many punitive exhibitions: executions, denunciations, trials of accomplices. Buvat, Marais and Barbier embellished their memoirs with long discourses about Cartouche and his gang; while tales spread, the events were acted out on the stage and in the streets, and the authorities disseminated discourses of their own.

Cartouche was highly visible, and so was the suppression of his gang; it regularly attracted public attention. Cartouche was the son of a Parisian cooper, who between 1715 and 1721 controlled a network of swindlers and fences, some three hundred in all. It was enough to worry anybody, including the police authorities, already alarmed by the collapse of Law's system (with its serious consequences for small shopkeepers), and by the difficult economic crisis following the end of the War of the Spanish Succession (1700–14). Cartouche's gang, which was fairly representative of society as a whole (it included a number of artisans, labourers and innkeepers), chose to fight against impoverishment by means of theft and the receipt of stolen goods. The gang had so many ramifications that it represented (or so it has been said) 0.5 per cent of the population of Paris. As Lüsebrink rightly remarks, 'This proves that the people's interpretation of the idea of "crime" was out of step with the official meaning given by the law and the judicial institutions.' Thus we can no longer really talk about radically criminal behaviour, nor of marginality; rather, people accepted, almost as natural, reprehensible acts committed in everyday life by perfectly ordinary people. In the confused world of the suburbs and the cabarets, the populace amicably received the receivers of stolen goods!

The police developed a strategy. Rather than coming to grips with a certain element in the population of Paris that impoverishment had made at home with theft and crime, they preferred to stigmatize all such acts, impute them to a gang, and give shape to that 'reality' by classifying it as menacing, dangerous and conspiratorial. The idea of a 'gang' carried an image which could produce fright and arouse rejection and vengeance. Thus the pursuit of Cartouche and his 'gang' would engage all the resources of the police, and the trials would arouse all the terrors inherent in the most exemplary punishments. This zeal for the suppression of banditry was also an attempt to recreate a consensus which had been shaken by the disturbances in the *parlements*, the Law scandal and the Parisian uprisings of 1720.

If this police strategy was to work, it required the consent of the principal defendant, Cartouche himself. And Cartouche, having remained silent throughout the investigation of his case and even under torture, decided to talk at the last possible moment, at the foot of the scaffold. His confessions lasted for more than twenty-four hours, delayed the execution and implicated more than ninety people, giving an impetus to betrayal which inevitably destroyed all the forms of mutual loyalty by which their criminal activities were sustained. Cartouche's resolve, on the threshold of death, to bring down others – comrades or distant accomplices – must have been motivated in part by the desire to show the strength of an organization which had defied the police for so long. He also wanted to reveal publicly the rottenness of society and the strange relationships which had developed between certain poor people, policemen, members of the military and craftsmen in the service of a sort of natural delinquency – which had already become apparent among the great of this world and their financial activities, when the Law scandal broke. The ensuing multiple denunciations produced a sum total of 742 accusations and 329 individuals brought to judgement, most of whom were condemned to death.

Cartouche having held the stage for a time, it was the turn of the police to parade their trials and executions. Police and people were inseparable in this context, and it was undoubtedly the former who began the process that turned Cartouche into a hero. This is attested by the interrogation of a defendant, Jean-Pierre Balagny (known as 'Capuchin'), aged twenty, an apprentice gilder.

> That in one of the rooms in the prison of the Grand Châtelet where there is a green bed, diverse actors suitably dressed came there and had all the accused brought in, questioned them and made them talk in their slang and made them walk in their usual way, exciting them to laugh, the king's procurator and the *lieutenant criminel* being present, pulled faces at them

and turned somersaults, and he helped the actors to make songs, and that
these actors kept giving him money. He thinks it was Master Legrand, the
actor, and his troupe, and that Master Le Comte, the *lieutenant criminel*,
burst out laughing when he heard the songs of Cartouche and said,
'Cartouche is sublime, if you do not count his crimes'; [that] the king's
procurator had bread and wine served by his lackeys to make them say
foolish things.[42]

This is confirmed by the chroniclers. A strange thing, that the police
themselves should ask for theatricals in a prison, turning the hero so
soon into a stage character, and the stage character into a hero. Theatre
and punishment were inseparable, as if there could be no punishment
save in the immense theatre of society. No sooner had the Cartouche
affair arisen than it became theatre, on the initiative of the very people
who denounced, persecuted and punished its protagonists. On the very
day of the execution it was acted out in a play called *Cartouche, or the
Robbers*. The delighted public wanted that drama of death to be staged,
and restaged.

The execution was a theatrical scene, a public performance, a spectacle available to all, but also a literary motif. In fact, it gave every
incentive to turn the victim into a hero. And it was the police who made
it so. Laments, poems, songs and stories spread rapidly from the very
day of Cartouche's execution (26 November 1721). The situations and
images which they included came from the traditional picaresque literature of the sixteenth and seventeenth century: Cartouche the king,
Cartouche the grandiose and terrorific bandit.

Though the whole process had been satisfactory – with the encouragement of the police and the co-operation of the accused and the
public at large – it was soon cancelled out, for not everyone perceived
its meaning in the same way. The police were worried by the spread of
printed accounts of Cartouche, for they glorified him far too much and
glossed over his abominable crimes; moreover, the glory went to simple
men who had used anonymity to keep themselves at a distance from
their enemies in authority.[43] The police were in danger of being robbed
of a hard-won victory, so they made distributing stories about Cartouche
into a crime. Distributors, street vendors, journeymen printers and pedlars
who sold the stories were arrested, and an official story was sold and
distributed which was supposed to frighten readers and bring out the
real moral in the history of the wicked Cartouche. This was the *Relation
véritable*, the authentic version. It emphasized the joy of society at being
rid of the thieves who had been poisoning social harmony.

But it was hard to control the effect of images which were flung at
the public, and in fact the populace had their own way of appropriating

myths, which did not necessarily accord with the way those myths had been peddled to them. Meanings could shift rapidly, especially as they were based on images of multiple significance.

In many texts, the name of Cartouche was the peg for a reflection on the causes of criminal behaviour and the legitimacy of hideous punishments. The *lieutenant criminel* had called the hero sublime, but in mockery; the populace, whose definition of sublimity was different, found him sublime in very truth.

At this particular period, the people did not actually intervene, but hijacked the meaning of something which had been roughly forced on them from above. This new meaning was based on their social and economic situation, and found space enough to give rise to vigorous criticism. Within a circle defined by police, defendants and the public, the police had tried to construct a meaning which balanced myth against the fear of myth; the public was minded rather to construct another meaning, in which myth was made to divulge the secrets of poverty and the misdeeds of the great.

King, court and princes: staging the Other

There is no subject who, from far or near, does not wish to have news of the court, and does not turn his eyes incessantly towards the king; he says to himself: who *is* this man who commands over 24 million men, in whose name all is done? All the pleasures of opulence surround him . . . what idea, from his elevated station, does he have of all that surrounds him? . . . We all employ ourselves in guessing what he is; in breathing (so to speak) the subtle emanations from the throne, to form conjectures which are almost always far-fetched.[44]

Everyone looked at the king, the monarch, his finery, his surroundings; everyone desired to know him, interpreted the signs he offered, sometimes meanly, sometimes generously – if not, at times, with trust or distrust. Chroniclers mocked at the popular enthusiasm for obtaining knowledge of or from king and court, as if they were oracles, and at people's lack of discernment concerning the king. Mercier notes with renewed amusement that 'The courtier follows him in the hunt, the soldier fights for him, the magistrate comes with remonstrances, the man of letters lies in wait for him, the philosopher laments for him, the people judge him by the price of goods.'[45] His judgement is more complex than can be understood from that one sentence: king, queen, princes and court were to Parisians an open book in which to read their hopes and their future.

Royal maladies were a cause of solicitude; they worried relatives,

imperilled the continuity of the reign, and caused anxiety to the populace, who were exhorted to pray when they came on and to rejoice
when they passed off. From childhood to adulthood, Louis XV had his
share of them: from 'king long-expected' to 'king of disappointment',
his health was often in question. By exploring this theme we can find
our way into the tangled skein of mechanisms for informing the public
and the attitudes which that public adopted. Police reports and news-
sheets offer a means of satisfying our curiosity over the manipulation of
public anxiety and the way the populace became aware of this.

In 1721 the king was a little boy; Paris adored him and 'waited'
expectantly for him. In 1721 the regent was vilified; after the Law
scandal, and because of the notorious debauchery of the court, pamphlets
– 'Philippics' – were circulated against him. In summer the little king fell
ill, causing consternation, but as August began Paris echoed with joy at
the news of his recovery. 'The shouting makes one dizzy,' said Barbier;
'The joy is unbelievable,' said Marais; 'One sees nothing but rejoicing,'
wrote Buvat. Truly, everyone was overcome with joy, and it was all
processions, illuminations, fireworks and *Te Deums*; cavalcades, dances,
'bourgeois and popular festivities' kept the city awake for several days.
There was shouting, drinking, rockets were set off and the people 'made
themselves a king', that is, paraded an effigy of him (one way of appropriating or making their own version of a king who had not yet
reached his majority and was eagerly awaited). The astonished chroniclers
stressed that such rejoicings had not been seen in living memory. It was
surprising to see how 'all estates and conditions of men' shared in the
public glee, bourgeois and poor folk expending prodigious amounts the
better to celebrate the event. The fishwives, who routinely played a big
part in official demonstrations, played a bigger part than usual: they
took carriages equipped with violins and bottles of wine, and went into
the Tuileries gardens to form long lines of dancers in front of the little
king's apartments. There was a crack in the fabric, however: it could be
seen (and heard) amidst all the dancing and the lights, for the regent,
it seems, was hated as much as the little king was fêted. The fishwives
cried, 'Long live the king, but to the devil with the regency!' At the
Palais-Royal they danced – while slapping their backsides and crying,
'That's for the regent!' When the regent entered Notre-Dame to celebrate
the *Te Deum*, there was an ominous and absolute silence. It was only
when the crowd saw the Maréchal de Villeroy, then governor to the
young Louis XV, that shouts broke out and lasted almost a quarter of
an hour, despite the pallor of the disconcerted regent.

The child once cured, a rumour soon arose and spread, causing no
anxiety but diffusing hatred. It gives an idea of why the regent was

unloved: Louis XV had probably been poisoned, and maybe by the regent himself . . . The anecdote was tantamount to a political analysis, as was often the case with stories and scandals. The rumour was taken up on every level of society; Marais and Buvat thought it had been fathered by the common people, while the Countess Palatine (mother to the regent) and Duclos,[46] in their *Memoirs*, tell of the endless precautions taken by the Maréchal de Villeroy to safeguard the little king's food, and of the incessant suspicion at court.

Poisoning was a familiar theme at the time, and it really happened. So, the crime was practised; but why should people have thought that the regent might have dabbled in it? Simple enough: he was interested in mechanics and chemistry, and in fact had a laboratory at court where he conducted experiments with the help of a Dutch chemist, son-in-law to the dauphin's doctor. Chemistry plus laboratory plus regent plus dauphin's doctor added up to quite enough to produce a rumour, orchestrated by Fénelon himself – Fénelon having sedulously suspected its existence ever since 1711–12, when the royal family suffered several bereavements.

In these conditions rumour, peddled by both great and small, could persist. It shows, and tells, how the people hoped in Louis XV and took vengeance on a regent whom they held responsible for poverty and increasing police harshness towards the poor and unemployed. It was a safe rumour: the populace could not be dismissed as naive when the great were also giving it credit. The (recent) Affair of the Poisons was there to help them. The motif was well established, and nourished a severe kind of public opinion.

In 1723, when the child again grew weak, the lieutenant general of police ordered his commissaries to go into every house in their district and tell the inhabitants that the king was out of danger. The commissioners' reports of these visits show the ostentatious personalization of the relationship between the king and his subjects, the wish to make the most of the 'advantages acquired' in 1721, meaning the people's love for their king.

In July 1726 there was another alarm: the king had a fever and a few spots on his face; the queen was very poorly. They both recovered, and the *parlement* had a *Te Deum* sung at the Sainte-Chapelle; fireworks lit up the city; the rejoicings, which were not particularly noisy, were disturbed by orders and counter-orders from the lieutenant general, but everyone felt involved and murmured 'that we are at the dawn of another great reign.'[47] Thus did they celebrate – and sacralize – their wait for a new king: it was punctuated by illnesses and recoveries.

In January 1729 the king was ill again – a slight anxiety which took on a shade of disappointment. Police inspectors garnered the Parisians' ill-tempered remarks.

> They say that it is his own fault, since he was taking no care of himself whatever; that it is, however, in the interests of the French people to have a king who will take more care of his health than Louis XV does. Others say that a man must value his life to the extent that he knows it is precious to him, and that it is not surprising if the king does not indulge in such reflections since he is still living like a young schoolboy.

It was a long wait. The king was not turning into a king, and bitterness was just beneath the surface. It was a long time since 1721.

In April 1744, at Metz, the king fell ill on his first visit to the front and the frontier, during the War of the Austrian Succession. The event was important for many reasons. It was at that precise moment that the feelings of the French towards Louis XV, henceforth to be called 'the Well-Beloved', reached their highest pitch; but at the same time a real disaffection from him was beginning. A detailed study of what happened between the king's departure for Flanders, his illness and his return to Paris will help us understand one of the roads of communication between the king and his subjects, and also show us the physiognomy of a public opinion which was attentive to the smallest detail and ready to emit a concerted and assured judgement on the king's conduct and affairs of state.

The year 1744 was an important turning point which was to puzzle people later on, as Mercier echoes in a few sentences:

> I saw the same king, who had been adored, die without a tear being shed. Was that the same people who had shown such enthusiasm for their monarch, who had made the vaults of the temples ring with sobbing and wailing to procure his recovery when he was ill at Metz? What had he done to deserve the earlier transports of feeling? What had he done to arouse feelings so wholly contrary? What was this man, now adored, now viewed with indifference?[48]

It is not necessarily to the man that we should look to find reasons for that alteration, but to a combination of situations and fact which produced first affection and then indifference.

There is a uniquely valuable source for what was subsequently to be called 'the episode of Metz': the news-sheets written by the Chevalier de Mouchy and kept in the archives of the Bastille.[49] Why are they to be preferred to Barbier's account in his *Journal*, or d'Argenson's, or the *Memoirs* of the Duc de Luynes or the Duc de Choiseul? Because Mouchy's news-sheets were designed initially for informing the police.

For this reason, they were later to become a principal source for official chroniclers. They show us how the police manipulated public opinion, and their minute and concerted examination of popular reactions to the event and those who gave information about it. They tell us the news, but also the news which was invented to influence the public; they tell of the bitterness of the lesser folk and their attempts to avoid being fooled by lying versions of what really happened.

Charles de Fieux, Chevalier de Mouchy, was born in Metz on 9 May 1701 into a noble but impoverished family.[50] He married a poor girl for love, and by the age of forty, with five children, he had to live by his pen, because he had no particular training. His pen was prolix and earned him a certain respectability, but also got him into a great deal of trouble. One example will suffice: in 1733, he wrote more than a dozen books on the most diverse subjects, but still could not meet all his family's needs. It was then that he decided to write news reports; and to eke out his narrative abilities, which were scarcely equal to those of an inferior novelist, he decided to profit from his own natural and insatiable curiosity by entering houses, great and small, to write his news-sheets. In 1741 came the first signs of trouble: one of his works, 'The Thousand and One Favours', was declared contrary to religion as soon as published, and Mouchy was sent to the Bastille for a month. The incarceration was short because Mouchy had succeeded in becoming an authorized newsmonger, that is, an informer with an official stipend.

He kept open house in his office, which was located on the Rue Saint-Honoré. There he was regularly visited by members of the public looking for news or bringing some echoes of Parisian street gossip – or sometimes a profitable 'advertisement'. His numerous subscribers received flysheets which had been, as was usual, corrected in advance by the police. Mouchy was a conscientious worker, an avid seeker-out of anecdotes of every kind who knew Paris inside out. Every day he wrote a long letter to the lieutenant general of police containing a careful résumé of his inquiries, conversations and political echoes which he had picked up here and there. He also passed on to the lieutenant all the critical remarks about the government and the conduct of military affairs. In fact, he was journalist and policeman in one, and zealous to boot. Despite his privileged position, in 1745 he got into fresh trouble for prevarication and grievous misdemeanours, and found himself in the Bastille for the second time. A few months later he was in exile in Rouen, whence he incessantly begged for liberty and permission to return to the capital. He dragged himself pitifully in the wake of Marville, the lieutenant of police, but was only restored to the police force much later, thanks to de Sartine. In 1763 he was again riding high, frequenting the circles around Bachaumont, whom he served as an informer. Bachaumont made frequent use of him; when he was being bothered by the police, he used Mouchy as a 'mole'.

Mouchy died in 1784, at the age of eighty-three. He and his operations are interesting for what they show about the way that authorized news and police information were combined. He gave his subscribers a normal service of news authorized by the police, but for a consideration he would also send copies of his secret reports, the ones intended only for the lieutenant general, to certain generals and high officers in the field. In return for services rendered, the secretaries of those officers would send him a detailed journal of military operations, and this was a godsend for his newsletters. The detail of these interchanges gives us a better understanding of the indistinct, underground way in which news-sheets were created, as secret reports intended for the police were sent to field-marshals who then sent more news to nourish the reports. Quite an imbroglio, in fact. The news-sheets for the years 1744 to 1748, concerning the king's illness, were intended for the police. Indeed, Mouchy had an authorized office at a well-known address, and was a police informer in any case. His writings give us glimpses of 'reality' across this double information level; we must not forget that his news would be used later as the raw material for chronicles and memoirs. This is the threefold reason why the chevalier's stories are something out of the ordinary.

In 1744 France entered the War of the Austrian Succession, and for the first time the king left for the front, to the great relief of his people who had been worried by his exclusive devotion to hunting. But not alone: he decided to take along his mistress, Mme de Châteauroux. In April he became seriously ill, provoking an immense wave of emotion throughout France which was prolonged and amplified by numerous ceremonies designed to induce heaven to bring about his recovery. After some hesitation, Bishop Fitzjames asked the king to expel his mistress publicly, so that he would not be in a state of sin when he received the last sacraments. The king agreed, which Mme de Châteauroux took as a fearful insult. Some time later, the king recovered; there was great rejoicing at the news; from that day forward, Louis was to be known as 'the Well-Beloved'. When his return to Paris was announced, in November, the joy first rose to a climax and then suddenly turned to dissatisfaction, for it was also announced that Mme de Châteauroux would be returning as royal mistress. Paris and her king were reunited amidst this atmosphere of intense disappointment. The king reacted with taciturn bitterness: he never again stayed in Paris, save for some one-day visits, and he kept himself as far as possible out of the Parisian eye.

How should we interpret attitudes to these successive events? Within a very short time (April to November 1744) a very strong relationship between king and people was forged and then broken. The phenomenon is worth attention. It was, in fact, a very mobile situation with many social characters: on to the stage came the king, his mistress, his councillors, the generals and marshals on the field of battle and an influential king's confessor. Moreover, ceremonies, speeches, prayers and commandments were combined into a policy intended to give the most impressive frame possible to the picture of the royal illness and recovery. To that we must add a news-hungry public avid for the smallest detail of that royal departure. Thanks to the news-sheets, we can discover what information that public had at its disposal, the means they used to keep up to date, the rumours which reached the capital and the reactions which were heard there day by day.

The attitude of the populace can be deciphered through a series of responses to events and ceremonial arrangements, and through their attitudes to something which occurred in the king's private life: his decision to take his mistress with him, followed by the episcopal decision to send her back again. Beyond the fear of losing the king another problem arose: could a king make love in time of war?

Mouchy's news-sheets follow the details from day to day with passionate interest and reflect the political conditions under which the information was transmitted. There is an evident desire to guide people's minds, and there is a closely woven network of discourse and prayer intended to create a common language in which subjects were to declare their unshakeable and universal faith in the king. But Mouchy, in his capacity as police informer, was also obliged to show, as it were in parallel, popular reactions which at times tried to constitute themselves outside that obligatory sphere. Otherwise he would have been useless to the police.

All in all, 1744 was an important year for Louis XV's reign: the moment which set a seal on the love between people and king, after a long wait, in between an interminable regency and a ministry which was to be oppressive. This was so evident that when, later on, it was thought necessary to revive the good relations between Louis XV and his subjects, 1744 was used as a fulcrum and a reminder. The joyful public mood of those days, the gratifying sobriquet 'Well-Beloved', were called to mind. Official reactions to Damiens' attempt on the king's life in 1757 looked back to the whole ceremonial sequence of 1744 in order to banish from simple minds the spectre of conceivably legitimate regicide. Discourse and strategic harping on memories would thus reconstitute a sort of popular unanimity, focused on the king, seamless and unchanging. It was then possible to write, 'The anxiety of the people is as great as in 1744, at the time of the king's illness.'

The good relationship between Louis XV and his people was forged with difficulty after a long period of euphoric expectation during the royal childhood. That childhood over, the people gained the conviction and 'sad opinion' that they were not beloved by the king. This state of things worried the police, and Mouchy informed them point for point. In 1722, the court returned to Versailles, and the king did not prove a regular visitor to Paris, while Fleury seemed to have acquired a bad influence over him. Louis XV, in retirement at Versailles, was far from living in public after the manner of his great predecessor; he was unapproachable, deserted the court, leaving the memory of his grandfather intact and fresh: absolutist the latter might have been, but he had always allowed his people some access to him. If the public wanted to 'see' Louis XV they had to be content with the military parades which took place twice a year on the plain of Les Sablons and at Le Vesinet, or with the occasional fleeting visit to Paris. Unhappily, on these various occasions Louis XV let scarcely anyone near him, and his guards kept the public firmly at a distance. Worse still, the king did not touch for the scrofula and did not take Communion.

Mouchy, ever attentive to popular opinion, ferreted out the signs of a change in attitude. He found them in the announcement of a public declaration of war on England and the royal determination to make the campaign an effective one: 'People are saying most positively', he wrote, 'that the king will go on the next campaign.' The image of the king going to war was a relief to everyone: at last he was in action, ready to enter upon one of the most essential activities of the monarchy, that of war.

> The news that His Majesty wishes to be present in person on every occasion when his enemies are to be combated has been received with much joy and assurance by public opinion; they are saying that acts of vigour and firmness are capable of spurring his nobles and his troops to prodigies of valour and the defeat of his enemies . . . These rumours have attracted the love of the people, who for some time had been most discontented.

The king's presence at the war was all the more striking in that the 1740s had seen a constant parallelling between the all-powerful image of Louis XIV and Louis XV, who did not shine in the comparison. The secret police reports were constantly repeating how all people in the cafés and the parks were sadly noting that the king was interested only in hunting, and was not taking the civil or military affairs of government in hand. Everywhere he was derisively nicknamed 'Louis the Pacific', or more mildly 'the Great Hunter'. Hunting was doubtless an important activity for a king, but it could only have real value in combination with the pleasures of war. Hunting was mimic warfare, it required war; without it, it demeaned both princes and kings. A warlike king was a strong king; Louis could not win a reputation for valour by chasing deer, especially as he was often accused of being rather cruel in the process. Such cruelty, exercised beyond the legitimate sphere of warlike exploits, destroyed the noble image of blood and war.

As soon as the king's presence in Flanders was announced, Mouchy started looking out for positive reactions, and offered the lieutenant of police a pretty turn of phrase intended to delight him: 'The king', he wrote, 'is on the brink of being much beloved.' It was an unsafe brink, and that potential joy was already mingled with some anxiety: already people were saying that Mme de Châteauroux might be leaving to accompany her royal lover to the front. This possibility, which was being everywhere discussed, disturbed the fragile balance of popular opinion. In time of war, it was necessary to safeguard the image of the royal couple. Fighting was an important function which must not be officially interrupted by the appearance of a royal mistress; there was no room on the great battle scene for private fancies. But the queen, at this crucial hour, seemed to have been thoroughly abandoned, not only by the king, but by his official entourage. On 23 April 1744, Mouchy noted anxiously:

> The closer we come to the departure of the king, the more reflections are made on the way it is being done. The public will be very surprised and displeased to learn that the ministers are not working with the queen and that on this occasion they are giving her no mark of consideration. The king is very ill advised, people are saying everywhere, to behave in this fashion.

Louis XV was transgressing laws of conduct which had been laid down a long time before: when the king departed for the front, the cabinet had to shift towards the queen to ensure the symbolic continuity of state business. The populace were astonished. All they could gather was that the king 'had had a sealed packet sent to the queen' with orders and letters for her and her children. It was not much to go on. Official disregard of the queen unsettled people's minds and augured ill for a departure for the front so disrespectful of custom. In a letter to the dauphin, which he refused to make public, Louis XV 'spoke of his love for his subjects'. This secrecy was damaging; Mouchy said as much to the police and stressed that the publication of that correspondence would at last have 'effaced the sad opinion which they almost all hold, that they are not beloved'.

This neglect of consideration (and of the rules) towards queen, dauphin and people was compounded by the official presence of the duchess at the king's side. The populace responded to it with a certain indignation, to the extent that the police were worried by the hostile remarks that were passed. Police and court then began to slip false news into the news-sheets, intended to reassure the populace: it was mentioned here and there that the mistress was not certain to go; a few counsels of prudence to the king were slipped in. The problem was clearly spelt out. Sex and war were incompatible, at least if it was desired to offer an official representation of the image of kingship. Not only was the current deviation culpable and likely to draw down a divine punishment ('We might lose the war!' said a few scattered voices), but also it opened the door wide to the most scurrilous of satires and pamphlets. The virile energy demanded by war, of which Louis XV had given little evidence hitherto, was suddenly put in doubt by his mistress's presence. It would have been better if the king had avoided mentioning her altogether, but after multiple changes of mind, he unfortunately ignored his counsellors and decided to make the illicit companionship public. It must be admitted that some of the counsellors had been in favour of the duchess's presence, on the grounds that without her Louis XV would take no interest in arms and the defence of his country.

The sovereign was playing on another popular feeling: he thought that the people would be happy to know that he was happy. He was wrong. The people had their own ideas about the reasons for that happiness. The rites of war were not easily transformed. To bring sexual diversion into them just when the favourable attention of the whole people had reached its height was a political error, compounded by the king's insistence on making it completely obvious by having an exterior gallery, connecting his apartments with his mistress's, built over the street of every town he went through between Paris and Metz. The image passed on to the populace turned out to be deplorable; and the chroniclers, Barbier among them, were harsh in their judgement of a king who had so clumsily defied the rules appertaining to so grave a situation as a departure for the frontier of war. His kingly function had been weakened twice over, by the effacing of the image of the royal couple and by the dysfunction this brought into his march to glory. It seemed very likely to lose him the war.

In order to express their uneasiness, the populace fell back on a number of anecdotes, scrupulously reported by Mouchy. It was said (falsely) that the Comte de Clermont had just died in the attempt to pursue simultaneously 'the charms of glory and of love'. He took his mistress, dressed as a man, to the front, and she fell seriously ill. She had to disclose her true identity, and the Comte de Clermont made himself scarce. He was said to be dead; on the whole people would rather he was. This story, though it lasted only the blink of an eye, said of Clermont what nobody could think or say about the king. But no one, count or sovereign, could infringe the laws of war and religion with impunity.

From then on, the news fed to the public was increasingly transformed and manipulated. The rumour was deliberately spread that the king was actually 'neglecting' Mme de Châteauroux, so that this appearance of disaffection might reassure an anxious public. On this point, Mouchy gives some interesting details: 'They are taking the greatest care that nothing hazardous should get into the news authorized by the court, and nothing is less haphazard than the bulletins which spread through the populace in the evenings.' He tells how people were chosen to write the news in secret, and how their stories were corrected and amended. The whole mechanism of manipulation is laid bare. Once again we observe the singular paradox whereby public opinion, which did not even exist officially, was treated with the closest attention – to the point of feeding it lies. Other bulletins elsewhere lauded the king and described the huge displays of applause and praise which greeted him wherever he went. Mouchy adds more detail: 'Never will a king of France be more beloved, but one should take heed that such sentiments are about to be contradicted by a fatal contrast.'

The king's illness and the removal of the Duchesse de Châteauroux came in the nick of time: at last, Louis the Well-Beloved became a reality. The cacophony of events (sick king, king at confession, rejected mistress, cured king) was orchestrated into a tidy sequence of public anxiety and public rejoicing. Some, however, did not at all approve of Bishop Fitzjames, author of the duchess's removal, nor of his calculations and his authority over the king.[51] Barbier fulminated, but contradictorily, starting with the rejected mistress and her suite: 'When they left the town they had to draw the blinds of their carriage, for fear of being insulted by the populace. They had only what they deserved, being driven out more shamefully than the lowest of wh—s.' A little further on he adds:

> In Paris, the news of these dismissals gave the public infinite satisfaction ... The public often wonders at great events without reflection. For my part, I take the liberty of finding that conduct most unfitting, and that public reparation an outrageous scandal. One should respect the reputation of a king and let him die in the faith, but with dignity and majesty.

What is the use of this ecclesiastical display? It would have been enough if the king had repented sincerely, in his heart of hearts, and the outward seeming had been hidden. It was very just that Mme de Châteauroux should not have reappeared, but her removal should have been arranged more tactfully ... I do not know what will happen after three months of perfect recovery, but I find this conduct light, imprudent and too gratifying to ecclesiastical authority over princes in critical moments.[52]

The last sentence shows Jansenist influence. Naturally, the party of orthodox religion, led by Bishop Fitzjames, saw it as a sign of heaven's opposition to royal adultery.

To the populace, the public confession and the mistress's removal restored an acceptable image of kingship; moreover, the king being now cured, he could be presented to the public exclusively as a warrior king, the vision they had long waited to enjoy. Once monarchic purity and the monarchic function had been restored, joy could be unconfined and the king well-beloved. This reveals a fairly obvious desire to return exactly to something known before – to the glorious and warlike age of Louis XIV. Not only had it become possible to gloss over earlier hitches, as when the king had refused to touch for scrofula or perform his Easter devotions; people could once again envisage a new, founding representation of kingship, and thus yield to one of the other functions of a king, which was to extract taxes from his people: 'Since everyone agrees that the king is adventuring himself for the glory and advantage of the nation,' wrote Mouchy, 'nothing is more just than to make every effort to put him in a position to bring such noble labours to a glorious conclusion.'

The ritual of ceremony lasted into October, restoring the king to the hearts of his people and constructing a memorial of the event. A king could not brush with death without result; his cure and his public atonement for his adulterous fault healed the people's wound and gave them, at last, a basis on which to love their sovereign. The political, social and textual strategy behind the ceremonial was directed towards a single end: to forge an indissoluble bond between the monarch and his subjects.

The die was not wholly cast, however, especially for the people of Paris, always so attentive to acts, gestures and signs from king and court. Between November 1744 and January 1745, Mouchy was again passing blow-by-blow information to the police. He observed that the populace kept at a distance from information received and tried to be sole masters of their own attitudes.

The king's return to Paris was announced for 14 November, and the police noted a febrile mood among the populace which had little to do with traditional manifestations of joy. It was a limited, precise kind of agitation which lurked in particular places such as markets, and concerned especially members of the lower orders. Mouchy prowled around such places to get a better idea of what was happening, and grasped that there was a new rumour going round Paris: that the king had 'taken back' Mme de Châteauroux. The irritated inhabitants were essentially getting together to decide whether they were going to give evidence of rejoicing or stay at home on the day of Louis XV's return; before deciding, they wanted better information. They were much less trustful of the rumour than might have been expected. Mouchy, with the aid of his cronies, observed that the populace were seeking more information, and tried to verify it. Parisians were well acquainted with the addresses of news bureaux and went there, anxiously inquiring. The market women organized a demonstration at Mouchy's bureau and demanded to see his agent, Augier, so as to get better information. This kind of organized, sceptical interrogation was something new. Faced with such approaches to the authorized news bureaux, Mouchy explains what the police had ordered him to do: his agents, for example, were exhorted to deny rumours of a possible return by Mme de Châteauroux. These denials were to be followed by appeals to the populace to emerge joyfully onto the streets travelled by the returning king. The agents, Mouchy insists, did their best to 'explain to them that they [here, the market women] should be thinking only of the joy of seeing the king whom heaven had been pleased to restore on the prayers of his subjects.' He noted, a little imprudently, that 'they left content.' This shows he did not realize that the events which were to come would mark a break between the king and his subjects. In reality, the king had indeed 'taken back' his mistress, and the Parisians most certainly did turn their backs on his road home. Only from the carriages accompanying him, so we are told, did anyone cry 'Long live the king'; but nobody was to be seen at the windows, and these were not even lit up. At eleven o'clock in the evening, Paris was asleep; even the Tuileries was in darkness, 'as if [harsh remark!] the king had not been there'.

Eight days later, Mme de Châteauroux died suddenly at the age of twenty-seven. Ill-natured remarks and placards in the markets greeted the news. The king was annoyed, and never again stayed in Paris; from that day onwards, he was very hard on any man, or woman, who dared allude to that particular stage in his life. In this connection the *Tanastès* affair is typical. *Tanastès* was a book written by a woman called Mlle Bonafon (or Bonafons), telling of the king's love for Mme de Châteauroux and his illness at Metz. 'This book', said the police report, 'was an allegorical fairy story in which it was easy to detect insulting allusions to the king, the queen, Mme de Châteauroux, the Duc de Richelieu and the Cardinal de Fleury.'[53] The king, highly displeased with this work (whose print run was 100 copies), had its author put in the Bastille and subsequently in a convent, where she was immured for fourteen years.

Under interrogation, Mlle Bonafon pleaded her need of money and said that she had only followed what everyone had been saying when she wrote her book:

> [That] she composed her work on her own; [that] she even bent her imagination upon it, but she admits that having her head full of what was being said in public about everything which had happened during and after the king's illness, she sought to make some application of it to her work, not at all realizing the consequences and having no evil intention, and declares that the more she is aware of her fault, the more she grieves at it.[54]

This Bastille dossier contains a long correspondence, lasting more than ten years, between the prisoner and the lieutenant general of police; this uninterrupted sequence of letters show how impossible it was to obtain a royal pardon and how serious was the breach which had opened up at that very time.

What to conclude? First, we must stress the fecundity of this theme of royal malady, how much it has to tell us about both popular opinion and the sorts of information used by the police authorities. For the populace it was a major preoccupation; for the authorities it was a way of understanding the populace, or rather of bringing them into the open. The period of a king's illness (or of any member of the royal family, to a no doubt lesser degree) is a chance to observe the dynamics of the relationship between the source of power and its subjects. Of course, we can seldom obtain as much information about every episode of a royal illness as we do about the illness of 1744. Thanks to the news-sheets produced by journalist-cum-police-agent Mouchy, we can use the singular event, the moment in time we have just described, to reveal the workings of an information system which was created essentially in order to steer public opinion in the right direction. The mechanisms stand so clearly revealed that we can grasp shifts of opinion at the very moment they are produced, and then see how (against all expectations) they fade away and escape the very people who seemed so eager to welcome them. Amongst the populace we can perceive a desire to distance themselves from the news that was fed to them, and from the hastier forms of collective negotiation (such as demonstrations in the market-place) which often established a certain mode of behaviour. Thanks to Mouchy's journal we can see more clearly both on and behind the scenes, detect the stratagems of the police and the people's struggle not to be taken in; we can unwind the skein from manipulation to information to receipt of information and see what Parisians really *did* consider as a good reason for judging an event, or even changing its course.

Such shifts of opinion were essentially discontinuous and contradictory. Sometimes the people expected the king to make the most traditional gestures; sometimes they demanded a visible break with the past; sometimes they expected the signs coming from the sovereign to coincide with their needs of the moment. Even when a general state of opinion did take shape, it was never to be relied on. Louis XV was to learn that, to his cost.

Exceptional inflections

The passage of time sometimes crossed a fault line which cast the peaceful progression from day to day into disorder. Wars, epidemics, religious disputes, changes of reign, were exceptional inflections which transformed the social and mental economy of the people and forced them into quick reactions to facts which were modifying the balance of their lives and aspirations.

Riots provided one such fault line. In the eighteenth century, sedition, bread riots, violent protests against child kidnappings, the 'Flour War', punctuated the course of time. These disturbances, less frequent and probably less violent than in the seventeenth century, have been many times described[55] and discussed by fascinated historians, who have worked on them from every possible angle. Should we look to them for the origins of the French Revolution? Did they make a major contribution to the forming of a political consciousness? My purpose here is simply to ask what they represent in relation to the shifts of opinion we have already sketched, how and on what basis they were organized, what was at stake and whether such irruptions of violence produced any more or less decisive changes.

Thanks to the police archives and accounts by politicians and chroniclers, we can examine the riots of April 1720, July 1720, 1725, 1750 and 1775. These five events are interesting because they were on the whole differently motivated. Those of April 1720 arose after the wave of repressive ordinances aimed at idlers, beggars and vagabonds; those of July 1720 marked the deep disappointment at the failure of Law and his economic policy. In 1725 it was a 'traditional' uprising caused by the high price of bread, while in 1750 it was a response to abuses by the police who were out to clear Paris of 'its rogues'. The riots of 1775, which were surprisingly serious, were linked with high prices, but still more with the new policy of free trade, including trade in corn. Even this rapid survey of the motives for subversion shows the variety of popular attitudes. They dispose of the traditional, and even then outmoded, explanations which could only discern public subversion when the public went hungry. The populace was more than a belly, a hungry body, and the uprisings of the eighteenth century are based on well-defined political situations and economic contexts. 'Any resistance offers a plurality of meanings,' as Jean Nicolas wrote in the preface to his *Mouvements populaires et conscience sociale*. Moments of anger recharged this community of meanings, but no meaning was given once and for all: mostly they were improvisations, half-excessive and half-rational, anticipating the future, laying down new rules while re-establishing old ones. It may be true that subversion has a memory, but this does not mean that popular emotions succeeded one another in a linear progression of consciousness, so that the events of 1775 were an elaboration of those of 1719–20.

April 1720

On 20 March 1720, there was a police ordinance for the severe repression of mendicity. Vagabonds and immoral persons were to be arrested, while 'those who were acknowledged to be able-bodied and of suitable age were to be taken to the colonies'. Thus began a wave of arrests in broad daylight and of forced emigration to Louisiana. This repression began in an uneasy social climate: poverty was widespread, beggars lingered on the highway, and the police showed an unpleasant visage well larded with embezzlement and misappropriation. A police commissioner well known to Parisians, Cailly by name, who had formerly been an inspector, held to ransom the upholstery trade and the rag trade, merchants and middlemen. He was put on trial. Working for d'Argenson, the lieutenant of police, he had been made responsible for distributing wood to the poor in the winter of 1709, but had not distributed it all. It was also discovered that he had made a good deal out of forced enlistments, demanding considerable sums from the prison officers with whom he was working. And yet the *parlement* freed Cailly and his henchmen and took no steps against d'Argenson. The populace was brought face to face with injustice; their regular close contact with inspectors and commissioners gave them a bitter vigour. Through the summer of 1719 there were uprisings among young men and women who had been carried off, while 150 women sent from Paris to La Rochelle rebelled against their escort of archers, who then fired on them. Six women were killed. There was high indignation in September 1719, when the first of a series of forced marriages was celebrated in public in the priory church of Saint-Martin-des-Champs. The public watched in horror as the young people, thus forcibly united, emerged tied two by two and chained: 180 young men united to 180 young women. Saint-Simon himself thought this a barbarous spectacle:

> They had taken not the smallest trouble to provide for the subsistence of each ... at night they were locked in outhouses with nothing to eat, and in the privies where there were any, from which they could not get out. They cried out in a way which excited pity and indignation. ... This inhumanity, together with the barbarity of their escort, meant that loud complaints arose.[56]

The ordinance of March 1720 provoked anger. More than 5000 persons were carried off in less than eight days, some from the families of respectable artisans. That was beyond the pale. The revolt was rapid, precise, brutal and localized. In the Rue Saint-Antoine, on the bridge of Notre-Dame, in the Rue du Roi-de-Sicile, archers and exempts were attacked and massacred, often with savagery. The corpses were horribly abused; one archer was carried, gravely wounded, to the Hôtel-Dieu and was finished off by the patients themselves. The people's violence brooked no negotiation; it was determined and precise. They knew they were right, a conviction which was shared *a posteriori* by the chroniclers. Saint-Simon we have quoted; Buvat expressed the same opinion; as for Delisle, clerk to the Paris *parlement*, he wrote in his notes that 'the people were right'.[57]

What was going on? It was an explosion of anger which expressed not only a collective sensitivity to injustice but an attachment to personal freedom which made it intolerable for people, however delinquent, to be forced to marry. Such an intrusion into private life was thought unacceptable, just as public rioting was unacceptable: the reaction was therefore rapid, savage and non-negotiable.

Eventually this state of affairs, in which many people were deprived of 'the public freedom to go outside without being arrested and sent to the Mississippi',[58] drew an intervention from the *parlement*. D'Argenson was summoned, and a new royal ordinance was promulgated which was outwardly just as severe: the king forbade 'on pain of death, all private persons, of whatever quality and condition they may be, to oppose the execution of the ordinance of 10 March or the present ordinance'.[59] But it was made clear that arrests could not be validated until they had been submitted to the commissioner of police (people in 1750 were to remember this stipulation). And to prevent abuses, the archers detailed to persecute beggars must keep 'in their brigades and wearing their uniforms'.

April 1720 saw a surge of violence in the face of injustice and police corruption. Few words were spoken during those days of revolt, but savage acts were committed. It was an isolated and fleeting instant. Thirty years later, when the police were again guilty of abuses, popular reactions worked on the memory of 1720; the path followed by the rioters of 1750 had been laid by the ordinance of May 1720; the victims (police inspectors and exempts plucked out of the crowd on the suspicion of kidnapping children) were dragged to the commissioner's house.[60] The betrayal of legitimate authority became an emblem. There was less immediacy; most important was that demand for legitimacy which had been decided in 1720, and the movement as a whole was organized around that mechanism of memory and rationality. In 1720 it was a hand-to-hand struggle prompted by the people's refusal to be treated like animals; to that, the rising of 1750 added memories, and a logic of its own.

July 1720

This time the emotion was quite different. It was born of an atypical economic and political experiment which had been intended to involve everyone. There are few traces of this uprising in the judicial archives; perhaps that is why Edgar Faure, in his analysis of Law's system, rejects the word 'revolt' and prefers 'incident', 'a spontaneous reaction of the collective psyche of an unclassified, and socially unclassifiable, mob'. Whether this was true remains to be seen.

Law's system[61] put the economy of the Ancien Régime in an unprecedented and original situation which was to provoke a mixture of hope and disappointment. It was a new and risky economic procedure: to reduce the national debt through an inflationary policy (which proved uncontrollable), stimulate the economy by flooding the market with banknotes guaranteed by the State (or more accurately, by a central bank), and concentrate in the hands of the authorities the bank, the issue of currency, indirect taxation and trade with the colonies.

Onto this policy were grafted three additional elements. Anyone could play a direct part in the operation as his own interests dictated, without distinction of class, nationality or even of sex – many women were to join the 'speculators'. The liveliest scenes of the early eighteenth century took place in the Rue Quincampoix, and it was all in public and in the open air. Everyone was infected with the frenzy: some speculated, others picked the pockets of speculators too preoccupied even to notice, yet others rushed to start little *ad hoc* businesses dependent on the reigning fever. Rue Quincampoix was both reality and illusion: it was crowded out every morning, and all those in the crowd thought they were playing an active part in the State, and without intermediary; this possible and actual participation by all acted like the mirage of a possible equality, or at least of a direct and self-interested sharing in the affairs of state.

The second element was the feeling that this new version of Fortune's wheel would turn to some effect. Everything happened in public, and day by day the ups and downs of speculation enriched some and ruined others. This high visibility increased the feverish excitement; hour by hour, for several days, one could witness fabulous gains and spectacular reverses of fortune. Money is always good theatre, but offstage there were many misfortunes and many excesses. Some were ruined and committed suicide; others, in their greed, perpetrated the most outrageous swindles. Moreover, the fortunes gained and lost did not follow the rules of traditional logic: the rich man could fall into misfortune, the poor artisan win three hundred *livres* in a single day.

The dream was within reach; the idea that the hierarchy of wealth could be overturned made the system very attractive. For a short time it was possible to believe in a different social order with no rule or law other than that of a fortune received or regained, as in a lottery. The greater folk were worried. 'I think,' wrote Mme Dunoyer in 1723, 'that if God had not set things in order, in the end valets would have become masters and masters, valets.'[62]

In Rue Quincampoix there was an impressive social mix. Churchmen rubbed shoulders with lackeys, rich women with journeymen and petty artisans – an unlikely situation which provoked a quantity of anecdotes, as unverifiable as they were plausible, which ran through streets and cabarets. The legend of the poor man making his fortune was the order of the day, as was the story of the little hunchback who offered his hunch as a desk for people anxious to make a deal; or of the silly parvenu who attended to his natural functions in solid silver chamberpots. Wealth overturned everything, but not all managed to shake off their earlier social habits. It was said that a lackey, dizzy with newly acquired wealth, had forgotten that he would need to change his habits and inadvertently climbed on to the outside of his own carriage ...

In these exceptional circumstances, disappointment was as profound as hope; hence the riots of 16 and 17 July. And they *were* violent. They took place in the very places responsible for the affair: there were skirmishes before the bank and before the Palais-Royal (where Law was living) – a corpse was laid out there.

The women were active and vociferous: 'They want to give courage to the men,' Barbier explained. At times, the populace joined with the guards to abuse the system and its creator. A fearful Marais describes what went on:

> Everything is in a state of extraordinary excitement. Law's coachman has been seriously hurt. His lackeys have fled; their master has remained at the Palais-Royal ... In spite of the guards, the people have broken the windows of his apartments, and the guards themselves supported the people, telling them that they would be the first to kill the old rogue ...

Order was restored later, and the chroniclers marvelled – as they always did – at the people's capacity to calm down. The uprising of July 1720 was not an isolated incident; its structure conformed to the forms of popular participation encouraged by the system itself. The anger of the Parisians had taken the same course as all their activities in recent months: first, the bank, then the search for the author of their misfortunes. Once the system had collapsed and its creators had lost power, calm returned and the relations between State and populace were 'normalized'. No longer could a simple artisan dream of a golden coach, and the habitual social distinctions were back again. In fact, they had never really been away.

July 1725, May 1775

These were two grave uprisings, separated by fifty years, which rocked Paris. Between them, in 1750, the city rose up against the police who were kidnapping children off the streets.[63] The riots of 1725 and 1775 had many aspects in common. Both were triggered by persistently high bread prices and the conviction that the shortages were not natural but organized to force up prices and swell profits. It was what they called the 'famine plot'.[64] The problem of these rumours and plots has been studied in detail; Steve Kaplan has shown the realities on which the rumours were grounded and later amplified, explaining that 'the accusations which were made lacked neither foundation nor credibility and were not silly denials', since in 1725 'the maximum priority was given to direct purchases of grain from royal funds or operations confined by the government to particular persons who, in theory, were working at their own risk.' Here I am more interested in discovering how these two sequences of subversion unfolded, and what their repercussions may have been.

It was in the Faubourg Saint-Antoine that popular emotion first erupted in 1725. The very place was emblematic. It had its own sovereignty, and its population was rather sparse, consisting of workers, artisans and farmers. It was a privileged enclave, outside the Parisian system of justice, a free territory which had no guilds and to a degree escaped the surveillance of the police and the constricting framework of professional community obligations. Thus it attracted beggars and criminals, who used it as a bolt-hole or shelter. Its remoteness from central authority gave Saint-Antoine a character of its own: the inhabitants, anxious to maintain their rights and privileges and a sort of highly prized autonomy, had developed a true freedom of thought and action, a critical attitude and a vigilant eye for the authorities.

Strong in this acute awareness of rights and liberties, the crowd this time took the initiative, became wrathful and refused all negotiation with the authorities. It all started with a women's quarrel.[65] A customer went into a bakehouse to buy a four-pound loaf of bread; the baker's wife tried to charge her 14 *sous*, but she refused to pay more than 12. The women rioted and refused to calm down on the plea of some of their menfolk; a full-scale uprising ensued, and when the guards began to fire, nobody was intimidated.

The police tried to negotiate peaceably, urging the crowd to pursue the path of legality rather than violence. The attempt failed. Mediators who had rushed to the scene, such as the parish priest of Sainte-Marguerite, were abused and even attacked; Commissioner Labbé had to flee. The populace refused to recognize any police or judicial authority; they proclaimed that they had their own rights and their own justice. 'There are no fair prices and there's no work,' shouted the rioters, expressing a feeling of collective outrage in connection with their legitimate rights. Since justice itself was in doubt, justice could not repair the fault: by a logical progression, mediation and negotiation were rejected by people determined to make their own substitute for an unjust justice which could never have become a worthy partner.

The outcome was repression and two hangings, and the crowd was forbidden to attend the executions. But the most astonishing thing must be the long-term repercussions of the uprising. For months afterwards, Paris was on a knife-edge, and the police reports bear witness to the popular discontent. Women took the initiative; their words and actions gave the city a violent atmosphere, and their main targets were the lieutenant general of police and Mme de Prie, the current mistress of the Duc de Bourbon. When the hated d'Ombreville died, in April 1725, he was replaced by Hérault, and the city was peppered with injurious placards warning the new lieutenant general 'not to contemplate appearing in public, for the women of the markets will pull his nose for him.'[66] Hostile speeches and insulting remarks were everywhere to be heard, while the women organized themselves and visited both the first president of the *parlement* and the lieutenant general to draw their attention to poverty and high prices; since they received nothing but the occasional flinging of alms from a window, they showed how weary they were of inapposite speeches and political gestures, and publicly complained of the arrogance of the great and the apparent indifference of the king. The Duc de Bourbon 'smiles when all others weep'; the king 'thinks of nothing and leaves Paris'; the lieutenant general of police, harassed in the market-place, replied, 'If you have no bread – eat cabbage stalks!'

At that, Parisians turned towards the queen, which was a logical attitude for two reasons. First, the king was a disappointment; second, the movement of 1725 belonged essentially to the women: the female element in the populace had assumed its responsibilities and entered upon both words and violence; naturally they turned towards the female element in power, towards the queen. To remind her of her role, to bring her into politics, was a logical gesture for women who had just assumed positions of their own.

It did not, however, stem the flow of placards and seditious remarks, and the lieutenant of police and his associates were worried. Duval, first secretary, wrote to the lieutenant to warn him of the unpleasant atmosphere that prevailed everywhere: 'You will soon see to what degree of rebelliousness we have come.'[67] Witness the following virulent 'Exhortation to the French People':

> Since the injustice of those who govern us has no bounds, it is up to us, the French people, to set bounds to their power. It is time to take up arms and abolish tyranny ... The remedy I am proposing to you is extreme, but when evil is inveterate one must apply steel and fire ... There is no other way, since all the remonstrances made by the *parlement* have been in vain.

This, then, was a year of violence and open criticism, when people were determined to make their way into the political and social debate outside the judicial and parliamentary institutions. It was long before they forgot the year of high prices, the year when they had tried to do justice for themselves. Repression extinguished the violence; there was no general conflagration, but the discourse of that time left its mark and went on developing, to be applied later to a new political situation: Jansenists and the *parlement* versus the king. After those hours of violence – which were extratextual and yet generated their own text

– thoughts and words, enriched by their experience of combat, transferred themselves onto the daily battlefield of the bull *Unigenitus*.
May 1775 was the time of the 'Flour War'.[68] Louis XV had died a
year earlier, unlamented. Terray, the comptroller general, who had taken
the control of the grain trade into his own hands, was hated; he was
often frightened to see how both the bourgeoisie and the common
people seemed convinced that one company had the monopoly of the
grain trade. He was accused of deliberately starving the people, and was
dismissed shortly after the king's decease. Turgot succeeded him and
introduced free trade, including trade in grain, and left the shadow of
suspicion over Terray's activities. When riots broke out in May 1775,
Turgot immediately thought that the instigators were his enemies, agents
of a former grain supplier. He was equally incapable of understanding
the real social tensions which had accumulated round the long history
of subsistence pricing. He thought rather in terms of plots, perhaps
instigated from abroad, and his convictions fed on a 'proof': strange
men and mysterious women on horseback had, apparently, been seen
scattering gold in order to incite the mob to rebellion . . .

Examination of the archives and more recent historical studies have
dislodged the revolt of 1775 from its former position and given it a face
rather different from the one which earlier historians were fond of
describing. It remains difficult to grasp, however, because the chronicles
and contemporary accounts by Métra, Hardy, Lenoir *et al.* all adhere
to the plot theory, and the police interrogations formulated their questions
to suspects on the basis of the conviction that brigands, agitators and
instigators had organized the whole movement. This makes it difficult
to discover from the transcripts anything other than the meaning induced
by the tenor of the questions asked.

However, the events of May 1775 can be fitted into a framework.
Paris knew that peasants from Dijon to Versailles had regularly been
gathering in unprecedented ways around the market-places, talking in
violent, and even threatening, terms against the government and high
prices. Some chroniclers were disquieted by the impressive number of
women who had taken it upon themselves to harangue the crowds: 'The
women . . . as everyone knows are more dangerous than the men in
crises of this sort';[69] but in the main, until they saw Paris submerged in
angry crowds, most people seem to have been resigned in advance to a
possible crisis, showing how accustomed they were to trouble from
people living on the breadline. 'The populace', Condorcet reported,
'were accustomed in moments of famine to visit their wrath upon the
sellers of grain,'[70] and Terray emphasized that this was a 'popular
movement, very common in itself, a dire and unhappy spectacle which

in the last years of the reign of Louis XV was seen in each of our provinces in turn'.[71]

Maybe it was an ordinary sort of movement, not to be chronicled with a trembling hand – until the unexpected happened: the crowds entered Paris by the gates of Saint-Martin and Vaugirard and marched on the markets, then the whole city and the suburbs, pillaging almost every bakehouse they came to. The surprising thing was that this sizeable crowd, composed mostly of women, carried out its business with calm, determination and even gaiety, meeting no obstacles: 'What was very difficult to understand,' comments Hardy,[72] 'was the sight of a mutinous populace absolutely capable of executing all that it had thought fit to undertake, without obstacle.' When rebels were merry, archers smiling and complaisant, and Paris invaded from end to end, the spectacle was quite sufficient to convince people that there was a plot, with instigators all over the place. Nobody, indeed, could think that the populace were doing all this on their own account, so the rumour spread that brigands and certain scatterers of gold were egging on the crowd. The police were criticized, and it was to be the last event in the career of the lieutenant of police, Lenoir, who was forced to resign and replaced by Albert.

In fact, the affair was more complex. In 1775 the people were nursing a great anger. Previously, at the only gathering before the royal château at Versailles, the peasants had called for the king to show himself on the balcony. Louis XVI spoke, so it was said, with 'unction and kindness', and promised to bring down the price of bread. He could scarcely be heard for the torrent of insults, while placards and lampoons sprouted everywhere: 'You have always ground the poor under your feet, but the time will come when we shall do the same to you.'[73]

Clemency, then, was already in the picture, and had been put there from on high, so it was not surprising if in Paris the police used a certain restraint; perhaps they were also intimidated by the sheer numbers of peasants who had invaded the capital. The commissioners (Desormeaux, Roland and others) had bread distributed in order to prevent trouble. The *parlement*, likewise very anxious, issued a decree intended to calm people down: it recalled that large assemblies were forbidden by law, but announced that it would beseech the king to lower the price of bread. This decree was posted in the evening and overnight, and all the people crowded to read it by candlelight. Turgot, worried by the turn events were taking, hastened to visit the king at Versailles and urged him to speak out with firmness, which he did. The next day, the *parlement* heard that the king, in a *lit de justice*, had abrogated its decree and licensed the *prévôts de maréchaussée* to judge the rebels. The *parlement* submitted, and things moved quickly thereafter. On 11 May there were two executions (a gauze-maker and a wigmaker). Condorcet drew the moral from this affair: 'For the first time the people saw the government insensible to any fear, following its principles ... and refusing to make to the prejudiced, or to *popular opinions*, any sacrifice contrary to justice.'

These 'popular opinions' (need we repeat?) often belonged to a context other than that perceived from above; moreover, some accounts of the affair, Métra's for example, have inconsistencies which allow something of this other context to show through. We may pursue our thinking along two lines. First, in 1775 the Parisians had just seen a change of monarch; disappointed by Louis XV, they had eagerly awaited Louis XVI and his first royal acts. Above all, they had fervently hoped that the king would have himself crowned in the capital; in fact, he chose Reims. Métra remarks in a footnote: 'Nonetheless, the king had resolved to go to Reims; his refusal no doubt pained the citizens, but had not given them any idea of revolting.' This may be true, but the disappointment was there, and certainly must have influenced the feelings and attitudes of the populace. At a time of such hardship, Turgot's decisions were incomprehensible to peasants and people of modest means. Freedom of trade, free trade in grain, sounded to them like a way of allowing the rich to get richer. For a long time the common people had been pleading, arguing and complaining about 'fair prices', in which they were supported by the *parlement*, a number of churchmen and some royal officials.[74] The sudden price rises of 1775 provoked a widespread movement of sedition, in which rejection of the new economic outlook mingled with the specific demand that the king should be a just monarch to his subjects. The march on Versailles, the king's appearance on the balcony and the decree of the *parlement* all revealed the people's desire to address their king directly, in which they had the support of the *parlement*; that desire was repelled by the attitude of the king, who not only supported Turgot but induced harsh repression, while himself remaining distant and aloof from the capital.

Holding the coronation at Reims was felt to be an archaism; approving of Turgot's over-innovative ideas was ill-omened modernism: here again, events unfolded against a background of contradictory reasoning, midway between the modern and the antique, around the compelling idea that it was *legitimate* to ask the king to ensure fair prices and maintain direct contact with his subjects.

As for the conspiracy theory, we may take leave to doubt. The archives show that out of 145 private persons arrested in Paris, 100 were paid workers, twelve small shopkeepers and fifteen peasants. The interrogations and police commissioners' reports reveal a 'merry and determined crowd' of working people. There may have been a few agitators and brigands, but it proved impossible to uncover the traces of a sustained plot; the instigators themselves, men and women, were of the common people.

If there is anything to be concluded from the violent crises which regularly rocked the eighteenth century, we might emphasize that neither the words spoken nor the criticisms (or insults) expressed were any more heated than at other, calmer moments. The uprisings (as far as the judicial archives can show) do not reveal any accentuation of the severity of people's remarks; the 'eruptions' were not on that level, and the riots do not seem to have acted as a safety-valve for words or opinions. Other, non-violent episodes show an equal verbal acerbity. The riots were also strikingly short, and their outcome summed up what the populace had long been thinking about their relationship with the king, the authorities, the economy and the police. The improvised expression of their wrath sprang out of their reflections on that relationship.

Their rejection of negotiation and obstinate refusals to yield show how greedily they seized on opportunities – however brief – to carry out 'legitimate' actions whose legitimacy was not measured against the discourse of power. Indeed, during the riots they turned their backs on the 'authorities' as a means of becoming the king's true subjects, directly, simply and face to face, strong in their legitimacy and their unashamed staging of their own existence before a king who seemed in danger of forgetting that they existed at all. 'Riot' could then be seen as a social being, a living person, partnering the king in a loving relationship of which he received regular reminders. When this king–subject partnership seemed to be back in balance (a result to which the usages and symbols of violence made a substantial contribution), riot could bow out and retire. This did not, however, mean that the people's political consciousness had progressed; nor had riot made the quantum leap towards the sort of discontent which worsens perceptibly from day to day. Riot was simply a convenient (and violent) way of summing up a situation which had been endured and ruminated on for some time; each riot may have been remembered, but the effect was not cumulative. Memory was ever ready to assume new attitudes and adapt to new challenges, which carried opinions and sentiments of their own.

Thus riot alternated with tranquillity. What astonished contemporaries – chroniclers, the upper classes and even the king – need not astonish us: violence might drive out violence, but that did not necessarily imply submission. The gestures and signs of riot could create enough meaning to ensure that the succeeding tranquillity was not, by comparison, meaningless. Moreover, almost every time, it was the authorities who retreated; the culminating emotion was fear, backed by an uneasy feeling that that fear might be well founded.

PART III

Speaking against the King, or Words from the Bastille (1661–1775)

Individuals who spoke or wrote against the king, or who invented or fomented plots against the king's person or his entourage, might be denounced as 'evil-speaking' persons and sent to the Bastille. There, they might explain themselves or beg for mercy, rave in anger or compose long speeches; the police might require them to elucidate their relations with the sovereign, but they never really listened to what was said, convinced that only folly or villainy could account for so abominable a transgression. Inside the prison walls was a mêlée of discourses which met only to clash. However, the police's insistence on reading every seditious remark as the beginnings of a decisive onslaught on authority eventually did allow long-term prisoners to attempt some kind of explanation of their outlook – always providing that the physical and mental deterioration induced by prison conditions had not blunted their intellectual edge.

Pierre Rétat, writing about Damiens' attempt on the life of Louis XV, said that 'Someone ought to ... do a systematic analysis of all the "seditious remarks" recorded in the archives of the Bastille and the Châtelet.'[1] He was right, and thanks to him I have had the chance to decipher all such data from the Bastille archives which are still in the Bibliothèque de l'Arsenal. I have gone further back, and ahead, in time than he originally suggested, for I have examined all the dossiers of seditious remarks from 1661 to 1775; but I have also narrowed the scope, since the vastness of the task made it impossible to include the archives of the Châtelet. Rétat speaks of a collective 'muffled clamour' emerging from these dossiers. I do not altogether agree either that there was a clamour or that it was muffled; what I do find, in these reasonable and unreasonable texts, is a chance to seize on particular moments in the history of the relationship between the king and his subjects, in all their complexity and in their absolute singularity – a singularity which is nonetheless linked to the collective perceptions of that period, or that moment in time. I also think that before we attempt to understand the contents of these ill-tempered outbreaks against the king, these treacherous and malign denunciations, we must first realize that this particular section of the Bastille archives reveals, first and foremost, the changing anxieties of the authorities over the criticism which periodically rose to confront them. An archive is not a mirror – the reflection would be too flattering – but a query: how was reality interrogated so as to produce the results we now read? After that we can start looking for thought processes, moments of fierce resistance and moments of submission, which can then be fitted in with the judicial apparatus which registers and punishes – or sometimes incites – them; and finally we can contemplate a public opinion whose elements are knowledge of an event, a perception of the king's body, the police viewpoint and the determination of individuals to be their own judges of public affairs. Thus opinion will appear to us as an emerging of needs and knowledge: some rooted in ancient symbolism, others in a radical perception of the self and the Other, the king and I. The content of these perceptions must of course be analysed, but without forgetting that the most important aspect may be the conviction of legitimacy which inspired them.

If the persecution of plots and seditious remarks reveals to us the full force of popular speaking, it is because of the way that the monarchy focused on them. If the authorities inquired into seditious remarks, they stirred up *ipso facto* a new set of seditious remarks which spread very promptly; on the other hand, if you had a grudge against somebody, there was nothing easier than to denounce him for making seditious remarks. In fact, the apparatus of repression encouraged what it sought to prevent: rumours true and false developed variously out of the very attempts to gag them. To a certain extent, repression unleashed words, and words, by a circular movement, went on to transform situations and the representation of them. Thus sedition was reborn of itself, repeated itself, transformed itself and forged images of royalty whose meanings were interdependent.

Between 1661 and 1775: approaches to a distance

This is a long period, including part of the reign of Louis XIV, the regency and the personal rule of Louis XV. He died in 1774; the Flour War occurred in 1775; then began the reign of Louis XVI, which would be well worth looking at, except that the Bastille archives begin to run dry during this period and dry up altogether in 1777. For the last years of the eighteenth century we should have to look elsewhere, in the

Châtelet archives for example, completing some studies which have already been carried out on lampoons and pamphlets.[2]

The Sun King was followed by a debonnaire and debauched regent, and the regent by the ill-beloved Louis the Well-Beloved. If it is really necessary to reduce to a simple schema the evolution of collective feelings towards the king, one might say that between the late seventeenth and the early eighteenth century the king changed from being glorious, intimidating and severe, but finally exhausting (Louis XIV) to being eagerly awaited (the regency and the minority of Louis XV) to being disappointing and later unkingly (Louis XV in his maturity, after the dismissal of Fleury); Louis XVI, first unkinged and then executed, got the worst of it. But this retrospect is too easy, and therefore unsatisfying, and that is not going to be my approach, because 'the truth of an event which is perceived by those who experience it, when they experience it, the truth which drives men to act, is not the only factual and "objective" reality established by historians.'[3] The historian, of course, sees the film backwards from the end, so that when he interprets the beginning his eye is inevitably fogged with memories of the film. Another method had to be sought, but it was often exhausting work; I have often dreamed of working in the archives unaware of everything that happened 'afterwards', with a sort of naive immediacy, relating to the texts in a utopian present, letting my mind discover facts out of nothing – facts forgotten or misunderstood by historians, but active in a reality which has never been delineated in the history books.[4] This falsely ingenuous, and doubtless artificial, way of looking leads to many questionings and turns all certainties upside down.

What was 'seditious talk'? Who talked sedition?

Under a cloak of homogeneity, the corpus of the Bastille archives and the Joly de Fleury archive[5] is in fact very heterogeneous: the rubric 'seditious talk, seditious remarks, seditious intentions' covers a quantity of differing facts and acts of varying importance. Under the same rubric go other headings for crimes we have already examined: injurious remarks, plots against the king, letters said to be 'reprehensible to the king', anonymous letters against members of the royal family, denunciations of invented plots, all kinds of blackmail associated with the king's person, ill-omened predictions or 'wicked' astrology, sending of alchemical objects and suspected poisonings . . . a long and variegated list to which can be added crimes of lèse-majesté and threats to kill the king, which made the authorities tremble. Evil designs and machinations could take the form of thoughts and unrealized dreams as often as that of actions, some contemplated, some actually carried out. It was a nebulous enemy for a power structure anxious for its own reputation.

This list of crimes omits the impressive number of hawkers arrested in 1726 and 1729 for offences such as selling evil (usually Jansenist) books; or the convulsionaries, male and female, who were locked up during the tumult provoked by the closure of the cemetery at Saint-Médard; or the writers of news-sheets, lampoonists and other pamphleteers persecuted during the 1760s, and again during the Maupeou affair in 1771. I have, of course, taken all these into account (one could hardly hope to understand public opinion without considering such specific examples of opinion in a heightened state), but I have not examined the dossiers minutely, since other historians have looked in detail at the convulsionaries and the crimes of the printed word.[6]

Not counting all the accusations of, and prosecutions for, seditious remarks after Damiens' assault in 1757, to which the Joly de Fleury archive is chiefly devoted, the Bastille archives contain more than 200 dossiers relating to the period between 1661 and 1775.[7] Most of them are voluminous affairs with intricate proceedings extending over a good many years. Once there had been an arrest the case was never closed: the police kept up the pressure, looked for accomplices, tried to find out all they could about the real motives for such evil intentions against the king. Inside the prison there was a whole system of interrogation and counter-interrogation, correspondence with the highest police authorities, information given to the king and memoirs written by prisoners to justify their position or express their repentance. It could go on for up to twenty years, and it is hard to guess why the treatment inflicted was so varied, almost arbitrary. Once the seditious remark had been uttered, or the plot denounced, one might have thought that that was the end of it; but it was only the beginning, and the dossiers show how difficult it was for the authorities to deal with 'seditious opinions', and how varied were the ways in which 'seditious' thoughts – if that is what we should call them – could be expressed.

Two hundred dossiers from 1661 to 1775: a figure from which it is impossible to make any sort of quantitative analysis. For thousands of other critical remarks were dealt with directly by order of the police or by *lettres de cachet*,[8] or were subject to an ordinary complaint before the police commissioners and a formal arrest.[9] Thus we miss the everyday opinion of the streets, though its echoes come back to us very distinctly in the secret police reports which I have used constantly throughout this book. Thus I offer no quantitative interpretation; only a few necessary indications of the social status of those who were suspected or arrested.

Let us begin with an obvious fact: women, despite their reputation for chatter and gossip, make up only a sixth of those found guilty. This, as we already know, quite fails to show how their more or less acerbic remarks rang incessantly through the market-places and the public squares; but such remarks were monitored and punished in a different way from the cases which went to the Bastille.[10] More surprising is the great variety of social status among the wrongdoers who did find themselves at grips with that fortress. There were, naturally, marquises and princes, clerks and priests from Paris and elsewhere, but there were also equal numbers of soldiers, innkeepers, lackeys, vine-growers and peasants, apprentices and waiters, artisans both male and female; not forgetting two socially important categories which we should expect to find: servants and domestics (Damiens was a domestic), and the imprecise and unstable world of gazetteers, public scribes, lampoonists and notaries' clerks – a galaxy of seditious pen-pushers.

The king – threatening and threatened

The king gave love to his subjects and demanded love from them, basing part of his power on this direct relationship entrusted to him by God at his coronation. All royal rhetoric was articulated on that ineffable love of the sovereign for his people, a supreme gift which could only become significant and operative if it was reciprocated: the subjects' love for their king had to be untouchable and sacred, whatever might befall. The king decided what form his love might take: wars, peace, taxes, domestic and foreign policy; the people could not so decide. This imbalance was never explicit. Monarchic rhetoric was one and indivisible, and the law of love between king and subjects, people and king, was inviolable. Not to love was treason, but it could only be judged in a subject. Thus the obligation to love the sovereign carried a penalty: not to love him was criminal and deserved extreme punishment, as ferocious and violent as for any infringement of the divine law. To deny love to the king or challenge his love for his subjects (via a critical opinion or evil action) was the act of a felonious and perjured traitor whose perfidy was equalled only by his disloyalty. Not to love the king was the impossible crime, a diabolical infringement of the supreme law.

Out of this symbolism, which underlay the whole policy of the Ancien Régime, emerged, more or less unintentionally, a two-sided king, at once threatening and threatened. Because subjects were punished for lack of love, the king felt persecuted, and so created a menacing image of monarchy which in itself generated menace. This meant that 'greatly

to love the king' or not to love him at all were two different versions
of a single imposed reality: the gift of, and demand for, love which was
the symbolical foundation of the link between king and subjects was
also, through the institution of punishment, a king perpetually threatened with withdrawal of love. Thus it can be suggested that the figure
of kingship played simultaneously on love and lack of love; because it
was based on love it provoked and implied love's inseparable contrary.

A reader's impressions

A first cursory read through these cases gives an impression of monotony: the dossiers seem to follow and repeat one another through one
unchanging structure, form and language. Insults, criticisms, threats and
recriminations, calumnies and machinations against the king seem
frozen in ways of saying and doing which one almost comes to think
of as invariable. It is as if, from Louis XIV's time to the end of the
eighteenth century, there existed accustomed ways of complaining and
accusing the state; as if a single topos of critical attitudes to the king
remained constant through time, so that 'political' anger always played
on the same words and assumed the same accents. The anger against
the king, the insults pronounced against king and princes, the hate-filled
threats against the sovereign's life, are indeed vigorous enough. This
anger seems to take the measure of a double reality: the real distancing
of the king's person (though Louis XV was not 'distanced' in the same
way as Louis XIV), which put his subjects outside politics; and that
imposing royal rhetoric which stressed the necessary symbiosis between
king and people and incessantly mimicked their closeness; there were
people to whom this seemed mere sleight of hand.

A more minute examination of the archives dispels the first impression of monotonous repetition and starts to reveal a disturbed and
contrasting landscape, in which two directions are already visible along
which relationships to the king and his politics are articulated. These
two directions co-exist through the years and are inseparable, but at the
same time very different. The first arises paradoxically from the very
exaltation caused by the fundamental and inviolable law of the realm
which dictated to its subjects their necessary love for the king. This
symbolism, which forced the people into awed reverence for their
monarch and faith in his holiness and inescapable wisdom,[11] fed a
persistent notion that to murder the king, while impossible, could be
both necessary and just. At the heart of submission to the king lurked
radical subversion; regicide had happened, it was still conceivable, though

unthinkable. That wild dream went on echoing from 1661 down to 1775: there might be those who preferred hell to seeing a people unhappy under their sovereign. It could be expressed in many different ways, it could be attempted, it could be done; it was a leitmotif. 'What is to stop me killing the king?' is one of the most astonishing ways of saying it, but we find that said in the archives. What *was* to stop them? It was a recurrent posture which could undergo many and varied modifications according to the course of events.

The second path, which is inseparable from the first, depends on other mechanisms of thought, which express criticisms, project new ways of relating to the king onto the political scene, oppose images of the king as inviolable and gradually transform the imposed figure of the sovereign. The king's reactions to such provocations were rather unpredictable; it could be said that certain exceptional events forced both king and people to alter, reciprocally but not equally, their idea of the bond between them.

The chronology of all this is not one of linear and progressive evolution; motifs shaped themselves in sequence, some lodging in the memory while others were forgotten. At the very least it must be said that the critical mechanism was in a state of unending development. There is a sentence from the archives, dated 27 April 1753, which aptly sums up this many-faceted second attitude: 'Your worthy subjects deserve a king who will surpass them.'

5

'Who is to stop me killing the king?'

They called him Champagne, but his real name was Joseph Botat. He was thirty-seven years old, footman to the Venetian ambassador, and he was in the Bastille. In the interrogation dated 30 March 1684,[1] the commissioner remarked that Botat 'had an extravagant way of talking'; he was in prison on that day because 'The Venetian ambassador was paying a visit to Mme de Bonettes, and Joseph, who had followed the ambassador into an antechamber near the fire, said in so many words: who is to stop me killing the king?' Most unusually, this affair seems not to have been much talked about, except to note that the prisoner had escaped; the news-sheets recorded that 'In the last few days, ten prisoners have contrived to run away from the Bastille; they broke the doors and windows.'

Killing the king ... 'It is no doubt a central feature of kingship that kings are so prone to be killed.'[2] No doubt it is also a central feature of kingship that subjects are prone to dream of killing their sovereign. There are, of course, famous historical examples – Jacques Clément, who assassinated Henri III, Ravaillac, the murderer of Henri IV – but that is not the most important thing. Sticking a dagger into the king was one of the images in everyone's mental repertoire, if only because the act fitted so logically into the rhetoric and ideology of monarchy. The king could, indeed, be killed without killing the monarchy:[3] the king's 'body politic' was immortal, as the state propagandists never tired of proclaiming. Moreover, the king, as God's vicegerent on earth, was the sole partaker of state secrets, the one who guided his subjects, declared peace or war, administered his realm according to an idea of bene-ficence which he seldom needed to account for to any other. The social

hierarchy was often represented by an organic analogy: the plebs constituted a body of which the king was the head. At any moment someone might arise from amongst the plebs to threaten the head, but the
body was nonetheless immortal. A desire to challenge the king and
oppose his private and uninfluenceable notions of love for his subjects
naturally took the form of a wish – which was and remained quite
conceivable – to murder him. The most ordinary, the most humble of
his subjects nourished this theme of royal murder all the more naturally
because their relationship to the monarch was one of forced immediacy,
forced by the exaggerated simplicity of the monarch's message to them.
Absolute royal power was proud and arrogant, intransigent and un-
bending. A typical example of its expression is the preamble to the royal
decree of 1719 concerning the reasons for the quarrel between France
and Spain:

> Kings are not accountable for their actions save to God alone, from
> whom they draw their authority. Called inexorably to work for the hap-
> piness of their peoples, they are not called to give reasons for the means
> they adopt to that end, and they can, as their prudence dictates, either
> hide or reveal the mysteries of their government.[4]

This excerpt, one among many and yet another which expresses a king's
love for his subjects, forces the individual into total submission; his
happiness is constructed amidst the most impenetrable secrecy. It is easy
to understand how such allegiance could be coupled with its radical
obverse: the subject kills the king, unerringly, and in performing that
gesture of paradoxical and absolute proximity, he knows that he is still
the king's subject. Subversion is the obverse of submission, although it
is also the most execrated of crimes, the crime that will plunge both
body and soul into hell as God's punishment.

Killing the king was an exacerbated form of social representation by
the humblest in society, further nourished by the idea, so often reiterated
by the monarchy itself, that the king was a presence, an approach to his
subjects, appearing to them on numerous occasions and healing them
by his touch. And his subjects, in their turn, sought out that symbolic
and physical link which gave meaning to them as subjects and meant
that their obedience could be rooted in a visible relationship. Subjects'
desire for proximity to their king is one of the consequences of royal
rhetoric, which never ceased to proclaim the king's affection for his
people. Here is Louis XIII explaining the measures he has taken over
the regency:

> The things which we have done during our reign have made only too
> clear the love which we have had for the preservation of our peoples and

the care we have taken in our labours to assure them of perfect felicity
and to give the most certain proofs of our love for them.[5]

Every sovereign had his own way of managing this affection and of
coming close to his people. Rather surprisingly, Louis XIV seems to
have been distinctly more accessible to his people than Louis XV, who
(as I have said) cut himself off from Paris and never went through it,
much less stayed there, after the child-kidnapping riots of 1750. The
desire to come close to the king was part of the theatre of monarchy;
the monarch simultaneously aroused and repulsed the desire, amidst a
complex symbolism stage-managed to a greater or lesser extent by each
successive king. The need to be close to the king was interiorized by his
subjects,[6] and found its way into many minds. If it brought hatred with
it, or the conviction that the king had gone astray and led his people
away from the principles of kingship which were part of the fundamental
law of the kingdom, the desire to approach the king could change into
a desire to touch him directly – with a dagger, with death. That inaudible
and unspeakable gesture was the mirror image of the gesture of veneration; king-loving and king-killing were the same attitude seen from
a different angle and generated by the very principles of sovereignty.

If people approached the sovereign it was at his own request, but they
could not go beyond certain limits which the sovereign himself set, and
outside of which he felt threatened. We have already alluded to this
duality of kingship: threatening and threatened, the monarch manipulated approaches from his subjects, and his own whim dictated whether
such approaches were normal or excessive. The experiences in 1684 of
a certain Marie-Geneviève de Saint-André are emblematic of the far-
from-simple mechanism whereby a desire to approach the king, which
he repelled, could amount to a serious crime of 'evil designs on the life
of the king'.[7] Marie-Geneviève de Saint-André, aged twenty-four, had
been in service in various great houses, but was now out of work. She
was from Normandy, and was lodging in the hayloft of the Pot d'Etain
(Cookpot Inn), near Versailles. She was at her wits' end, and lent an ear
to a 'tall young man' who advised her to go to the court and see the
king, and to borrow some decent clothes for the occasion. The young
man added that he had just come from there and was sure that the king
would ask for her. Trusting in this, she managed to get into the guard-
room. In an introductory note to her dossier (for she was later imprisoned
in the Bastille), Ravaisson commented on the case: 'We have already
pointed out the facility granted to the people of approaching the king.
This is a simple servant-girl, she entered with ease, and she was only
forbidden to enter the dining room for fear of poisonings.'[8] Once she

was in the guard-room, the door was shut on her and 'she remained there, warming herself, for three hours; then the guards brought her out and gave her some money, for she had nothing.' In the courtyard, feeling desperate (as she said later), she climbed into the queen's carriage and broke the windows, and had to be forced to get down. This misdeed brought her to the Bastille, where, under interrogation, she said in her defence that if she had come to Versailles 'it was to see the king dine and find out what His Majesty wished her to do; that it was her intention to speak to the king and that she would then have fallen on her knees before him; that she never thought any evil against the king.'[9] This (surely genuine) desire to approach the king and be saved by him turned to frustration and violence; the king felt threatened, and punished and imprisoned a woman who doubtless had intended only to 'speak to the king and fall at his feet'. The story of Marie-Geneviève de Saint-André contains elements from that part of the public imagination which authorized every person to see the king – and, if disappointed, to hate him. This strange relationship, generated by the very essence of kingship, reveals a threatening underside.

An obstinate theme, 1661–1775

There were people who wanted to kill the king and felt themselves bound to carry out that horrid intention: the motif endured over the years, through reigns and regencies, becoming reality when Damiens attacked Louis XV in 1757 and leaving its traces from dossier to dossier in the Bastille archives. They are violent traces. The intentions were unambiguous, the decisions firm, the risks consciously accepted. People called on the name of Ravaillac, or Jacques Clément, or the unhappy Damiens, whose end had been so horrible that surely he could not have wholly deserved it; people used arguments going back to antiquity, to show that parricide could sometimes be necessary and regicide salutary. Time seemed to make no difference; even if some of the facts are peculiar to our period, the motif of the murdered king dwelt almost atemporally in certain minds, and regularly gave rise to the same expressions of ill-concealed rage:

... spoke very angrily against His Majesty, saying even that in the countryside behind him, La Grandeur and three others were there in a wood and if the king had passed there or nearby, they would have killed him. (1678)

... said, 'sblood, I would not have missed him, I'd have let him have my musket on his head. (1679)

... that he would stab the king. (1684)

... that he wanted to go and kill the king and cared little if he were cruelly put to death. (1687)

... that he would not do as Ravaillac did. (1687)

... that the king must be killed, and the king's army. (1701)

... stab the king, that rotten carcass. (1703)

... if I die, I die; let the king die. (1710)

I would not miss him with a pistol-shot. (1716)

... that I must find a disguise, appear before the swine and stick a dagger in him. (1722)

... wait for him in the wood to fire a pistol at him, even if he is torn apart for it, for he is a dog. (1722)

... gouge his eyes out. (1752)

Damiens must go to Paradise, the king must be murdered. (1758)

... maintains the murderous and parricidal doctrine, counsels its practice and forms the execrable desire for a fatal revolution against the precious life of His Majesty. (1762)

... admits that he had formed in his heart the execrable design of immolating to his wrath the Lord's Anointed. (1765)

The reader will have guessed that these rawly expressed desires co-exist with other, more complex formulas and political arguments anchored in social reality. But it is interesting to study the 'raw' motif whose forms remain so similar over time; in fact it relates to an archetypal scene which sometimes seems to have come straight out of a popular tale.

Cold steel was the preferred weapon; one waited for the king hidden in the woods where he was expected to pass with his court or army; one was certainly not going to miss him and one always had to strike oneself, without intermediary (poison, for example, would not do); there was no possibility of negotiation, for one fatal blow would strike him dead. It was an immolation, a shared sacrifice, for he who killed the king would die and knew it, and the punishment did not matter: 'if I die, I die, let the king die'. All these details go to make up the potential history of the man who dared to strike the king to the heart in a mortal ambush from which no one could emerge alive. The ensuing punishment – execution, tearing apart by horses – would not mean hell for the person willing to endure it: 'Damiens must go to Paradise', and the man who killed the king must save both kingship and his own soul. The outlines emerge of a hero beyond the law, beyond God and beyond suffering: a hero created by a savage understanding of the mystique of royalty and its symbolism of love-given and love-denied.

From secrecy to secrets

'The royal authority is accountable only to God for its successes and the execution of its designs. However, kings ... are sometimes willing, out of kindness, to make manifest the reasons for their actions.'[10] In general, who said king said secret: affairs of state were the king's own affair, and he was never obliged to discuss them in public. Thus the king was exposed and manifest, but secret; and Habermas's researches have shown that the elites of the eighteenth century made enormous efforts to lift this veil of secrecy from public affairs, to appropriate many aspects of them and to create a critical public sphere in which 'things' of state could be discussed. Even justice, normally conducted in secret, was finally revealed, and judicial reports broadcast, with passionate eagerness, everything that was said and done in court,[11] giving an enlightened public the means to understand and discuss. This was not pleasing to the royal judiciary, who preferred to prepare their cases in secret and veil certain orders for detention in the deepest darkness. The police dossiers are affected by this compulsory silence; it seems that there were words which could not be recorded without some danger, especially if they were words against the king which ought never even to have been heard. A short dossier from the Bastille shows the secrecy surrounding detention orders: in 1678 (the exact date is lacking) Nicolas Martin, a vine-grower from Saint-Cloud, was put in the Bastille for speaking evilly against the king. On 1 March in the same year, he was taken to the Petites-Maisons at Bicêtre; there is no trace of any interrogation or materials for a case; the only annotation is that 'his seditious speaking made one shudder and one did not wish the words which he had said against the king to be known to anyone'.[12]

The obsession with secrecy and the way it was elevated by the monarchy into a principle of government had an effect on relations between king and subjects. There were many people who were convinced that they bore an important secret which could be told only to the king, necessitating a private interview, a tête-à-tête with the sovereign. This attitude is often encountered, but it was of course inadmissible; it frightened the authorities as much as people who wanted to kill the king. To have a secret which the king did not know was a serious insult, a crime, even before it became a threat. Kingship could receive secrets from nobody; it was treason even to believe oneself equipped with greater knowledge than the ruler. Thus between king and subject there appeared a real and symbolic representation whose consequences were contradictory: the king could receive no secrets, but the subject thought he could approach the king only if he were equipped with a secret whose contents, if revealed, would admit him to the king's own sphere.

What the secret actually *was* mattered little; its owner and would-be transmitter was in any case guilty, harmful to the royal destiny. Some found themselves accused of *lèse-majesté* because they had had 'evil dreams concerning the king's person' and had tried to shake them off, first by going to confession, later by going to the king. Others spent a long time in the Bastille or Bicêtre for saying that they had secrets which would make the king rich and show him where to look for mysterious and fabulous treasures; lengthy punishments could also fall on those who desired secretly to reveal to the king the name of someone who wished him ill, or knew a sure way to kill off the court or the king's army. In this domain, nothing could be inoffensive. Not even the 'stubborn' astrologer who 'took his ridiculous and criminal curiosity to the point of measuring the lives of princes and kings'.[13] This was in 1701, and François Henry de Bardy, the astrologer, was imprisoned in the Bastille for a year and then expelled from Paris with the woman who lived with him. His interrogation is very revealing: 'Was he not aware of the laws forbidding the application of astrology to kings, which imperceptibly edges people into impiety and, so to speak, subjects the life of kings to the comprehensions of astrologers?' To which Henry de Bardy replied that 'if he drew up the king's horoscope, it was above all with the intention of presenting it to him and laying before his eyes the events illustrating his reign.' That was the crime and the impiety: the king was *of* God, and his future could not be at anyone's command, for that would subject him to fluctuating laws and human principles which did not apply to him. Bardy was criminal in his insolence; nobody ought to dare to predict the events of the king's life, still less its duration. The case outlines a new form of proximity to the king, the dream of a subject which was an actual attack on his kingly function.

The secrets – some derisory, others deceptive, some sincere, others astrological – which people wished to divulge only to the king were monstrous in the same way as evil designs and the desire to kill were dangerous; they were one of the most disquieting derivatives of suchlike devices and desires, and the monarchy persecuted them in all the forms they took.

Vision and genius, alchemy and poisons

We should feel no surprise at kingly prejudice against revelations, secrets and bad dreams. At the heart of Louis XIV's reign there came a massive upheaval known to history as the Poisons Affair, which has caused as much spilling of ink as the Man in the Iron Mask or the kidnapping of Louis XVII. However, this grave affair, which lasted from 1679 to 1682, was not merely anecdotal, a matter for historical reviews of the more sensational kind. It was not so much an 'affair' as an exceptional social climate which generated manifestations of credulity and criminal behaviour involving those closest to the king, and perhaps even the king's very person.

I do not think it necessary to recall the facts, except briefly (there is a more than copious literature on the subject).[14] People in the mid-seventeenth century were haunted by the fear of poisoning. Great poisoning cases, such as that of the Marquise de Brinvilliers in 1676, reverberated through the realm: the sole topic of public rumour was poisonous powders and mysterious crimes by women against husbands whose brutal behaviour, after a long career in the royal armies, apparently sickened them. In fact it was a crisis of extreme gravity which affected every level of society, from the court to Paris and from Paris to the provinces. The Dutch War of 1672–8, which ended with the Treaty of Nijmegen, had bled France white. Meanwhile, 1672 saw the end of a long series of witch trials:[15] Louis XIV ordered the prisons to be emptied even while certain *parlements*, such as that of Rouen, were still filling them up with sorcerers. Sorcery was no longer a crime, but belief in the Devil, in astrology, in magic powders and in alchemy was still very much alive, in the hands of tricksters and charlatans and in the minds of the credulous individuals who were to be found in every social milieu. This very exceptional situation has been described as a 'mentality of magic'; but that divided culture might be better seen as evincing a profound anxiety over the social and religious upheavals provoked by the advent of a 'rationality' which enabled people to dismiss the crime of sorcery as a superstition, but not to shrug it off altogether. At court, as in the country villages, they believed in spells, in insolent demons, in love-restoring or wealth-restoring philtres. The rigid framework of the court, the stern etiquette and the remorseless competition for the king's favour engendered irrational fears of abandonment which a host of soothsayers, charm-sellers and tricksters from outside was always ready to exploit. All the charlatans who had been living quite openly off dubious alchemical dealings – since they were immune from persecution as witches or sorcerers – were now exposed in a society which still needed them, but was gradually and quietly discovering other forms of reason. Amongst the most deprived levels of the population there were strange networks of quack-doctors-cum-soothsayers who were resolved to rise in the social scale by means of sulphurous practices, black masses and child sacrifice.[16] There were no 'expert' doctors at the time, and the official pharmacopoeia remained a strange mixture. As in the fifteenth or sixteenth century, people believed in the medicinal virtue of the livers, lungs or brains of healthy animals; similarly, the same organs taken from sick animals were believed to cause sickness. People made mixtures of herbs and chemicals which could be easily procured from apothecaries or pharmacists, the latter often doubling as spice merchants who brought in spices from distant countries for use in medicines. 'In the absence of suitable regulation, anyone could buy the most dangerous substances on any pretext whatever.'[17] Judicial dossiers are full of complaints against irate neighbours who went out at night and poisoned the cats, dogs or herds of people they did not like.

The police authorities were on the watch for crimes of poisoning, rumours of which came indistinctly to their ears. It might be a whisper from the confessional, or a tavern rumour. La Reynie, lieutenant general of police, was on the alert; he was the first lieutenant general to be appointed in Paris, and was acutely aware of the poison problem, which he suspected to be a serious one affecting large sections of the population. His researches and his vigilance against coiners had already brought him into contact with gangs of evildoers who, under cover of magic and alchemy, worked both on counterfeit coin and on poisons. Things became more serious, especially when he noticed that every poisoning case revealed the involvement of ladies and gentlemen of quality, sometimes even from among the court nobility. The *parlement* seemed to be quite taken aback by this, and let itself be swayed by intervention from powerful individuals. Louvois then decided to create a special commission, and asked La Reynie to carry on the project. 7 April 1697 saw the birth of the Commission of the Arsenal, better known as the *Chambre Ardente*, an extraordinary tribunal from which there was no appeal and which conducted its business in secret. The *chambre* created by this remarkable procedure went on, between 1679 and 1682, to arraign 442 persons and pronounce 104 judgements, including thirty-four death sentences and numerous consignments to the galleys and elsewhere. During those years suspicion was thrown on numerous prominent persons, but it was scarcely possible to punish them as one would some vile poisoner from the lower orders; they were imprisoned, by *lettres de cachet*, in fortresses such as Belle-Ile, Salins and Salces. The net was cast very wide. Mme de Montespan was accused of using criminal methods to detach Mlle de Fontanges from the king, and even of trying to get rid of the king himself. At that point La Reynie, worried by the breadth of the investigation, and under orders from the king, halted all the proceedings. The *Chambre Ardente* was dissolved on 21 July 1682; its work remained unfinished, having been made impossible by the king's alarm at all the abominations going on around him, which he could not bring himself to make visible or public – or even to believe in.

Society as a whole emerged shaken from those dark days. Reading some of the interrogations, we can see how events were pushed to a climax and how they imprinted people's minds with a mixture of religious intensity, witchcraft and atrocities. We hear that on 9 March 1681 La Joly, a glazier's wife accused of crimes against children, told how she saw lying in a tin bath

> the bodies of two children aged seven months or thereabouts, who were two boys cut into several pieces, which had been brought close to one another in very red, fresh blood, and at that having touched the bodies of the children, she noticed that they were still warm and [that] she asked La Mignot if the two children had been alive when they were sacrificed.[18]

We can see that the Poisons Affair was more than just an affair, or even a skidding off the social rails. This lurid world where God wallowed in blood along with the Devil, and even the monarchy could not quite keep aloof, showed up a quantity of fears and familiar obsessions which were beginning to cast a raw new light on the space left vacant by the abandoned witch trials. The change was slow and profound, and all through the eighteenth century we can discern the traces left by that troubled period. They are of many kinds. As early as 1676 the people of Paris were rioting intermittently, thinking that their children were being kidnapped, for there had been many a dreadful bargain, and many a child had disappeared, during those dark years when aborted foetuses or sacrificed children were used in black masses. Later, in 1720 and again in 1750, Paris rioted once more, and rumour spoke of a compromised police force and a mean-spirited king thirsting for innocent blood. The shift from the tubfuls of blood seen by La Joly to the image of a bloodthirsty Louis XV was slight, but significant: public opinion and shared consciousness were still in that same sphere, where the sacred consorted with the diabolical, but the crime was now audaciously ascribed to the king himself – which, of course, offers quite another image of monarchy than that of Louis XIV, thought rather to be under threat from his nearest and dearest and their criminal allies from among the dregs of the people.

This difficult episode bequeathed ways of relating to the king whose themes and practices were borrowed from the world of alchemy, of talismans and visions. The Bastille dossiers throw up a regular, though steadily decreasing, supply of people accused of 'evil designs against the king', meaning nothing other than a suspicion of poisoning – by means of cakes laced with arsenic, or handkerchiefs impregnated with a deadly poison and left for the king to find. In 1683 Jeanne Roland, a baker's widow, was suspected of 'evil designs against the life of the king, having taken marzipan and cakes to Fontainebleau for His Majesty, and in order to get them served, used the arms of the Abbey of Longchamp and carried a false letter which she said was from the lady abbess.'[19] In the indictment they did not even bother to note the suspicion of poisoning: in 1683, an attempt to give the king some cakes was self-evidently criminal.

In 1687, they arrested a German who had come to watch the king at supper; among his papers he was carrying evil secrets to make women barren, or make them abort just before giving birth.

Such conjectures reappear from year to year; most of them are unproven, but all carried a severe punishment. A suspect visitor to the king, or a few cloths left about in the chapel at Versailles which was regularly visited by Louis XIV, had a smell of plots about them; talismans and pretended sorcerers were hunted down, and there was an attempt to regulate the apothecaries' stock-in-trade with its excess of remedies both true and bogus. This anxiety may have faded with the years, but it resurfaced from time to time, reflecting both monarchic fears and the mental furniture of a certain section of the population. Especially it surfaced in times of extreme deprivation: thus the winter of 1709, and the famine which followed it, engendered a goodly number of accusations of commerce with spirits and designs to kill the king by means of secret alchemical procedures. For example, La Doublet spent a long time in the Bastille for having protested against arrests of poor folk in 1709, and uttered death-threats against the lieutenant general of police; to which was added her dubious identity as a pretended witch, treasure-seeker and friend of demons. From the heart of poverty and deprivation came forth revolt, feeding on the ever-present remains of very ancient beliefs.

'You will murder the king . . .'

It sometimes happened that an individual thought he had been charged with the mission of killing the king, perhaps (he would claim) by a dream or personal vision. After a somewhat calmer period during which the stream of dangerous visionaries into prison began to dry up (there was only one serious incident during the regency, in 1721),[20] Damiens' attack on Louis XV started the process all over again. It was 1758, and the social landscape was, to put it plainly, one of multifarious anxiety. To the fears for the king's life were added furious arguments between those who blamed the Jesuits for the shameful crime and those who blamed the Jansenists. Against a background of political disturbance, 1757 had seen a breach in the collective imagination: the king's death was possible because Damiens had approached the sovereign and committed his act by means of a pocket-knife; the king's death remained impossible because the king was not in fact dead, the blow not having been hard enough. In this clearly defined space – defined in part by direct lines to the most ancient beliefs, and in part by links with the most recent events and the most immediate reality – social representations moved and had their being: the possibility and impossibility of the king's death were there in a confrontation which gave life and body to a double attitude, of aspiration towards a death which was covered by an absolute taboo. Amidst this confusion, while the police deployed every possible strategy to unravel all the threads of the plot which was thought to have been woven against the monarchy, there arose an affair which seemed of no great importance but which was immediately to unleash concerted action from police, doctors, judges and bishops. As we follow this case we come to understand the entanglement of rational and irrational forms taken by collective thinking under invasion from that most disquieting of all political adventures, the death of the king. Even more interestingly, we can grasp the way in which a single and singular individual calked his personal history on that of the highest authority in the realm – the natural way in which he linked the ups and downs of his personal history with that of the collectivity, weaving his own words and ravings around the figure of a murdered king.

Here are the facts. The story unfolds over twenty-one years, from 1758 to 1779, through a set of voluminous dossiers in the archives.[21] Thorin, aged twenty-six, was a native of Gruyère in Switzerland, a domestic servant, and had been living in Paris for only five years, serving the family of M. de Foncemagne, deputy governor to the Duc de Chartres. He was very attached to his mistress, Mme de Foncemagne, and grieved very deeply at her sudden death. It was this loss that started the whole affair. One night, Thorin roused all the other servants: he was in a state of shock, declaring that he had heard the bell ringing insistently from his dead mistress's bedroom, and that he had heard her calling him by name. Lying near his mistress's bed, he signalled to the other servants, who had come running, that he had lost the powers of speech and hearing. He asked for writing materials, and from that night and for a over a fortnight thereafter he told what was happening in a kind of phonetic writing used by a certain number of illiterates.[22] Through a strange question-and-answer system he explained that his mistress's voice had ordered him to fast for forty days, to pray to the patron saint of Paris, Saint Geneviève, and to have Masses said. She had added that he would only be healed when these things had been done; at the same time he revealed that he had a secret which he could not divulge. The case became an 'affair' at the precise moment when Thorin announced that there was a secret, and on this frail basis, over twenty-one years, the affair became more and more complicated. In 1758 (perhaps especially in 1758) the supposed secret was still an object of anxiety which no ecclesiastical, police or medical authority had yet been able to elucidate.

A doctor was brought to Thorin and adjured him to reveal all; the doctor called in not Thorin's own confessor, but Fitzjames, Bishop of Soissons, who since 1742 had been the king's principal almoner. He was famous for having refused the sacraments to Louis XV, lying ill in Metz, unless he sent away the latest royal mistress, the Duchesse de Châteauroux. We should also recall that in March 1757, two months after Damiens' attack, Fitzjames had unequivocally accused the Jesuits of complicity.

Under intensive questioning, Thorin explained the secret whose importance had been suspected by all around him for several days. He finally wrote what his mistress had ordered him to do: 'You will murder the king and as a proof that it must be done, you will remain deaf and dumb.' He immediately explained that he would not accomplish this act, seeing that it would be such an 'unspeakable crime against religion', as he himself put it. The unspeakable but spoken secret brought Thorin under some astonishingly heavy fire from all the Bastille authorities (he was already in the Bastille), plus the bishop (seconded by two priests), the lieutenant general of police in person, the first secretary of state for the police and the famous Commissioner Rochebrune, widely known for his skilled interrogations of reputedly dangerous criminals.

For two years the dossier continued to swell with correspondence among the authorities, police notes and medical reports. Every couple of days another important item was added to the pile. After that the notes became more infrequent, but they were added to regularly until 1779, when Thorin, worn out by his captivity, ill and almost out of his mind, was freed after his father's death and at his mother's request. He was first moved to the castle of Vincennes, and finally exiled to his native Switzerland.

If the procedure lasted so long, it was surely because the authorities were bound to connect it with the fatal year of 1757. It was also because at the core of the universal social obsession with the king's death was an establishment floundering in a system of proofs and counter-proofs, trials and testings: an establishment which was thus unable to follow the paths of logic and rationality and had no grasp of the kind of social disturbance which had hatched Thorin's visions; indeed, the establishment had never quite extricated itself from the world of dreams and visions in which Thorin himself dwelt, as if it were still an exhalation of truth, or could transmit a genuine message. The mental outlook of the judges and doctors was still contaminated with secrets and visions, despite the efforts of the former to seek out imposture and detect fraud, and the inclination of the latter to declare Thorin a madman. These representatives of the establishment were never able to link Thorin's history with that of the society which had produced it, and their arguments, as they searched for the truth, operated in several different registers; starkly revealed is their own uncertainty and inability to fit the event into a political logic – which would have immediately made it look less serious.

It is most striking that here, in the exact middle of the eighteenth century, we find all these doctors, priests, judges and high politicians who were never able to agree on a 'name' for what had happened to the humble servant, Thorin. Up to 1672, the crime of sorcery had been a convenient label for many a doubtful and dangerous activity. In 1758 there were still people in society for whom killing the king was a dream, a desire or a reality, and the desire was still fed by dreams and visions; but the establishment had lost all capacity to put a name to such things, for it was still spreadeagled between a supernatural world and a set of procedural realities which would not fit that world. Thorin's affirmations were, perhaps, sufficiently 'probable' to batter a breach in the categories – part new, part traditional – of medical, ecclesiastical and judicial expertise.

The only solid reply they could give was twenty years' imprisonment: that, at least, had a name. If the thing itself could not be named, and therefore could not be judged, it could be sternly set aside. The reprisal took the form of the exhaustion of the body and mind of Thorin.

Nevertheless, every section of the establishment had tried to respond to Thorin's case: the doctors thought of imposture, but never managed to prove it; the Church, in the person of Bishop Fitzjames, was convinced that there was a plot to poison the visionary domestic, make him deaf and dumb and impel him to commit the horrid act. The plot, as Fitzjames exclaimed at the end of a long address to Thorin, must have been 'devised by the Devil', a phrase which betrays a lingering belief in the existence of diabolical activity. As for the police, they were very much at a loss, but had the safest means of dealing with it: the fortress of the Bastille. The inquiry focused, as such inquiries traditionally did, on the attempt to elicit a desired admission. If there had been secrets or visions, there *had* to be an admission; but this attempt, too, faltered as Thorin passed from admission to counter-admission, and never actually admitted anything which could really enable justice to be done on him.

One day Commissioner Rochebrune, in a police note, wrote: 'This villain wants to make a scene in Paris.' However, he never pursued his inquiries in that direction, nor did he try to understand on what social and political stage the servant was acting out his secret; he was simply brushing aside all real danger, using a dismissive formula to recall that Paris would make a scandal out of anything. The astonishing sentence which closes the dossier, and which was written in 1779, significantly sums up the police inability to know or recognize anything about the affair: 'He was a madman of a very *dangerous* kind, and although he was more or less an *imbecile*, he was not incapable of *imposture* and has caused much *anxiety* over the person of the king.' There was no more to be said, but the sentence meant nothing: the vocabulary of 'explanation' scatters Thorin's act limb from limb in a web of classifications in which every term ought logically to exclude every other, but which cumulatively obviates any need to give a name to the affair.

A close reading of the writings and declarations made by Thorin reveals other elements which clearly show how certain subjects could connect their private history with that of the highest in the land. When Thorin enumerated his reasons (as best he could), and tried to explain himself convincingly, he could not be understood, because he took only a few elements of his private life into account: elements which could *not* be taken into account by the police, who were out to find either a plot or an admission of imposture. When he declared that the command to do murder neither astonished nor disconcerted him, he meant that once the scene of the murdered king had been acted out, the death of a king would become possible – but as far as the police were concerned, that scene must not even be heard.

Moreover, when Thorin heard his mistress order him to commit the worst of crimes, he interiorized the order as a deserved punishment for him in his personal capacity as sinner. Mme de Foncemagne had always wished him well, so her order could not but answer to the state of sin in which Thorin knew himself to be. Two years ago (he declared), while he was betrothed to a girl of his own country, he had greatly desired another, married women. God had subsequently punished him for that evil thought by subjecting him to the supreme test of murdering the king. He explained that mind-boggling truth as a temptation which had to remain impossible, and from which he must preserve himself by prayer and holiness.

Finally, for Thorin the death of the king, which he had been commanded to perform, was 'tempting' in the same way as those ardently desired relations with a married woman – and also as unthinkable and transgressive as any such liaison would have been. Painfully to the point of madness, Thorin integrated the ups and downs of his private life with the great stage of royalty and politics, which was still trembling under the shadow of Damiens' assault. Here we have an antinomial coupling – king's death possible, king's death impossible – onto which Thorin seems to have grafted another motif – king's death tempting, king's death desired – and in so doing he participated in a widely shared mental schema. What is interesting about his story (and probably many others) is its profound integration with public perceptions, not only within the collective structures of his time (the king's death, for example), but also within traditional realities (sovereign, desire, woman) and values, such as honour, which were respected by all.

The word and its history had crept onto the field of collective history and borrowed acceptable social images. In this sense, it was quite true that Thorin was 'making a scene in Paris'. That scene was dangerous, because it provoked anxiety about the king's person; but it was unlikely to be much heard by the representatives of power because it had made itself part of a popular consciousness whose forms of reality were unknown to them. What Thorin said could not be received by interlocutors who were unable to decipher the meaning of the events. Thorin had no secret, but he was 'the Other' who, as a subject, was feebly and clumsily trying to connect his story with history, and who, for that very reason, could not be heard.[23]

The impossibility of innocence

This 'who is to stop me killing the king?' was a motif around which gathered acts, denunciations, ruses and false opinions which the monarchy treated with the same rigour as if they had been real threats. Anyone who, even out of a conscious or declared loyalty,[24] falsely accused anyone else of talking sedition against the sovereign was himself a criminal. Anyone who, whether cunningly or naively, used the figure of the king's death was criminal. For anyone who toyed with that motif, punishment was inevitable and often took the form of lengthy imprisonment. An accusation of wishing ill to the king was a topos which contaminated all who touched it, either to win reward or to do harm to a neighbour: the fact that they might have been trying to draw the king's attention to their admirable conduct, by defending him against real or imaginary plots, did not save them from being swept up in the ensuing repression. No one could touch, even remotely, an evocation of the king's death without being swallowed up in the malevolence of the theme; one could not touch pitch without being defiled. He who brandished a loyalty that flirted with its opposite would stumble into subversion; in no case could love for the king be compatible with the manipulation of sacred motifs which it was guilty even to mention. This made innocence impossible; here again, throughout the reigns of Louis XIV and Louis XV, we can follow the traces of those individuals who thought they were drawing closer to the king, only to be cut off from him for ever.

In 1671, Marguerite d'Anglebermes, an apothecary's daughter from Orléans, sought to draw attention to herself by accusing herself of a 'design to attack the person of the king'. The exempt who arrested her and the commissioner who interrogated her realized that it was an imaginary crime which existed only in her weak and somewhat naive mind. Over twoscore years we find her in the Bastille, then in prison at Angoulême, and finally in the house of the Filles de la Charité in Paris. Her health was ruined, her eyes could scarcely see. In 1716 she wrote to the regent:

> that she was arrested in 1671, then again in 1682; that during this long interval she spent more than twenty-four years in the Bastille or in the prison of the town of Angoulême and the rest in the Christian Union, and in this community of Saint-Chaumont where she is at present in frightful poverty; she asks for leave to retire to whatever place she may think most suitable to her sorry state.[25]

The regent granted her request: after forty-five years, Marguerite d'Anglebermes was set at liberty. In the margin we read 'for accusing herself of an imaginary crime'; the dossier is filed among the crimes of *lèse-majesté*.

Jacques Vigier, a lawyer for the Paris *parlement*, was accused of pretended designs on the person of the king and was arrested on 3 March 1694. On 2 May, Pontchartrain wrote to the governor of the Bastille:

'He will see none but Monsieur de La Reynie [at that time lieutenant general of police], but I am nevertheless repeating it to you in this letter and telling you that you must take particular care that he sees nobody, not even the officers of the Bastille.'[26]

On 21 July, Vigier was allowed to take a walk on the terrace; however, it was soon discovered that someone had been plotting his downfall. And downfallen he remained, because it was said that he was involved in 'obscure private affairs'; in 1789 a note was added to his dossier: 'It is not known at what time he left the Bastille or if he died there' (much good it did you to be innocent!). Accusations outweighed denials: both Vigier and Marguerite d'Anglebermes were stained by the idea of an abominable crime and could never be cleansed.

The populace knew well that the motif of 'the king's death' was mud which stuck to whatever it touched, and they reacted with a vigour which could sometimes be taken to extremes. In 1703, a cabinet-maker became worried about his nephew, apprenticed to a master who often inveighed against the king. Convinced that the master's notions would inevitably make the apprentice guilty in the eyes of the authorities, the cabinet-maker panicked and denounced the master, in order to save his nephew from any contamination by this limitless crime, which affected even those who were in no way responsible, who had merely happened to be present.

In 1705 a young man sought to murder his parents, using neither dagger nor poison, but a weapon which he knew (or thought) was still more efficacious. He accused himself of trying to murder the king on their instigation. He was imprisoned in the Bastille, and later transferred to Bicêtre; whether he was eventually freed we do not know.[27] This topos of 'killing the king' must indeed have figured powerfully in people's minds if it could induce someone to make an attempt on the lives of his own nearest relations, with the mere multifarious evocation of it as his only weapon.

Much later in the same century, and even after Damiens' assault and the ensuing suspicions and accusations (including accusations against those who claimed they had heard seditious talk), we still find the same inability to establish one's innocence once one was caught in the net of groundless denunciation. The extravagance of the accusations against Adam Bunghert is so patent that we can scarcely believe what he had to suffer. He was a German, deeply religious and with small knowledge of French, a servant in a college of Capuchin friars. One day he was warned that the friars were in danger of being turned out, and he burst out in abundant lamentations. A man who was listening thought he could make out from the scarcely comprehensible mumblings of the servant that he was talking about murdering the king. In the Bastille, it proved difficult to interrogate Adam Bunghert, given his limited acquaintance with French; but he denied everything, telling about his past, his humble origins and the profession of coopering which he had hurriedly adopted. He spent most of the time crying, wherefore the following question was asked of the commissioner who had come to interrogate him: 'Are not his cries, and the affliction in which he is, proof that he has repented of his evil thoughts against the king, for remorse is awareness of a crime whose punishment one fears?' Adam spent a long time in prison, writing letters in German and others in almost indecipherable French. A translator transcribed them: 'I was born in poverty and my heart is timid and afflicted, and knows no politeness or civility.' Smitten with periodic despair, and not wholly in his right mind, he wrote curious missives in bad German mingled with words of Latin and French, notes of music, unknown characters and illegible scrawls. Later he was transferred to the house of the Frères de la Charité, where it was noted that he gave vent to fearful howls. The director asked for medicine to be given to him, and this request closes the dossier of a servant who did not even know French, though someone believed he had heard him blaspheming against the king.

Innocence was indeed impossible for the man or woman who ventured on the death of the king, either attempting it themselves or hearing others attempt it: all such acts, whether imagined, insinuated or only dreamed of, could come only from the minds of monsters. From time to time the police readily found words for those monsters, whose mentality fascinated them and gave them such assurance in detecting the causes of crime. This is Benjamin Crutz-Crosnier, accused of harbouring evil secrets against the person of the king in April 1684:

> Medium height, hair very black, very thick, curly but nevertheless very long. He has a very long face. He is badly pock-marked, especially around the nose, where he has a sort of leathery ridge higher than the rest of his face. He has very small eyes, very black and bright, his eyebrows are quite thick. He has a square nose and very pronounced nostrils so that one seems to be looking right into his brain. He has a very uneven mouth, the upper lip being much thicker than the lower. He has very white teeth, very fine and very small. He has a very sharp chin. His physiognomy gives him a very abrupt imagination which is always capable of depicting objects to him in the worst possible light. He has an impatient spirit and some quite good flashes of wit, but is incapable of reflection. He has all the turbulent passions but nothing of them shows, since his physiognomy is so bent on cruelty and the pleasure of vengeance.
>
> I had forgotten to say that his linen is grubby and that he has an unbecoming cravat with a very low edging of lace tied without a ribbon.[28]

6

'Your worthy subjects deserve a king who shall surpass them.'

While the 'death of kings' is a leitmotif traversing the entire period, we must not deduce from this that the relationship between king and subjects was fixed in immovable configurations. Far from it: between 1661 and 1775 there were numerous transformations, resulting in an uneven terrain on which the populace, grappling with puzzling events, built new sentiments towards the king and new representations of what his image should contain. These inflections were ordered (or disordered) according to diverse directions and did not necessarily build themselves steadily into storm-clouds (as it were); they formed part of a wild and varied landscape in which there was room to build criticisms which co-existed with more conventional attitudes. The study of those long years is valuable for the rich palette of opinions which it reveals: opinions organized both chronologically – in line with successive occurrences and political situations – and according to less mobile schemas whose roots lie in a definite tradition.

The co-existence of certain permanent themes (the king's death is one, the good but ill-counselled king another) with fleeting and constantly changing views attaching to the present event means that different notions of time intersect. Representations of the future built on the upsurge of the present, and the instability of opinions, so often criticized by the authorities, was really a reshaping of the sphere within which public affairs were, in some fashion or other, being appropriated. The appropriation was vociferous, sometimes tumultuous, and always disputed, constantly reorganizing the way in which the populace looked at events.

The figure of kingship was firmly set within specific parameters, and yet it *was* transformed, even quite violently. Let us examine some particular instances of these changes, and so take the measure – not of a inexorable tendency to desacralize the king (a theme recently explored by other historians), but the shifts of opinion whereby the populace legitimized its appearance as actor on the social scene and would-be interlocutor (though the term may be a trifle anachronistic) in a political universe which it was beginning to make its own. The progression was a jerky one, through a series of periods of repose and shared disappointments, or expressions of loyalty to the sovereign which assumed different approaches to his role and authority.

Thus themes and chronology go together; the king's place is always central, even when his function is under dispute. All reactions and criticisms focused on that place, bringing even the king to the point where he had to defend himself or modify some of his actions. The dossiers of people sent to the Bastille for seditious talk help us to understand the anxieties which weighed on the monarchy and the changed intentions which strengthened the resolve of the populace. These words and acts, rejected by the king, allow us to examine a series of images of the monarchy and of politics. This is especially true in and after 1744, the year when the king fell ill at Metz, when the Jansenist dispute was at its height and relations between Louis XV and his people were in a particularly delicate state, though this was before Jansenists were refused the sacraments. At this stage, mid-century, there appeared the idea that subjects had enough brains and resolution to judge a king whose actions sometimes invited them to cast off their traditional duty of subjection. Later, the troubled and violent year of 1757 (Damiens' assault on the king) reveals the anxious state of police opinion, while events from 1762 (expulsion of the Jesuits) to the Flour War show a volatile state of affairs, with many people openly proclaiming their views. Thus the present book, from its opening pages, has been ranging across several reigns according to a chronology which intersects with a series of themes, each richer than the last – or, at least, their content becomes ever more complex and diffuses rapidly into every level of society. The surface of society is agitated by the uneven but lively courses of opinions and spoken words, between forgetfulness and memory, conviction and enthusiasm, and particular moments in history at which the king's subjects acted sometimes indifference, sometimes legitimation – when they were not humming the discordant jingles of protest or anger. Such moments are not always the ones which have been officially recognized in the textbooks, because the momentary lived experience of reality has a sharp-edged instantaneity which the historian can seldom perceive. But it is precisely this rather exceptional chronology, itself an actor on the social scene, which concerns, and surprises, us here. To end with a fresh surprise, we shall inquire into the forms of and reasons for repression (which in their turn disturb the forms of reality), and the way in which the long years in prison led some of the prisoners to produce very lengthy conceptual elaborations: for their dossiers, full of letters and memoirs written in the Bastille, reveal a concentrated meditation on politics which also sheds light on attitudes outside the walls.

From 1744 to 1749

The period immediately preceding had seen encounters between two types of collective attitude which were diametrically opposed, but logically comprehensible. The repression of Jansenism, the surveillance of churches and priests, the attitude of the *parlement*, had generated a whisper (and sometimes a written opinion) that respect for the sovereign meant going against his orders. The bishops 'appellant' who had quarrelled with pope and sovereign, and the remonstrances of the Paris *parlement*, offered the populace a new field of thought: if they could pass judgement on their priests and magistrates, the forms of action taken by the latter could also provide the wherewithal for passing judgement on the king. We have already remarked on the surprise it was for police and monarchy to find the populace not only determined, but with attitudes of its own towards anything and at any time. Some element in the link between the monarch and his subjects had apparently been suspended.

However, in 1744 the king intervened personally in the war, and this aroused extraordinary impulses of love, fidelity and pride focusing on Louis XV. The sudden onset of royal illness produced shows of grief and outpourings of more or less accomplished hagiography.

Forever lost this precious Treasure lies
Though never was it dearer to our eyes . . .
The universe of its good fortune tires,
And Discord wakens, breathing angry fires;
Ne'er did the Hero's splendour shine more bright!
All Europe trembles as he moves to fight,
As from the Scheldt he comes to Rhinish brink,
And impious Furies from his visage shrink . . .
O heavens! Now we view a scene of doom:
There the triumphal car; here gapes the tomb . . .
Protecting Virgin, our Parisian wall
Now guard, as we thy children on thee call.
But what new horror now doth bring us low,
What sad and august spectacle doth show?

A wife goes forth in grief, what fate to meet? . . .
Nature is quenched, and Art is stricken dumb . . .
A new Ezechiel, upon the field
He falls; with modest courage Death he braves,
But seeks it not, and pities us, his slaves . . .
Most nearly was eclips'd this rising Star.
What ardent transports, what rejoicings then
When mortal Fear fled from the hearts of men!
Now happier yet, with yet more hymns of praise
To Heaven let us prayers and incense raise:
The Senate, organ of our laws, doth say
We should be merry: blithely we obey.
The Hero and the Father of this land
Is now restor'd by God's almighty Hand.[1]

But, perhaps because to speak out and pass judgement had already become a habit, the unhappy and humiliating episode of the king's mistress, the Duchesse de Châteauroux, and her dismissal on the orders of Bishop Fitzjames blew a chill wind over the king's return, especially when Parisians learned that the duchess had been more or less restored to favour. 'This news has been received with infinite disgust by all the people of Paris, and the news is of Mme the Duchesse de Châteauroux, concerning whom comments of all kinds are made by all, though they should be treated with circumspection if one wishes to avoid the Bastille.'[2] The murmurings did not last long, for in December the duchess died 'in astonishing agitation . . . they say it was a deposit in her head, caused by a suppression of her periods which is attributed to the chagrin of her disgrace, or the joy of her restoration.'

From 1723 to 1744 was a key period for the opposition, a singular and autonomous period during which opinion fed on new elements. After the first outburst of enthusiasm for the king's warlike image, disapproval of his anti-Jansenist policy was compounded by disappointment in him personally. The motif had its subtle aspects: it was compounded of traditional images (at last the king had gone to war, as his great-grandfather Louis XIV had so often done), plus disappointment in his physical and amorous capacities (the king had had three sisters, one after another, as his mistresses, all of whom had died an unpleasant death), while the pressure of a popular opinion which remained unheard began to disturb the political atmosphere. The Bastille dossiers are full of cases of repression against Jansenism, that is, attempts to dam innumerable streams of words. The police were seeking the best way to 'stem the course of this diabolical impetuosity'.[3] There had to be examples to deter those who talked or wrote out of turn: there were numerous arrests, especially as 'it was not only against the minister, but against the king that offensive speeches were quite openly made'.[4] News-sheets and the *Nouvelles ecclésiastiques* were seized; a decree issued by the Paris *parlement* on 18 May 1745 'forbids any person to compose or distribute any writings described as gazettes or news-sheets'. The repression was already well launched, for in 1744 Modeste Brunet, usher to the Cour des Monnaies, was accused of writing an abominable history called 'The Carthusian Porter'. In fact, he had merely copied out that supposedly scandalous pamphlet, for which crime he was put in a dungeon for eighteen days before appearing before the Chamber of the High Police and being condemned to imprisonment in Bicêtre by sentence of M. de Marville, the then lieutenant general. He was not freed until four years later, 'Aged 59 years and 4 months, incommoded with an oppression of the chest which he contracted in the dungeons and other places of his first detention'.[5]

Writing, speaking, anything could be held against the transgressor; but a Jansenist priest could scarcely have thought that he might some day find himself in the Bastille on a mere accusation of 'making faces during Mass' and on possible suspicion of possessing copies of the *Nouvelles ecclésiastiques*. He wrote to the lieutenant general:

I cannot be accused of a crime for having made faces during Holy Mass. If I did happen to do this, which I do not admit, the faces were not voluntary, but caused perhaps by a sudden intense itch or pain, or even a distraction which I would rather have banished and the effort to do so may have appeared a little on my face. As for having put some of the precious blood on my eyes, I can assure you that I never even thought of it, let alone did it.[6]

After several years he was sent back to his home region of Blois.

Thus, through those years, we find nothing in the Bastille archives but pedlars, pamphleteers, carriers of the *Nouvelles ecclésiastiques* and seditious talkers 'desirous of knowing the pros and cons'. Besides them there was a cohort of deserters and swindlers who got out of the Bastille by agreeing to join the army.

The atmosphere in 1748 was stormy; the repression of Jansenism was increasing, especially as the new archbishop of Paris, Christophe de Beaumont, enthroned in August 1746, was accentuating the repression of Jansenist priests and parishes. According to d'Argenson he behaved like 'a raging wolf',[7] increasing the universal impression that he felt personally attacked, that the inviolability of his innermost convictions was threatened. There was one comforting sunny spell, when in May it was learned that preliminaries of peace had at last been signed after a congress at Aix-la-Chapelle, whereat all Paris rejoiced. The rejoicing did

not last long, for a rumour (and, alas, a true one) ran that France was
'giving up' all the captured towns and would not profit at all from the
sacrifices she had willingly made: did the king care nothing for his
country's blood? In Paris, the stinging insult à la mode (originating, it
was said, with the fishwives) was 'You're as stupid as the Peace!'[8] It
became an ironic and universally accepted password.

One unexpected event cemented the ensemble of individual opinions
and turned them into one deep impulse of dissatisfaction. In 1748 a
crack appeared which, although deep, has remained imperceptible to
historians, and justifies those who think that outside traditional chro-
nologies there are forgotten moments of history in which a whole people
may forge its certainties and fix new models of itself and its government.
One of the clauses in the treaty of Aix-la-Chapelle, scarcely noticeable
at first among the highly visible clauses annihilating the French conquests,
demanded the expulsion from France of Prince Charles Edward Stuart,
the 'Young Pretender', who was seeking to regain the throne of England
and whose unsuccessful venture into Scotland in 1745 had been assisted
by the French state. The prince, thus abruptly humiliated, started a
campaign. Not only did he refuse to leave Paris; he immediately put up
a printed protest at Aix-la-Chapelle, under the noses of the assembled
ministers. Moreover, he circulated pamphlets which irritated the king,
who was more inclined to bankroll the peace between England and
France by acknowledging the Hanoverian succession.

This was international politics, over which ordinary subjects of course
had no authority; but the truth was that the prince was extremely
popular in Paris, where he enjoyed living with ostentation, generosity
and conviviality. Here, there or at the Opéra, he presented a spectacle
which Louis XV refused to offer his city, and the people repaid his
affection with friendship, giving him that part of themselves which they
had always reserved for princes. Prince Charles Edward was well acquainted with the Parisian mind, and entered with relish into the game
of 'city versus court'.[9] In the cafés, taverns and public squares, everyone
was talking about him and had a chance to read the 'Official Protest'
which he had produced[10] and which the authorities did not dare pro-
scribe, feeling that the atmosphere was not at all in their favour.

'10 December 1748. State event': this was how Barbier began his
narrative of an event which was to scandalize people generally and lead
them towards a representation of the king in which contempt outweighed
mere disagreement. Prince Charles Edward went to the Opéra, as usual,
and did not notice the guards camouflaged in civilian dress. 'Seizing him
by both arms and both legs, they lifted him up, and threw over him
and immediately tied round him a silk cord which incommoded and

compressed both arms.'[11] As he was being conducted to the fortress of Vincennes, thirty-nine members of his suite were taken to the Bastille:[12] 'from place to place along the road brigades were posted, for fear of violence.' The minister for foreign affairs was uneasy about the conduct of the affair and the rumours it might create. On 15 December he wrote to Berryer:

> The king having been forced to have the Prince [Charles] Edward arrested, it is only too likely that, either from ignorance or with evil intent, people will attempt to attach to this event rumours contrary to the exactness of the facts and the motives which occasioned it. It is in order to put you in a position to forestall or destroy these false imputations that I hereby add a historical detail which contains the principal circumstances preceding the arrest of the prince and the consequences which it has had up to the present time; however, when making use of this memoir you will be careful not to give a copy to anyone whatsoever or allow anyone to take a copy, and to gather together most carefully the different impressions which this event has made, and the discourses which it has prompted.[13]

There follows a memoir noting details of the operation, the forcing of seals and the impounding of the prince's personal linen. At the end are these words:

> The king, who could no longer defer the execution of a solemn treaty ratified by His Majesty, still less tolerate a procedure which had become so scandalous by reason of the Prince [Charles] Edward's determination to show himself at the theatre and in all public places, as if he sought to create a party for himself in His Majesty's capital and under His Majesty's nose, was finally compelled, albeit with regret, to have the prince arrested.

The prince's arrest was perceived as a kidnapping, and everything depended on that interpretation. Kidnappings had been frequent in Paris for some time; priests and Jansenists were well acquainted with that unpleasant experience. The populace were uneasy, threatened in their innermost religious convictions. The kidnapping of the prince hardened this discontent: the arrest, which was secret though it took place in public, and was organized to happen by night – albeit at the Opéra where idlers loved to watch their prince and his suite leaving their carriages – was exactly what was needed to crystallize rancour and anxiety. If the king could secretly kidnap a prince, it meant that everyone was under threat and that there was no limit to royal audacity. This gave birth to mixed feelings, a bold and archaic combination of two elements. The first was rooted in the admiration traditionally given to princes, even foreign ones, and in the laws of hospitality which any decent country must respect (it was not done to 'kidnap' a prince, especially if he was not local). The second took contemporary happenings (the repression of Jansenism) as a foundation for the idea that the monarchy became abusive when it invaded the inner domain of consciousness. The king, already perceived as arbitrary, now began to look like a traitor, a felon, one who secretly brooded on dishonourable acts. The images which this brought into people's minds were all the more forceful because they were backed up by ill-natured writings in which the king was compared to a tyrant, and the peace he had concluded was called not merely stupid, as formerly, but shameful. Which mattered more: the people's law or the king's law?

It was a curious atmosphere; the admonition quoted above showed how frightened the authorities were of the excitement caused by the whole affair. To forestall disturbances, festivities were organized to mark the peace. Barbier and d'Argenson noted the crowd's reactions: nowhere did they cry 'Long live the king!', and in places the decorations were burned or broken down in the midst of seditious mobs. The populace waited eagerly for the remission of a tax, the 'tenth', which Louis XV had promised if peace returned. Fearing lest it should never happen, printed pamphlets urged people to refuse all payment. The ministry told the *parlement* to have this infamous proposition burned; the *parlement* did nothing. The government made a medium-term concession and reduced the 'tenth' to a 'twentieth'; after a royal pronouncement the *parlement* was obliged to submit, but the public were loud in their complaints. On 16 June 1749 an inspector, d'Hémery, sent the following observations to Berryer, the lieutenant general: 'Mairobert said in the Café Procope, speaking of the reform which has been carried out, that the court ought to be f—d up for good and all, since it has no other pleasure but to devour the people and perpetrate injustices.'[14] Elsewhere, Inspector Duval was making reports of a similar kind; here, an officer waxes too talkative at his wigmaker's:

> This officer was at Gaujoux's, the wigmaker's, and recited in the presence of M. d'Azemard, an invalid officer, a writing hostile to the king, in which His Majesty was accused of being led by ignorant and incapable ministers, and of having made a shameful and dishonourable peace by returning all the places he had taken; that the Queen of Hungary and the Duke of Savoy, on the other hand, had always behaved with wisdom and prudence and that their ministers were much more enlightened.[15]

There followed remarks disapproving of the king's conduct. These notes by Inspector Duval were to be followed by a goodly number of others on the same lines, as well as by records of imprisonment for writing insulting letters about royal morality. And indeed, since 1748 Mlle Poisson, wife of M. Lonorman, the Marquise d'Etioles de Pompadour, had been the king's official mistress, the woman

> whom every man would have liked to have as his mistress and who was very tall for a woman, but not too tall. A round face, all the features regular, a superb complexion, very well made, a superb hand and arm, her eyes were rather pretty than large, but with a fire, a wit, a vivacity that I have never seen in any other woman. She was rounded in all her forms as in all her movements.[16]

Thus Dufort de Cheverny, the incumbent ambassadorial master of ceremonies, a function which made him one of the king's nearest associates, a central personage at court. Not everyone admired the marquise as he did – far from it. Around the Marquise de Pompadour there grew a seething hatred which engendered both pamphlets and ill-natured wordplay in public places, buildings and market-squares. Everyone spoke against her and Louis XV. Thus to political disappointment was added contempt for a tyrannical and immoral king: his love affairs were never to be respected as those of his predecessor, Louis XIV, had been. On the contrary, they were excoriated because the king was inept enough to disdain Paris, to 'rid himself' of popular princes, to indulge in secrecy and kidnappings at a time when his people were already becoming conscious of their rights and some of their desires. Louis XV's amorous activities, seen through eyes filled with a new critical spirit which daily became more confident in the support of a bellicose *parlement*, assumed the appearance of a defect and a sin. We must not forget the still-vivid memories of an episode in which the king had had three successive liaisons with three young sisters – interpreted as incest, that gravest of lapses in moral conduct. From then on the reproaches burst forth, bitter and severe:

> [That] the king who had had to do with the three sisters was scandalizing the people by his conduct and would draw all manner of misfortunes upon himself if he did not change his life; [that] the king despised the queen, was an *adulterer*; [that] France would be sunk in tormoil, [that] the king had not made his Easter devotions, and would draw down on his kingdom the curse of the Lord.

Thus the clamour rose and spread like a powder-train, putting the finishing touches to an alarming representation of the king, one of vice intertwined with wickedness and contempt for his people. It is scarcely necessary to enumerate all the scandals with which the names of king and marquise were linked in 1749 and 1750. Some wrote satires, others hatched plots; a few, seeking reward, claimed knowledge of fallacious designs on the life of one or the other and expressed themselves with relentless severity, as in this phrase taken at random from the archives: 'When a prince is sunk in debauchery, crime becomes a duty, or at least one dares to commit it publicly . . . this prince brings shame upon love and upon the nation and would bring shame on himself, if he were capable of feeling it.'[17]

For the record, let us mention one man: d'Allègre, a tutor at Marseilles. No one, save for a few scholars, now remembers how he was imprisoned at the end of 1749 for denouncing a non-existent plot against the life of the Marquise de Pompadour,[18] or that he was rediscovered in 1789, wasting away at Charenton, where he died a few months later. A few people would probably have recognized him in passing, for in the Bastille he shared a cell with a certain Latude, with whom he escaped in 1756. Having heard that the hated 'twentieth' had been imposed through the influence of the marquise, he had had the idea of protecting her by means of a stratagem which proved his ruin. Wishing to inform Mme de Pompadour of the danger which pursued her, 'he planned to express in the form of letters certain comments which were current among the public and to insert in them a kind of plot against her, making out that Maurepas was the author of the plot.' The detail is significant: d'Allègre composed his story out of street rumours. He was not a pamphleteer, merely a listener who put what he heard into verse (as best he could) – another, singular way of disseminating opinions which does not quite fit into the traditional schema of the author transmitting his thoughts to a passive readership. D'Allègre, from his prison cell, tried to win a pardon by writing heart-rending letters to Mme de Pompadour. The police note which accompanies this correspondence puts an abrupt end to the case: 'This man has become violent and unruly. He does not lack wit, but he is of an evil quality, restless and accusing. He is better suited to Vincennes than the Bastille.'[19]

Thus in 1749 a sheaf of events accumulated around one arrest (that of Prince Charles Edward) and provoked a unique political climate. Its leitmotif was essentially ethical: public life ought to be moral. Since the king gave the lead, the king ought to offer worthy images of himself and his entourage. Everything which was helping to create a real, but inchoate dissatisfaction in individual minds (the Jansenist troubles, the war, the unsatisfactory peace, etc.) was hardened by the arrest of the prince and turned into a collective feeling supported by remarks both written and oral, against which the police, for all their severity, were powerless. Therein lies the interest of this precise but fleeting moment: we can observe the sudden formation of a new state of beliefs about oneself and the monarchy, a new state in which each man thought of his own self-image while reflecting upon the Other – the king – and his actions; in which individuals required the monarchy to compose an image of itself, an honourable image which was all the more necessary in that for some time, the king had been trying to root out what belonged most intimately to them (his repeated refusal of the sacraments being the most obvious example).

It is into this context that we must fit the sentiment, 'Your worthy subjects deserve a king who shall surpass them.' Here, many ideas are expressed in a few words. Observe first of all the consent to the monarch, whose image retains its vigour. There is no subversion, no insult in the words; but they are subtended by the beginning of a powerful criticism. The phrase as written must mean a rising disappointment; the king has withdrawn from his duty. Loyalty to the king is still present, but accompanied by severe injunctions: the king *must* surpass his subjects. The idea is so normal, so ordinary, that it would pass unnoticed were it not preceded by the expression 'Your worthy subjects deserve'. Here the king's subjects look on themselves and find that they are good; they *are* worthy, and nobody has the right to rob them of that description. They had made war; they paid their taxes; they were learning, through parliamentary disputes, how to resist orders from above; they defended their clergy and their ways of believing; they loved their king. From the inner conviction of this worth came the idea that if the king was really the sovereign they had a right to expect, he had to surpass them in honour, honesty and scrupulousness. The pairing of 'worthy subjects and king who surpasses' has the traditional form of gift exchanged for gift. But here, the gift comes from the subject, and the king must respond with an unsurpassable ethic. The subjects and their worthiness initiate an apparent reciprocity which, because it is uneven (the king surpasses), maintains the integrity of the monarchic function.

'Your worthy subjects deserve a king who shall surpass them' expresses a situation in which sameness is newly allied to dissimilarity, and the (almost archaic) tradition of a strong and just king is re-expressed in a new framework where the thinking, acting, and therefore deserving, subject assumes his rightful place. Thus disposed, the motif of kingship changes shape, even if it still contains many of the usual ingredients of the king–subject relationship.

1757–1760: concerning the Damiens affair

Here I shall briefly lay aside the Bastille dossiers and take up an archive, now in the Bibliothèque Nationale, which forms part of the important collection associated with Joly de Fleury, procurator general of the Paris *parlement*, and is entitled 'Seditious talk concerning the Damiens affair'.[20] This does not in the least imply that no individuals were sent to the Bastille at that time for having spoken out of turn. But the six manuscript volumes of the Joly de Fleury archive offer a clear and valuable overview of the strategic positions adopted by the highest authorities of state just after Damiens' attack on Louis XV on 4 January 1757. They contain police reports, correspondence between the procurator and the intendants (provincial officials) and governors of the realm, rumours picked up here and there throughout France and denunciations of seditious remarks overheard in high places.

Scarcely had the knife struck than orders went out from Paris to provincial intendants and commanders to stop false rumours and listen for seditious remarks. Thus quantities of information came back from all the towns in France, furnished with obvious zeal, carefully sorted into chronological order by the procurator. Deputy procurators wrote about the atmosphere in their little towns; intendants and provosts drew up detailed reports noting what their subordinates, sent out to hunt sedition, had ferreted out in the countryside, in towns or even by the roadside. Reading between the lines, we can guess at quarrels over competence and serious rivalries among all these authorities on their various levels, all under orders to get the situation clear. When quarrels between rival authorities come to a head, we can read the responses from Paris which attempt to soothe down jealousies and exhort all and sundry to keep their eyes on a single goal: tracking down seditious talk. Paris and the provinces wrote to each other almost daily throughout 1757, less frequently thereafter, expressing anxiety and an eagerness to repress which was equalled only by the extraordinary numbers of or-ganized public prayers, Masses and *Te Deums* which were offered for the king's fortunate escape from assassination. The mechanics of it are startling; it is astonishing even to see how vast quantities of corre-spondence could amass around tiny incidents based on nothing more than a few vague overheard remarks, of which most were quite in-consequential and well-nigh uncontrollable, and could not be subjected to any real proceedings. Indeed, this very insubstantiality provoked a great deal of remark, reflecting on the safest ways of fighting against a vagueness of speaking which was impossible to pin down. Surveillance was exercised on every walk of life, as if the whole of France, in her houses and her churches, in her fields and on her mountains, was suspected of voicing abominable sentiments against the king, under the guidance of organized parties (Jansenists or Jesuits) who were resolved to pitch the kingdom into disorder.

Contrary to expectations, what emerges most strikingly from a cursory perusal of the six volumes in the collection is the very constitution of an archive which is entirely concerned with repression and not in the least with reflecting any opinion, or even the tenor of collective representations. The discourse it enshrines is the product and the effect of a hastily constituted strategy. These bulky volumes show something other than the mere existence of seditious pronouncements: they reveal the tangled and contradictory intentions of the monarchic system and how, once again, the eradication of popular 'ill will' was pursued in a way which actually aroused or invented it: the authorities were building unstable castles of mistaken conviction upon sand. Thus it can be said that the Joly de Fleury collection, a product of the Damiens affair, is a pure archive product, a result of policies adopted, rather than giving any idea of the state of France at the time. It is also, logically, a product of words, the words which the authorities were absolutely determined to prevent or punish; the dossiers are clear on this point. Information networks, designed to gather seditious whispers, often functioned as an incitement to the production and diffusion of such whispers. The archive is full of denunciations, hearsay, empty rumours which feed on themselves, becoming part of a vast mutual inquisition, everyone alert to their neighbours' whispers, even the expression on their faces and their vague indications of annoyance about any subject whatsoever.

On these fragile foundations correspondence and police proceedings developed at inordinate length without any feeling of astonishment at their own prolixity or any doubt of their solidity – and supremely unaware that their very existence was inciting words which would otherwise scarcely have been breathed to become real, alive, perhaps genuinely dangerous. It was a way of alerting the hidden organizations which directed the state to what could never be verified but could always be condemned: words, words, words. The true status of such words mattered little; they were quintessentially suspect, and moreover, they could only be 'breathed' by parties opposed to the monarchy. The Joly de Fleury collection was a way of getting an administrative, juridical and repressive perspective on what was perceived, from above, as the product of the noxious malignity of such parties. There was no idea of clearly revealing what subjects were saying, or even investigating the political and economic circumstances which could have made them say it. The drama was played out elsewhere, far from the common people, though they were the sole subject under discussion. It was played according to a schema which had its own preconceived reasons, motives and convictions, and which passed fractured sentences, overheard rumours and vague exclamations through its mesh without bothering to ask what their true foundations were.

Having explained the exact nature of these archives and situated ourselves *vis-à-vis* both their structure and their content, we are now in a position to look critically at the whole mass of reported words and investigate the facts and incidents which are mentioned. The discourse and the words which are recorded, and the happenings which are denounced, are heterogeneous and come from widely differing places; I have therefore decided to treat this disparate collection of more or less disjointed situations as one event, resulting from a plan of action by the police, within which I venture to look for meanings, for embedded signs of pre-existing social attitudes, attempts to imagine a possible future, postures and forms which may lead to the discovery of original forms of popular speech, however they may have been truncated or engineered. In attempting to explore the content of the collection I shall constantly bear in mind the matrix of police and administrative activity which produced it.

Circumstances producing seditious discourse, as classified in the archives

It was imperious fear which encouraged people to reveal conversations which, it seems, really had taken place. It made little difference where, for those who revealed them were so frightened that they made little distinction between what might be said by drunkards in a tavern, parishioners after Mass or partakers of a private meal who, surely, might have been allowed to speak freely. Some even reported what they had heard in the fields when the seasonal workers were getting in the harvest, punctuating their labours with more or less good-humoured remarks about current events. Others had, while on a journey, picked up seditious insinuations in a stage-coach, or noticed someone suspicious-looking. Elsewhere, employers negotiating for the hire of workmen had noticed an unpleasant attitude to the pay, the conditions of employment or just poverty.

Friends and neighbours who had witnessed some suspicious scene were quick to report to the provost or his deputy. Their motive was not so much to get the other person punished as to protect themselves against attitudes which they feared might stick to them and so put them in danger. Damiens' assault was another thing: in that case, it was not so much the shock of his action which stuck in people's minds as the effect of that shock when the authorities began to perceive it as a serious threat. Everybody knew that no one could really be immune after such attempts on the king's life. What you really thought mattered little; what was urgent was to avoid getting involved with the police, who were known to be not only intimidating but also harsh. No one must think or suspect that by overhearing seditious remarks or witnessing scenes of latent opposition to the monarchy you could in any way be regarded as being in agreement with such ideas, or worse, suspected as having shared in the opposition. The idea behind this anxiety was that if one person makes a remark, the person who hears it perforce becomes involved. This notion of social relations does not seem so very disconcerting once we know how far people's way of life and surroundings engendered a way of looking at the Other which chained them all together in a cascade of actions and reactions, solidarity and counter-solidarity, which shaped the forms of social intercourse in both town and country. Knowing about the Other, passing on a neighbour's news, contributed to the populace's self-image and made them feel a part of all that was said – or denied. Therefore, in 1757, the thing to avoid at all costs was seditious talk, for fear of being contaminated by the ill-omened shadow of Damiens' act. The kind of denunciation we see here is indeed the fruit of a clear understanding of how politics works.

The remarks which were reported fit into three different schemas spanning a long period of time, from the event itself to 1765. At first they cluster round the observed signs presaging the actual attack; then they focus on the procedures against the accused and his eventual punishment; later, between 1760 and 1765 (and even as late as 1770) they question the whole royal policy, as well as the person of the king.

'In a little while you will hear something terrible': these words were written by Fidèle Amable Chauveau, a shop assistant in the Rue Saint-Etienne, to his parents, to the canon of Péronne and to Mlle Couvent, a spinster who lived in Soissons.[21] He wrote on 2 January; in February he was denounced. Before then his aunt, Mlle Couvent, had made this brusque and nervous answer: 'I beg you not to write any news at all to us, save about your state of health.' Better no letter than words which might bring ill fortune to the recipient.

So great was the fear that some people sought in their own memories for something written or spoken which might have foreshadowed what was to come. On 9 July 1757, a tavern-keeper, name unknown, made a deposition before the provost of Mitry. He knew no more than his wife had told him, but that was so serious that he rushed to reveal it.

His wife told him, some weeks ago, that she was very anxious about a harvester, unknown to her, who came asking for drink which he drank

along with a good many other harvesters; this man had made unfitting
remarks, saying that he had had a spell cast on him and had gone to
consult a man to attempt to be freed from it, and that he had told him
that to remove the spell, he would have to do much harm to, among
others, the royal family, which he says he is very far from doing, but
[that] she was very much frightened by these words.[22]

The harvester was swiftly tracked down and arrested; his name was
François Lépine.

People remembered about evil spells; they dredged up vague memories
of stories which were told – at a wake, perhaps – concerning nocturnal
assemblies, secret conspiracies, masked parties making darksome plots
against the ruling powers. People denounced those story-tellers, those
poor narrators of tales as old as history, in which devils and evil spirits
destroy the order of the universe. In 1757 it was a certain sign of guilt
to have talked so much about things which were really quite unex-
ceptional. The authorities who received such denunciations had little
critical sense, even if they sometimes had their doubts. Twenty days
after the attempted assassination, an intendant wrote to the commissioners of the *parlement*:

> Perhaps the revelation which I am about to make has no direct bearing
> on the Damiens affair; nonetheless, it is of some consequence, and de-
> serves no less attention for that. I hear from Bouchier de la Timonière
> that from 1750 onwards he had been warning the king that he had had
> wind of plans to make an attempt on the king's life. Some fanatics had
> caused a little palace of gilded wood to be constructed as a hieroglyph,
> in which they placed on a throne a waxen figure representing the king,
> and stuck daggers into it while uttering curses on His Majesty.[23]

We may wonder, too, what to make of those who were denounced
for having (so it was said) egged on Damiens to strike his blow at the
king; to this end, they had made a theatre with people in masks and
disguises, of whom one played the king: '[that] to give Damiens practice
in shooting with the bow they had brought in specially a savage from
the islands to train him; and [that] he who played the part of the king
was injured, and was not pleased about it'.[24] News reliable, news highly
unreliable, the authorities accepted it all eagerly; they entered readily
into an illusory world of stories in which prophecies and devilries were
more prominent than any sort of reality. Once the events were over,
writings and remarks made long since were treated in the same way as
those belonging to the present. Some of the king's subjects were so
frightened that they would rake in their memories for any scrap of a
reminiscence which they could set off against a chronic potential for
guilt.

Later on, in the years between 1758 and 1760, the questioning turned to the activities – festive, ecclesiastical and punitive – which had marked the event, and focused first on the king's recovery, second on the execution of Damiens. Since the king had not died, had it really been necessary to expend so many prayers on a wound which had not, after all, proved very dangerous? Those who had been merely indifferent to the public demonstrations became suspect; some were accused of having gone on working in the fields while the village bells were calling them to join in the rejoicing at the king's recovery; neighbours suspected one another of having failed to shed a tear on hearing the news of the attack. Now, they were spying not on words but on faces, making belief to remember an expression from long ago. An artisan wondered to see a woman in tears; she retorted, 'that he surely did not know that the king had been murdered.' Surprised, the man replied that 'it was not such a great misfortune that she need be so saddened by it.' He was arrested some weeks later. Other examples show that indifference could be supplemented by anger. The interrogation of Jean Mirault, a carpenter aged fifty who lived near Tours, has a particular resonance, for it is echoed fairly closely from every corner of France. He was accused by Roger, his neighbour, of speaking ill of the king while he was repairing a clock: 'The day on which we began to pray about the attack, he was in the workshop of M. Bauger, a locksmith, talking with Roger, and they did not hear the bells of Savonnières ringing; Roger explained that it was for the prayers, and he replied, "What! The damned scoundrel missed him, then?"' Mirault's denials fell on deaf ears; Roger stuck to his guns and accused him of adding 'that there was a passage in Holy Scripture which said that men had asked God for a king and that they were quite mad to have asked for one because God replied that he would give them one, but they would be sorry for it.' A few days later, hearing that Louis XV had recovered, he incautiously remarked that 'If he had died it would have been no loss.' Jean Mirault never admitted to those words, even when locked in the Bastille.[25]

The punishment, too, was resented by some – and it could be a good idea to denounce anyone who had expressed some misgivings about the excessive severity of Damiens' execution and the scant attention which had been paid to his declarations, which had explained some of his motives. What the police condemned, and people in consequence often denounced, was popular resistance to the mood which the state wished to arouse, that is, immense grief over the king's wound, hatred for the abominable Damiens and unfailing love for Louis XV. Not everyone was convinced by monarchic propaganda; and as soon as one's words and gestures ceased to conform to requirements, one became a potential criminal. If one failed to hear the church bells, or to weep, one was vituperating against the king. In other words, love for the king, in such an ominous hour, had to be made visible. Indifference was a crime, and a neighbour could denounce his fellow for failing to show affliction, or for not turning up at the obligatory spontaneous public demonstrations. The language of loyalty was called for, and not to use it was a crime. Each and every person was enjoined to concentrate all his feeling on the event and to fill his thoughts with veneration for Louis XV and opprobrium against Damiens; silence on these matters could be interpreted as a form of disloyalty.

As 4 January 1757 receded into the past, the denunciations focused rather on genuinely political attitudes. The authorities' fears had shifted slightly; it was no longer necessary to persecute people who failed to turn up for ceremonies, and it was more urgent to check the development of any thought directed against the king and his personal or political preferences. Thus the final volumes of the Joly de Fleury archives contain denunciations based on criticisms of royal justice, or the king's latest passion for Mme du Barry. Here and there a disquieting rumour emerges: sometimes people were heard to murmur that it would be better if there was no more king, and that if another Damiens were to appear, it would not be such a bad thing ... The authorities had never taken so grave a view; perhaps we can perceive, for the first time, a realization by deputy prosecutors, provosts and police officials of every kind that France was seeing the organization of a collective feeling of detachment from the king: a feeling which could no longer be treated in the same way as formerly, when it had seemed quite sufficient to deal with malicious gestures, uncalled-for remarks or the occasional indifferent expression on someone's face. The stakes had risen, and the authorities seem to have been aware of this. No longer was it enough to rely on individual denunciations, of which there was an inexhaustible supply; they had to do something about an obviously deteriorating mental climate.

If fear was one motive for denunciations, malice was another. In such cases the accusations were often false, but the process of denunciation was often so powerful that the man or woman unjustly accused nonetheless bore the consequences. In those years, there was nothing easier than to destroy someone: the strength and efficacy of words had increased tenfold; the power of words, already so strong earlier, drew its intensity from the heart of the apparatus which had been set up to harass and repress every suspicious utterance. A word was like an arrow fired at an adversary's heart.

This brought long-standing private feuds into the open; one of the adversaries, profiting from the current situation, would try and do harm to his old enemy. The process is well evoked in one astonishing story. On 18 February 1770, the lord of the château at Coudray wrote a long report against 'his' priest, Father Blancillain. For a long time the two had been accustomed to have their Sunday supper together and gossip about current and local events. So, one evening when the lord felt a little piqued, nothing was easier than to inform on his priest. He described how, for years, Blancillain had been on the side of all malcontents, and on the pretext of an unimportant disagreement, pushed his accusations to the limit. The quarrel was over the building of a new mill: there was some grumbling in the village and the lord presumed that the priest had a finger in this disputatious pie. The lord wrote:

> In the course of conversation he reproached me for having just had a mill built in which, he said, I wanted to force them [the villagers] to have their corn ground, and because I had just set up a new smith near my château for their convenience and my own; which was prejudicial to the Rabiés family, also smiths, who for some time had been giving me poor and expensive service . . . he pushed his audacity to the point of telling me (I shudder to recall it) that my father and ancestors were honest men who would never have done all that, that I would be hated by all my subjects, that my house would catch fire, that nobody would put the fire out, that the kings themselves had narrowly escaped assassination, that I ought not to think I was safe . . . He could bring everyone to revolt, for he is a cabbalist, the son of a street entertainer, a Judas. Under the specious pretext of attracting to his parishes the devotion of the faithful, Father Blancillain is abandoning regular worship and divine service at my monastic church at Coudray and often does not say vespers there on a Sunday and on feast days although the entire office ought to be said there according to the foundation deed of 1156.[26]

Inquiries into such accusations often seemed to substantiate them, and through a subtle mechanism, aroused fresh suspicions or reinforced the earlier ones. Women of easy virtue, for example, readily attracted suspicious eyes; they had dealings with so many people that they were thought to be at the heart of the most malign conspiracies. In Paris, many of the letters to the lieutenant general of police came from private persons of dubious honesty, denouncing prostitutes who were accused of being a crossroads of subversion. 'The State must be purged,' proclaimed one of them, before launching into a great diatribe against a washerwoman who 'receives all sorts of men into her bed'. 'Purge the State' was an expression often used at that time by people of modest social pretensions (merchants or clerks) who would go to any lengths to gain the reputation of being loyal to the monarchy. Another described the situation of a little lace-seller who spent too much time entertaining Jansenists, and was herself suspected of attending assemblies of convulsionaries and gave her body freely; the fact that this was apparently an act of private vengeance did not deter either the informer or the investigators, who would follow any clue which came to hand. The informer's final argument for arresting the woman brings out the pernicious atmosphere of such arrests:

> She has the clap and is contaminating the whole of Paris. A commissioner ought to visit her and oblige her to name all her acquaintances; if she declares them, many truths may be discovered which may concern the State and the safety of our monarch; if she does not declare them, her refusal will declare her to be very guilty herself.[27]

This was signed: Raspoutel, master of arts.

Denouncing women of easy virtue was one thing; denouncing one's own priest was surely quite another. It happened frequently, however: many villages in France complained about what their priest said in his sermons. In 1763, at Laval, a Recollect friar, who had given a lecture in the parish church of Saint-Vénérand, was accused of having shamelessly violated the secrecy of the confessional. In fact, he had ardently defended that secrecy, even adding that if Damiens had informed him of his terrible plan, he could have prevented him from carrying them out, and deterred him from his act, without breaking the secrecy of the confessional. This was too much for the audience; one of them, a minor worthy of the town, immediately wrote to the bishop:

> Although it appears that this friar had no other design than to inspire confidence in the penitent, this lecture, My Lord, seems very indiscreet, and I would even call it very reprehensible in that the proposition is contrary to decisions on this matter, and to the law of silence imposed on regicide.

The Recollect spent a long time away from his parishioners as a punishment for venturing onto ground which, in whatever way, was contaminated – in which every word spoken automatically turned against its author.

Some people concentrated on theology and dogma and denounced what seemed to them contrary to the faith; others, more energetic or more malevolent, invented seditious remarks supposedly made by their priests in order to settle a score with a man whose authority in the village was, as is well known, quite often resented. Thus, a few days after the assassination attempt, Lesnier, priest on the ducal estate of Piney, was accused of saying the following in his sermon for the second

Sunday in Advent: 'that in these days we could see prophets in prison, Herods upon the throne who had no scruples about helping themselves to the wives of their subjects, and that nothing was commoner nowadays than adulterers among the nobles of the court.' The informer's letter ends with revealing naivety: 'I heard this story from M. Gayat, procurator fiscal of Piney, and his wife, who were at Mass that day.' This time, the authorities were suspicious of the affair from the beginning: the expressions seemed too violent, quite unlike the habitual tone of a sermon (especially a sermon for 17 January 1757); moreover, the informer had not even heard what he affected to report. An inquiry was quickly set up in the village, which split down the middle: some of the inhabitants tentatively confirmed the denunciation, while the majority reported different words. No, Father Lesnier had not talked of Herod that Sunday, but rather about 'Solomon and his impurities; he never made any reference to the court.'[28] The matter ended there; a note says that 'In fact, after investigation, we noticed that the agents of justice at Piney have a quarrel with the priest and the matter does not need to be followed up.'

Through this labyrinth of reports, memoranda, denunciations, anonymous letters and forced accusations we can discern a people divided, their divisions made more acute by the events of 1757. Echoes from the villages reveal inner opposition between villagers and their lord, villagers and their priests; or lively ill feeling among those in authority. Here, the police officers hated their priest; there, the priest and the lord of the château were at each other's throats. As for the ordinary inhabitants, they were often torn between fear of repression, sincere alarm at what had happened, indifference (so often counted as a crime) and also a certain amount of deference to the monarchy. In both letters and memoranda one can discern a genuine attachment to the king and expressions of profound loyalty, even if these are sometimes accompanied by criticisms or anxious complaints about the hardness of the times. One personal letter and a collective opinion from the poor of Tours will give some idea of how such people felt. Their remarks are touching, and the clumsy expression only increases our impression of the torment of indecision which some individuals seem to have suffered. At Poitiers, a nun felt the need to write, in simple terms, to her bishop to tell him that her heart was confused because, in spite of herself, she felt very far distant from the king, 'that poor majesty bereft of religion'. She admitted that she did not at all like being in the convent and being influenced by her sisters, who spoke against the king and the *parlement*. She did not well know what to think, save 'that many things were being hidden in the novices' house and that girls are being made unhappy there who would be of more use to the State.' She demanded that little girls should cease to be told 'that it is a beautiful thing to be a nun.' This singular letter expresses, with naive fervour, the situation of women kept in infantile subjection in convents, but who were still critical of current events, though they were immediately seized with remorse at their boldness in having had any thoughts about the State.

In 1765, the poor of Tours sent the king a collective address. Subtle and ambiguous, it began with protestations of loyalty to the sovereign mixed with disapproval of the public mood. 'It appears, following what all the people are thinking, that they no longer feel the respect which is due to our good monarch and well-beloved king!' The next sentence contrasts with the first:

> The whole people is at the end of its tether; the yoke is too heavy, it can no longer be borne, the countryside is utterly desolate, the peasant has nothing to eat, the prelate cares not at all, every priest sees himself as a prelate and never ascends to the pulpit save to insult his parishioners out of self-interest, because they refuse to pay him sums which are not due to him.

There is 'loyalty' in this speech, and the reproaches it contains are aimed at the ecclesiastical authorities, but the reference to a general lack of respect for the sovereign has an ominous ring, and suggests that the poor people of Tours were not far from a darksome kind of criticism. Some of the poor were more explicit, crying out in their misery and accusing the king of fomenting it, wishing that the king and queen could be reduced to ashes 'much more so than Damiens'. And there were beggars who had been arrested, humiliated at having been caught asking for alms and insulting the man who had forced them into that unhappy fate, hoping he would soon die, regretting that the attempt to murder him had failed and crying out that it would be enough for 'France to be lacking two eyes' for everything to get better.

'Something has been lost which will never come again', wrote Michel de Certeau with reference to the mystics of the sixteenth and seventeenth centuries. In the present case also, something has been lost which will never come again. The words we have heard spell out a lack, an abuse, the beginnings of a separation, a gulf opening in people's consciousness. But we must add that 'something remains', and we must know what that something was. There *was* still a relationship with the king, even if it was chiefly notable for its contradictory place within people's minds. In 1757 all thoughts *were* focused on him, the failed or absent sovereign, the well-beloved, the ill-beloved. The relationship with the king, caught up in a two-way process which simultaneously tightened and slackened its articulations, broke up into multiple images. It was those images which simultaneously revealed and created political opinions, one might even say a politics. Something had happened some time ago (1757 merely emphasized the fact) which had allowed the people to enter into politics while the authorities were still straining every nerve to imagine public opinion as something changeable, following blindly after self-interested and malicious factions. The people were somewhere else entirely, and the more the idea that they could be politically minded was denied, the more it developed, refining itself in the very midst of its stumblings and hesitations. If it were true that the people were politically involved with certain factions (the example of the *Nouvelles ecclésiastiques* is illuminating here), we can scarcely remain unaware that they had already shown themselves quite capable of making up their own minds.

Having read the Joly de Fleury archives with some care, we may now advance a hypothesis, and take issue with the tendency of recent historians to see 1757 as a turning point. If we are careful always to link the contents of subversive discourse with the circumstances which produced it, and examine the Fleury archive as a product of administration and repression, we can shake off the idea that the concepts it contains are wholly new. We must remember that this archive is the first of its type, and that the police authorities had never, before 1757, conducted such inquiries, so massive and so clearly repressive. The secret police reports and the imprisonments in the Bastille do not relate either to the same intention nor the same plan of action, and up to now, few historians have paid attention to either of those sources. That is why the Fleury archive looks so much like the reflection of a fundamental change. Archives can entrap us, and documents are deceptive. Like it or not, they are part of a theatrical production; and we must take a good look at the production details before we try to detect the elements which are disguised or tamed by the performance.

I was not much surprised by what I read in Procurator Joly's archives. To a great extent it agreed with the backwash of whispered opinion from the political events of preceding years. Of course, Damiens' assault was not a negligible event, for it reactivated that ever-present part of the collective imagination which was alive to the idea of the king's death. But the attempted regicide does not seem to have added anything fundamental or definitive to opinions already circulating in writing, in song or in whispers. We need only look back to 1748 (the peace of Aix-la-Chapelle), 1749 (the arrest of Prince Charles) or to the refusal of the sacraments and the bull *Unigenitus*. For the authorities, 4

January 1757 may have been a key date which changed their entire outlook; for the people at large, that accursed (or long-awaited) day came rather as confirmation of something they had long known in secret, even if some wept at it while others flung their indifference in a neighbour's face.

The failed murder of Louis XV had a ready-made place in public opinion; it tells us more about the monarchy's reactions than about any new and original turn of popular thought. The machinery we discover in the procurator's manuscripts has been swamped by its own abundant output: the dossiers are incoherent, the proofs are lacking, the legal proceedings are not followed up, the correspondence files are fat – more substantial than the cases which fed them. It is hard not to see that Fleury's proceedings unmask, primarily, an illusion: the illusion that there was a network of evildoers attached to malign factions with an influence on popular opinion. In fact, no such network was there to be dismantled, and no plot was discovered; the archive shows, amidst an astonishing degree of disorder, the seriousness of governmental anxiety, but cannot offer the curious eye even the beginnings of an accurate map of any network of influences. The only visible influence is fear. Everyone – authorities and local lords, priests and farm labourers and even beggars – was afraid.

The outburst of opinions expressed indicates that reasons for disapproving of or hating the sovereign had for a long time been crystallizing around ordinary themes such as injustice, poverty, religion; and within frames of thought in which the image of the king had been doubly manipulated. He was a contemporary figure who could be held responsible for the misfortunes of the times and criticized for his religious, political and personal conduct. But he was also that impressive and mysterious personage who went back into the mists of time – into sorcery, prophecy and myths which bred freely in the imagination. Both near and distant, contemporary and mythical, the king sometimes assumed the aura of that apocalypse so often evoked by the Jansenists. The pragmatic outlook which held him responsible for the misfortunes of the times – poverty and war – was juxtaposed to traditional ways of relating to him as a figure of legend; but those traditions themselves were beginning to break up under the redoubled onslaught of the Jansenist challenge and the emergence of individual consciousness.

The Fleury archive testifies to a general state of fear: the failure of the authorities to find what they sought, a deliberate attempt to influence public opinion. It witnesses in its own way to something which had been many years in the making: autonomous thinking which adjusted as best it could to events; a varied discourse of mutually illuminating criticisms. It does not license us to speak of a shift in opinion, or even of a sudden sharpening of consciousness after Damiens' assault. The archive has played a neat trick on historians by providing them with a kind of 'seditious talk' which has to be read in the right way, not only in a long temporal context, but also in the light of the other sources with which it belongs, and, especially, in the light of the circumstances which produced it. And if it is read in this way, it looks very different.

1760–1775: the flight of a king

I return now to the Bastille and its prisoners. The dossiers are numerous, indeed copious, and in them I read yet another history, the history of a society whose reasoning was based on the conviction that putting people in the Bastille was fair and reasonable; of a king who, albeit unwillingly, was slipping daily further away from the image he had had in the first days of his reign and further into the image of a man ('In a king I see no more than a man, my equal in nature as in civil status', as was said during the Pelissery affair) and who was to expire amidst general indifference.

Damiens: the aftermath

The political climate was a difficult one. It made itself felt through a series of minor *affaires* in which notables complained of disrespect or insubordination from their inferiors, feeling that certain social groups had distanced themselves from them. Their traditional authority can no longer have seemed sufficient, for they appealed directly for justice to the lieutenant general of police. On 4 July 1758, Mme Hatte de Vauné made a complaint against her own servants, who were imprisoned, to be released a few months later. Her letter has the vehemence of those who feel themselves insecure:

> I demand justice against two of my servants, who are husband and wife, their insolence has become quite bare-faced, there must be exemplary punishment, they must be taught the lowliness of their estate and respect for their masters, I remember having been in much the same case in the time of M. Hérault [the previous lieutenant of police] who answered me: The only women who do not get justice are those who do not ask it of me, social distances must be maintained and the inferior must bow to the superior, this principle is fair and wise.[29]

Mme de Vauné's wordy protestations betray a certain anxiety. It was, in fact, seldom that a quarrel between master and servant reached so high a level; such incidents normally went to the commissioner of police. The appeal for an order of imprisonment without trial shows a slight disturbance of normal habits, and probably a more agitated social atmosphere.

The same phenomenon must have been at work when on 26 July 1758 Mme de Sénac complained of the officers on the Saint-Victor gate when she passed through in her carriage on the way back from Fontainebleau. Showing her scant respect, the 'visitors' on the gate searched not only the carriage, but also Mme de Sénac's person, an action which she found unacceptable and brought to the attention of the king's first secretary.

> They paid no attention to my name and rank, which M. Arnoult [her son] declared and repeated to them several times, nor to the indignation I expressed to them for a personal insult so contrary to my station and so unnecessary. When M. Arnoult told them who I was they replied in so many words that they did not care in the least. I really cannot tell you with what vehemence these visitors insulted me.[30]

An inspector arranged a face-to-face interview at which the 'visitors' denied having been in the least insolent, though they admitted that they had interfered with Mme de Sénac's carriage and effectively forced her to alight. As so often, a brief note in the margin reveals the climate in which the event took place: 'Prompt proceedings in this affair'. In 1758 it was unsafe to let such incidents lie, for there was no way of knowing how dangerous they might be.

The atmosphere was complicated by the number of complaints against the police. It is true that they were making their presence strongly felt between 1758 and 1760, and this pressure provoked a chain reaction. Even within the police force there were denunciations, while calumnious notes found their way into certain offices. Cadot de Condé, a police officer at the prison of the Bastille, sent anonymous letters to the lieutenant general about several police officers. He was in turn denounced by an inspector (M. Hamard) and was condemned to nine years in the galleys after three days in the pillory. He made a preliminary stay in the Bastille, where he was interrogated by Commissioner Rochebrune, a great specialist in such affairs, about the 'evil letter' in which he had harshly and crudely criticized his subordinates, inspectors or exempts. They seem to have been a queer lot.

Roullier: deceived Berryer.

Bourgoin: an apprentice wigmaker who fancies himself as an inspector and supports his local brothels.

Coutailloux: the worst rogue in Paris.

Buhot: his father is a mere porter.

Villegaudin: once expelled from the royal guard.

Durocher: the greatest pimp in Paris.

Mouteront, Dunous, Roussel are ex-lackeys.

Ferry brings girls to his house to service men in religious orders.

Marais [a very well-known inspector]: a domestic.

d'Héméry [also very well known and a terror to the book trade]: a bastard.

Arborat: a lackey.

That is a portrait of the officers whom you have at your command.[31]

The punishment was all the more severe because Cadot de Condé was made an example of. Bertin, lieutenant of police, explained his policy to the *lieutenant criminel* de Sartine.

> You will recall that a few days ago I informed you and M. the King's Procurator that we were inundated, both at court and in Paris, with anonymous papers, threatening letters, false or calumnious messages in which the most respectable persons are not spared, and we considered that it would be necessary to make an example of someone to put a stop to such criminal licence. Here is a favourable opportunity, we have good evidence for doing it.

Is it so certain that the example was heeded? A police report suggests the opposite, noting what happened on the first day of Cadot de Condé's exposure in the pillory.

> Last Wednesday, Condé was brought out and put in the pillory at the Pont-Neuf where he drank a half-bottle of wine; the officer took off his hat which he put at his feet on the pavement and it was completely filled with small change given by passers-by. The same thing happened the next day in the Place de Croix-du-Trahoir.

Often, repression provoked irony and derision; when it became cruel, it aroused general indignation. 1758 was not a good year for making daring remarks, as the bailiff M. Moriceau de la Motte learned to his cost. Dining in a tavern in the Rue Saint-Germain-l'Auxerrois, he spoke bluntly about current affairs, got carried away and unwisely opined 'that in truth one ought to love one's sovereigns, but only when they deserved it'.[32] As we know, these opinions were shared by many people at the time. But someone told the lieutenant general of police. Perhaps it was the innkeeper, Paillard, himself – if we are to believe inspector

Coutailloux, the man whom Cadot had recently described as 'the worst rogue in Paris'. Moriceau de la Motte was arrested, transferred from the Châtelet; being further suspected of possessing and fabricating insulting placards (which he always denied), he was condemned by decree of the *parlement* of Paris to be hanged and strangled in the Place de Grève, which sentence was carried out without delay on 11 September. Under interrogation by Commissioner Chenon, Moriceau had elaborated on his reflections about the sovereign, declaring that the French were 'not at all obliged to obey a king who was only in that position by birth'. The police, still with the idea that examples had to be made, assured themselves that their punishments were effective: 'We must silence these unhappy Frenchmen who, despising their own honour, glory in insulting the king, his ministers and his *parlement*; impunity engenders and hardens criminals.'

Severity engendered and hardened ill-feeling. There was a sizeable crowd at the Place de Grève on the day of the execution, and Barbier devotes more than three pages to the affair, stressing that it was being said, sometimes out loud, 'that you could not put people to death for words or mere writings.' That was indeed the problem of those years: would what you said be the death of you? Moriceau betrayed no accomplices. He prayed for a quarter of an hour at the foot of the gallows before meeting his end at five o'clock in the evening. Barbier adds that 'People say that on leaving the Châtelet he asked people to pray for him, saying that he was a victim of the circumstances of the times.'[33] He was quite right, especially in view of the number of seditious placards which were stuck or posted up in all the main squares of Paris during the next few days. Elsewhere, others were constantly speaking against the king and Mme de Pompadour: here again there were persecution, repression and another series of anonymous letters which sent the police into a panic and increased the number of judicial investigations. It was the beginning of a new wave of announcements and denunciations of plots against the king and his 'infernal' mistress; people prophesied rains of blood and strong poison to be used on the marquise, who was blamed for everything that went wrong, in particular for the Seven Years' War, which was bitterly resented by the people. Orders of imprisonment provoked protests which in turn produced more *lettres de cachet*.

This could have gone on for ever, but some people were more affected than others: people such as M. Tavernier, imprisoned for moral misconduct in 1749 and sent to the Iles Sainte-Marguerite in 1750.[34] His foolish imprudence earned him the distinction of being the last remaining prisoner in the Bastille when it was stormed by the people on

14 July 1789. In 1759 he had attempted to sue for pardon and gain his freedom; it was an unfortunate choice of date, but in the Iles Sainte-Marguerite he was scarcely in a position to know the exact state of opinion in France. He had sent long vehement letters, complaining of his situation, calling for vengeance and expressing his dearest wish: 'I shall have all *lettres de cachet* against young people of good family revoked, they will be used only for criminals against the State'; and he had been embroiled in a plot against the king. He was accused of imposture, which could only make his situation much worse; he was put back in the Bastille, and, since he had no more to lose, he spent his time writing – rather well, with a heated, sinewy style, sometimes the style of a sick man, for he found prison life exhausting. He wrote insultingly against his father and mother ('that madness in the womb whence I was born') and against his king: 'It is quite astonishing that Louis XV, who has acquired the title "Well-Beloved", should make the condition of the men he has the honour to command more deplorable than that of the boars and stags in his forest; at least they are not skinned alive.' In 1775 came a brief letter saying, 'I have water on my chest and have lost a good deal of blood.' In 1784 the governor of the Bastille sought a letter authorizing Tavernier to take a walk for half an hour each day: 'This prisoner has need of it, I think, not having left his room in the twenty-five years he has been in the Bastille.' In 1789, the doors of the Bastille opened for him; he was completely out of his mind.

These descriptions of atmosphere are not mere indulgence in anecdote. True, the Bastille dossiers are so rich and laden with emotion that it is hard not to be laying them constantly before the reader; but that is not our chief concern. It is more important to understand how, in 1760, a process was taking shape by which words, writings and placards acquired a life of their own, which the agents of repression occasionally touched on (a hanging was never an unimportant incident), but never really grasped. During those years the process was cruising on at a speed which nothing could halt: Paris and the court were indeed deluged, day by day, with anonymous libels; some deplored it, others approved. The great show trials and punishments did nothing to stem the flood, and the political climate settled into a period of permanent criticism shared by all, great or small. Everyone *assumed* the right to speak and think, and this universal self-licensing, punctuated by a repression which did nothing to weaken it, gave rise not so much to new forms of subversion as to a refinement in cognitive and reflective capacities. The originality of this period lies in the forms taken by discussion and criticism rather than in their actual content. Louis XV began to count for less and less, as if it were no longer really his position or physical person which was at stake, but another kind of politics, removed from him, which interested everybody. To see how this came about, we must pay attention to the great public events which shook France during this period.

War: 'an army of automata bringing ruin upon us with their endless trains of servants'

The aim was to destroy the king of Prussia, and this meant maintaining and strengthening the alliance between France and the courts of Vienna and St Petersburg, while trying to maintain the independence of Poland, whose king and queen were related to the dauphine. A shock development: Frederick II invaded Saxony, and Louis XV proclaimed his readiness to help, saying that he would send 24,000 men, though the king's council did not seem in much of a hurry to perform this task. A second treaty of Versailles was signed on 1 May 1757, leaving France with heavy obligations and few advantages, but Louis XV was attempting to crush Prussia while trying to establish a '(Catholic) Franco-Austrian continental condominium which would turn the Low Countries into a vassal of his kingdom and leave him free to turn all his strength and resources against England', as Michel Antoine clearly explains in his biography of Louis XV.[35]

The call to arms was criticized on placards which appeared in many places; and the 24,000 Frenchmen, ill-prepared and without the personal encouragement of Louis XV (who could not leave the State), suffered two severe defeats alongside their German allies. The first, at Rosbach, against Frederick II in November 1757, provoked sorrow and anger as the weakness of the troops and their officers' lack of talent speedily became apparent. A new and worse defeat occurred in June 1758 at the battle of Crevelt. The moral effect was deplorable, for the obvious superiority of the Prussian army was clear to all eyes, especially when it was faced by allies who could not agree amongst themselves. The discontent was entirely turned against the court, which was held responsible for all the misfortunes and humiliations, especially when an edict registered with the *parlement* in September 1758 demanded a free gift from every town, suburb and borough in the kingdom. It was perhaps not wise to speak of it in public, but people had got past thinking about that; they cursed and wrote anonymous letters to the king. Silence had had its day. In the letters to the king one can still sense a certain veneration (unless it is simply a strong respect for phraseology), as well as an underlying conviction that it was a grave misdemeanour even to address him. The sovereign had been so 'distant' for so long that the tone of the letters bears witness to the fact. Maître Touche, a graduate in law, was arrested for writing to the king.[36] He had taken oratorical precautions: 'I know that a feeble mortal is unworthy to speak and write worthily to the greatest of kings, and that one would need a mouth of gold to accomplish it,' but this did not prevent him from giving forthright expression to his thoughts.

> If divine and human laws were religiously observed, would we hear in every province the lamentable cries of oppressed and ruined people, who, reduced for the most part to a despair whence they cannot arise, prefer to abandon their labours and their cottages and let their country become desolate, and expose themselves to the harsh necessity of begging their bread? The disorder and vexations which have prevailed in your armies, the nakedness, the hunger, the miseries of so many kinds, make a most natural picture ... Ah, Sire! I will say no more, I fear to displease Your Majesty if I continue, and to betray you if I cease.

The dilemma is clearly seen: not to speak out is self-betrayal, to speak out is criminal in the eyes of the king. This fundamental experience of impossible silence irradiates all those years and gives a frantic edge to words – and to pens.

On this theme of war and misery, writers of fiction and persons of all social degrees never seem to have been deterred by the threat of the Bastille. That threat could fall even on a centenarian: Constans, an author aged 109,[37] never lost his verve, and when in February 1760 he wrote

> In this realm, the prince has everything: fair palaces, vast forests, good hounds, and additionally ministers who relieve him of all cares and courtiers who amuse him, sleek and fat and always gay, while the countryside, it is true, offers a different spectacle. There we see only pale, fleshless bodies which could be taken for skeletons; but at court they are made to laugh and in the countryside to go hungry –

he knew that it would take him to the Bastille. Not for long, it is true: in view of his age, he was set free in April.

A sort of indifference to repression could come over the bravest. In 1761 Pilon, a receiver of income at the Hôtel de Ville, complained bitterly about the taxes and fulminated against the king who 'eats the child in its mother's womb'.[38] A neighbour sought to silence him, but without success, for Pilon answered spiritedly, 'What will they do to me? They will put me in a dungeon, but I care not at all, for they will not say that I am a rogue.' There is an awareness that speaking ill of the king may be punishable, but confers no mark of infamy. The distinction, though probably seldom expressed, is an important shift, another way of conceiving the relationship between the king and his subjects. The Bastille may have been a prison, but it was not necessarily full of miscreants, and Pilon was not alone in thinking that seditious talk of this kind was a crime only in the king's eyes. Many others would go to the Bastille or to Charenton for protesting against that 'imbecile' war and that king 'who no longer seeks the happiness of his subjects'. Yes: the king was elsewhere, and by shrugging off his duties amidst one of the most symbolic of kingly activities, that of war, he was granting his people the freedom to criticize.

1762: the expulsion of the Jesuits

This rang out like a victory: in April 1761, the Society of Jesus was on trial. Father La Valette, Mission Superior in Martinique, had been engaged in an enormous trading enterprise with businessmen in the south of France. He went bankrupt, and the creditors appealed to the *parlement* for compensation; on 8 May, the Great Chamber decided that the Society of Jesus should pay. For several months, crowds had been invading the Palais de Justice where the case was being heard; they did not disguise their glee, clapping and jeering at the few Jesuits who were present. In the course of this debate, the magistrates criticized the statutes of the company. After lengthy deliberations, the *parlement* pronounced two decrees which dealt the society a mortal blow: twenty-six works by Jesuit authors were burned, and the king's subjects were forbidden to attend Jesuit schools. In Paris there was noisy rejoicing, and everywhere the *parlement*'s decrees, dated 6 August 1761, were snatched down by eager readers. Barbier, of course, was there to tell the tale: carriages jostled one another outside the printers', and travelling salesmen ran out of stock, so many were the clients demanding to have their own copy of the decree. Every night the printers went to work again to satisfy a public which cherished lively memories of the hatred of the Jesuits against the Jansenists. On Sunday 9 May, everyone was queueing to get the decree or get someone to read it to them. Despite the decision of the *parlement* and the public expression of a glee which some people thought indecent, it remained dangerous to speak out too loudly, whatever the view expressed. Those who spoke up for the Jesuits were punished as much as those who spoke against them. The event stirred up the discussions which had already taken place many a time over the attack by Damiens; once again there were arrests of plotters or those who carried ill news concerning the king's life. Jacques Ringuet, an abbé, declared himself a Jesuit and proclaimed, rather too loudly, that he had been a party to the attack in 1757 and had defended that murderous and parricidal doctrine. He was hanged on 29 December 1762.[39]

The expulsion of the Jesuits set words free; it was therefore not surprising if the king's death and the memory of Damiens were once again present in people's minds. Some exclaimed that 'Damiens was a saint', others that 'if they could be sure that by hanging God Almighty, the king would suffer as many torments as Damiens, they would hang God Almighty.' Once the Jesuits were gone, people thought it safe to heap the same opprobrium on both God and the king, both of whom had been under their baneful influence for so long. The vacant place left by the Jesuits was a symbolic space; the real events – the public book-burnings, the closing of schools, the Jesuits packing their bags – were relatively unimportant. Other things emerged from the mere fact that the event had taken place: the *parlement* victorious, the king and Rome at last confounded, God restored to His faithful people, the conviction that they had been right all along, the triumph of the people's will. The place vacated by the Society of Jesus was filled with a boiling excitement which almost transcended the actual object of the quarrel and the expulsion. That is certainly how the episode ought to be viewed, as the dossiers of prisoners go to show. Repression was still hounding anonymous letters, hostile remarks about Mme de Pompadour, visionaries and budding Damienses, much as in previous years. However, when we look more closely we notice that the police were persecuting not only acts and writings, but an attitude, meaning (as they themselves put it) 'the lively and exuberant imagination' of the people at large, which reinforced the mood of rebelliousness. That having been said, the excitement was persecuted; but the more tenacious the investigations, the greater the enthusiasm. I shall pay some attention to a single example which I think is emblematic of this period: the case of Pierre Dayrivier, arrested on 26 November 1762 by Inspector Delahaye for what he had been saying in cafés against the government and ministers.[40] There is no doubt that Dayrivier had been talking loudly, and pejoratively. They did not know his station in life; he might have been 'employed in provisions for the last war', but nothing was less certain. In any case, he incessantly criticized all the operations of government and wasted no time in denying it. He had to be made an example of, and Commissioner Rochebrune exchanged notes about him with the Comte de Saint-Florentin: 'If he were not punished,' wrote the count, 'it would increase the number of troublemakers, which is already considerable.' The notes on the inquiry which preceded his arrest are clear: 'This man has for a longtime been interfering with too many things; moreover, he is fiery and enthusiastic and thinks he has more intelligence and reasoning powers than unenlightened persons, and this has apparently induced him to fail in his duty either to the monarch, or to the government.'

Enthusiasm and reasoning were on trial, as they would be in many more cases; gradually, things were changing, positions were shifting. As criticism became more and more overt, in the assurance that it was justified, the police responded by putting most of the blame on 'reasoning'.

1763–75: 'Pray to God for the king who is blind, deaf and dumb' (placard displayed in 1768 at a time of high bread prices)

1762 saw the publication of Rousseau's *Emile* and *The Social Contract*, and the first appearance of Bachaumont's *Journal*, which continued up to 1779. It should be recalled that these printed memoirs, though known under the title *Journal*, were written by three different authors. Bachaumont wrote five volumes; Mairobert composed ten before killing himself in 1779 after being censured in a decree of the *parlement*; the rest are the work of Moufle d'Angerville, a lawyer well known for his *La Vie Privée de Louis XV*.[41] Thus the *Journal* begins with the expulsion of the Jesuits; and Bachaumont, who had a keen appetite for anecdotes, scandals and interesting details, greatly enjoyed describing the whole comic, disorderly and festive side of the affair. He made note of the songs, the insults, the parodies, the caricatures of fleeing Jesuits, and filled his pages with all manner of notices conveying the noise and excitement of the event. What he really enjoyed was emphasizing the public excitement – the very thing which so confounded a government shaken by the unpardonable misfortunes of the war. His pages express the pleasure of hearing people speak freely, whether in salons, in books or on benches in the public park. Bachaumont celebrated the celebrations of the mind, and his news items, which were keenly appreciated, went with feverish speed. In fact, they caught the public fever, and showed the public its own image, critical and impassioned. The *Journal* invents nothing, but reproduces, in a disorderly way, the animation which had seized on minds tossing between disappointment and hope. The king was near; the king was far; the king was near.

Perhaps that was not the best time to set up a statue of the king on horseback on the square opposite the swivel bridge of the Tuileries. It was February 1763; the operation took three days, and a large crowd gathered to watch. Mockers and troublemakers, accompanied by the usual informers, played their accustomed part. Say out loud that the king was going nice and slowly, laugh at the king and his horse, and you would find yourself in the Bastille for several months. The climate was once more swinging towards war between king and *parlement*; new taxes were in the offing, but no one knew exactly what. The secrecy maintained an atmosphere of anger, and there was talk of remonstrances, perhaps another *lit de justice*. This did take place, on 31 May 1763; the king came to the Great Chamber of the Palais de Justice, the highly official ceremony attracted a number of spectators, but no one came out with the traditional cries of 'Long live the king!' The people still knew nothing of what exactly was being planned. In fact, old taxes were suppressed and new ones added. The people were indignant at this new action by authority, which they held to be unjust, and acclaimed the *parlement* when it brought out a decree declaring that these forced registrations 'tended to the subversion of the fundamental laws of the realm'.[42] As well as this decree, the *parlement* began to gather critical documentation against the state of public finances. France had been worried about her finances for quite a time, and especially about the secrecy shrouding budgets, expenditure and income. As far back as 1759, a Swiss, Rudolf Effer of Sybourg, had been arrested and taken to the Bastille by order of the king[43] and under the following accusation: 'pamphleteer on the finances'. He had been distributing round Paris copies of a manuscript entitled 'Present state of the secret and general affairs of the finances of the realm of France' (1759), and from then until 1767 he made the acquaintance of various prisons: the Bastille, the Châtelet and Bicêtre. Something of a poet, something of a tragedian, his comments on that act had broken the silence surrounding one of the monarchy's best-kept secrets. The contents page of his manuscript is a piece of audacity in itself. It reads:

Ordinary revenues of the king
Total of revenues
State of the ordinary expenditure of the king
Recapitulation of expenditure
Balance of revenues and expenditure
Royal revenues assigned for a limited period
Recapitulation of revenues
Royal revenues alienated and assigned in perpetuity
Extraordinary transactions performed in France since 1755 concerning the war with the English and other matters

The register itself contained a strict account of expenditure and income, organized in columns and without any kind of commentary. Even so, it was a great deal too much.

Then there is a brochure of 1763, which was distributed free to the public and was entitled 'Riches of the State'; it proposed a plan for taxation, quite simple and apparently equitable. It was the work of a counsellor of the *parlement*, who narrowly escaped the Bastille and was warmly welcomed by the public, delighted at being able to debate a subject so serious and so important, with which they had never before had the opportunity to become acquainted. 'The populace themselves were discussing it and wished it to be put into effect,' noted Barbier. Bachaumont observed the same popular enthusiasm for anything which could keep them up to date with what was most dear to them (in every sense of the word): taxes.

Amidst this surge of opinions one is struck by the detailed way in which quite simple folk managed to express themselves. Talk reported as seditious at this time contains lengthy disquisitions on people's viewpoints; they confer a very different tone from that of the simple insults or hasty exclamations aimed at a bad, faithless and debauched king. The story of Anne Apoline Josèphe Chevalier, wife of Nicolas Renard, who sold tobacco in Reims, gives a good idea of people's ability to judge public affairs.[44] This ability to generalize puzzled the commissioners and the lieutenant general; we already know that they believed that they, and the aristocracy, were alone in possessing that ability, and they were now astonished to find it, or scattered traces of it, amongst the simpler folk. Renard's wife was denounced in December 1765 by Gabriel Piot, a clerk in the offices of the city of Reims. He declared that he had heard her in her shop 'interfering deliberately in affairs of State and of religion'. From this denunciation onwards, there was clearly a resolve to show up the woman's determination to 'reason'. She said that she had heard the news that 'M. the Dauphin was very ill, and that she would rather the king died than the dauphin because if that prince were king he would bring the Jesuits back to France; added that the king and the *parlement* were atheists.' The next day, in spite of her husband's attempts to silence her, she said that she had received further news and was now sure that the dauphin, still very ill, had been poisoned 'on behalf of the *parlement*'. She was conveying a good deal in a few words: she preferred the dauphin's life to the king's, set king and *parlement* down as atheists, wanted the Jesuits back again, and reawoke the spectre of poisoning, harking back to the height of the Poisons Affair . . .

As usual, Commissioner Rochebrune conducted the interrogation in the Bastille. Renard's wife expressed herself with precision (and caution) concerning her original and iconoclastic way of showing attachment to the king, giving us a singular sketch of the sort of relationship which could arise between king and subjects. Yes, she did love the king with all her heart, and knew that that love must be shown in speech (here she was repeating what she was expected to say: it was not enough to love the king, there must be words and gestures); every morning and evening she never forgot to pray for him, but she could not but be anxious about the health of the dauphin, knowing that he had 'in his chest a pocket which filled and emptied alternately'. She further explained that she could not understand how the Jesuits, 'after having been so well thought of at court, have had such a shameful sequel' and had been forgotten by everybody. She maintained her loyalty to the king, accused the clerk of having exaggerated some of the things she had said, and ended with an allusion to sacred history: 'She remembers, she says, that she has read there that the chaste Susannah was accused of adultery by two elders who were put to shame by Daniel.' Thus she defended herself stoutly, but the rewards were meagre: she spent a long time in the Bastille, her husband went mad and she herself was afflicted with 'a prolapse of the bowels'. In 1767 she managed to have herself and her husband admitted to the 'married couples' quarters' at the General Hospital 'to end their unhappy lives and mitigate their affliction'.

One may, of course, find Renard's wife less than convincing and think that her protestations of loyalty to the king do not fit in very well with her peremptory judgement on his 'atheism'. In any case, when up against Commissioner Rochebrune one had to 'hold on' and excuse oneself as best one could. However that may be, Renard's wife, consciously on the Jesuits' side, perceived quite clearly the complex trade-off between king and *parlement*, even if she added to her reflections the old terrors of assassination and poisoning. Where she was rash was in imputing atheism to both king and *parlement*; monarchy and magistrates were very sensitive on that point. The case of the Chevalier de La Barre, which occupied the headlines for a time and aroused the wrath of Voltaire, is proof enough: for his impiety and sacrilege (he had mocked at a crucifix) he was beheaded at Abbeville on 1 September 1766, after the *parlement* had confirmed the initial sentence.[45] The evidence against him was notoriously extracted from a populace which was never allowed to express its real thoughts, but was required to express its horror of any disrespect for religion. Equally notorious is Voltaire's exclamation: 'The inquisition is a feeble thing in comparison with your Jansenists in the Great Chamber and La Tournelle . . . We have been delivered from the foxes and thrown to the wolves.'[46] Here Voltaire put Jesuits and Jansensists on a par; and he went on to attack public opinion, unfortunately without paying much attention to the way in which it had been elicited.

The years from 1764 to 1775, which saw events as striking as the famine of 1768, the scandalous liaison between Louis XV and Mme du Barry, the suppression of the *parlements* by Maupeou and the king's death, were recorded with persistence and consternation by a right-thinking, conservative chronicler: Hardy, the bookseller, whose manuscripts are kept in the Bibliothèque Nationale under the title *Mes loisirs*.[47] His regular observations of street life are of great value; he notes in detail all the placards which appeared in the capital, and describes the street scenes and the crowd movements which accompanied various events, including public executions. His style is nothing like that of Bachaumont; violent, disorderly, fevered or agitated, he complains and sometimes breaks into lamentation. But he was a faithful friend of the *parlement* and flung himself whole-heartedly into the struggle on its behalf; his sorrow was boundless when he witnessed Maupeou's *coup d'état* in 1771, though he remained respectful towards the king. As the placards became more and more insulting and Paris was drowning in anger against Maupeou, Hardy wrote:

> All placards found in various places in Paris prove how far the excitement had gone, and how desirable it was that some angel of light and peace should come and unseal the eyes of our monarch by showing him the height of the precipice from which he was about to cast himself without knowing it, believing that he was increasing his authority.[48]

The precipice got higher even as celebrations were being organized to give an impression of rejoicing, and Hardy sadly recounted those parodies of collective consent:

> 1 March 1772. Today, the Sunday in carnival week, we saw in the Faubourg Saint-Antoine . . . a very great number of masques, and an even greater crowd of benevolent spectators, foolish individuals such as are picked out of the life of the people, and almost all in the pay of the police. There is every reason to believe that more money than usual had been distributed to the populace so that they could rejoice and dress up in various ways. We were assured that certain persons had been told off to ensure that they were making proper use of the money they had been given, according to its correct destination. We were further assured that all the maskers had gathered on the boulevard opposite the door of the lodgings of the commander of the watch, before they went off in procession. Why they had been subjected to this sort of parade or inspection, we were not told. It was also said that several disguised persons were going to appear and make a spectacle of themselves around the mansions of the chancellor and the lieutenant general of police in the Rue Neuve-Saint-Augustin. Might we not suppose that the intention of the minister, and especially of the chancellor himself, by this conduct, was to make sure that the king could be told that never had the citizens of his good

city of Paris given so many signs of rejoicing and content than during the
carnival days of the year 1772, although a good many people were saying
that all His Majesty's subjects were suffering greatly from the disastrous
revolution that had just been brought about in the various bodies of the
magistracy of the kingdom?[49]

It was an ineffectual masquerade; as Hardy had noted, many individuals were suffering, first from famine, second from the decisions of
Maupeou, which were robbing the people of the magistrates from whom
they expected support. Paris was seething with hatred of Maupeou;
everyone, from the working class to people of good family, was making
allusions to history and the law. Women also took part, as often in
times of crisis when major upsets were in prospect. Pamphlets were
circulating, some opposed to Maupeou, others written by his supporters.[50]
The return to absolute power, without the traditional mediation of the
parlements, was coupled with a notable reaction from the Church. The
clergy were delighted, and the Jesuits were soon back again. There was
no stopping the deluge of pamphlets which was flooding over France;
and from then on, persecution of individuals became more and more
frequent. There were arrests in Paris, and houses were searched. Anyone
carrying a pamphlet risked severe punishment.

All these upheavals are, of course, documented in the archives of the
Bastille, where the detainees were numerous and their dossiers bulky.
Looking in detail at these arrests, their motives and the type of seditious
discourse reported, we see that the debate has changed its form, or
rather its very nature. Of course, there were still naive individuals ready
to denounce their neighbours, or their nearest and dearest, for insulting
the king. Such was Louis Laporte, an assistant tailor who had retired
to the poorhouse at the hospital of Bicêtre; he was in unrequited love
with a nun called Henriette, a servant of the mother superior.[51] Having
been spurned, he decided to cause trouble for the nun by writing under
her name a letter addressed to the councillors of state and filled with
insults against the king. He was soon found out and put in the Bastille,
whence he wrote to the lieutenant general, de Sartine, a letter so moving
that I cannot pass it over in silence.

If I cannot get her [Henriette] back, I want to destroy myself or get myself
hanged; the world without her seems to me terrible and fearful, as if I felt
the earth trembling beneath me; I want to let myself go to heaven or hell,
to see if my soul is there.

In his delirium, however, he maintained that if he had written as he had
against the king, it was because he was 'angry to see that the king

governs justice so badly, having suppressed the former *parlement* which had more wits than he did'. History was within him, clothing his passion; in that sense he bore some resemblance to the visionary, Thorin. There were Laportes and Thorins all through those years, sadly mingling their faith, their loves and their disappointment in the king; despite all the shifts of opinion they show how the king was ever-present in the crises of their lives, at the turning point of their personal histories – pathetic, derisory or tragic.

But the general run of Bastille prisoners between 1768 and 1775 were of another sort: prisoners who had clearly advanced to a state of mind in which criticizing the king seemed such an obvious thing to do that they wasted little time on it before going on to clamour for 'the right to speak and write on any matter of State'. The vocabulary changed, and the political reflection became more sophisticated, day by day; they even spoke of resistance to despotism and of a king whose authority came not from God but from the consent of the nation. Sometimes they even dared to say that subjects had a perfect right to demand accounts from the king!

Most interesting of all is the desire, expressed as a right, to be acquainted with what was going on and to deliver their own judgement upon it. The figure of kingship which was being constructed at that stage was, perhaps, of little importance (it was not a very impressive one); the urgency lay in the conviction that to speak out was not just a legitimate act, but an inalienable right. The affair of the Abbé d'Iharse, who was arrested on 7 April 1771 'for having spoken offensively against the king in a café',[52] gives a good idea of the fundamental change in opinion which took place during those years of Louis XV's reign. What the Abbé d'Iharse actually said is of little importance; the problem no longer really lies there. His interrogation, on the other hand, which is dated 21 April 1771, shows the problem with marvellous clarity. The police asked him, in substance, how he could reconcile his attachment to the king with a 'spirit of curiosity'. The commissioner's question reveals the clash between two irreconcilable attitudes, for in 1771 loving the king and being up to date with the news were mutually antagonistic:

> Asked him if he is attached to the king and if he does not, in a spirit of curiosity, make a point of visiting private persons in the town and then going to cafés to inform himself of current news, true or false, which he recounts with vivacity without reflecting that it is not for a subject obedient to his sovereign to excite his mind with news.

We can see that the abbé's reply was not unsubtle; he readily and openly took up the distinction between king and court, admitted that he liked reading foreign news-sheets (we know what was in *them*) and looked for the remonstrances made by various *parlements* in the kingdom; and he proclaimed 'that a heart can be open to the praises of the king and still complain about the court'. The letter of supplication addressed to de Sartine by the abbé's brother is clear on this point: the brother saw nothing wrong with speaking freely about current affairs and asked what was reprehensible about such an attitude. He added slyly, 'Unless you consider guilty a man who, reading the decrees and remonstrances which fill the foreign news-sheets, might be capable of saying "That is well written."' This puts the debate in a new setting, and the struggle moves onto hitherto unexplored terrain. To the people, hearing and judging news were normal acts; for the police, as for the monarchy, eagerness for news was tantamount to treason.

After this it would be tempting to think that public opinion was born at just that time, as it laid claim not to its objects or its content, but to its own existence. It would be rash to do so, however. For a long time, as we have tried to show in this book, individuals had been reflecting on events, fabricating morsels of personal opinion on the basis of precise facts. Now they were considering the monarchic system, brushing aside a king who they thought was absent from himself and, especially, breaking the fetters into which the monarchy had compelled them, in the belief that not only were they equipped to speak out, but that they had a legitimate right to do so, and must exercise that right openly. Secrecy was out of fashion: the secrecy of king and counsellors, but also, and more so, the secrecy which compelled individuals either to whisper, in constant fear of spies, or to be silent. This attitude undoubtedly represents a major shift away from the position of those – probably still numerous at that time – who boasted of having a secret which they would tell only to the king. But most of the people had moved on, to a place where they had access to other forms of identity; where new situations, each more novel than the last, could be created. The gulf opened up by this realization revealed new possibilities to anyone who had come to dwell in that place with the conviction that he had a right to do so. Such a man, no doubt, was M. Lombard, clerk to a former procurator of the *parlement*, who found himself in the Bastille on 14 March 1772 for distributing pamphlets and being friendly with Chartier, an usher 'who likes everything that is new'.[53] Lombard was captured by Commissioner Serrau, and explained himself a few days later in a vehement and unequivocal letter.

Of what am I accused? Of having pronounced opinions. Ah, Monseigneur, who has not? I do not know what I should think of one who, seeing so extraordinary an event [Maupeou's reform], remained unmoved. What, in fact, did I say? A few vague opinions which could not have influenced the plans of the government in the slightest degree; opinions which, like many others, will be lost in the narrow sphere which they have traversed.

Lombard puts matters clearly. How can one not think? What should one think of those who do not think? How can one believe that anyone's thinking is essentially subversive, threatening, or even influential, since it is so easily lost among so many other thoughts? The public mind had its own vigour in 1772; opinion was beginning to seem both a right and a duty. We are far from the definition of public opinion given by Michel Antoine in a recent book on Louis XV, where in a section entitled 'The phantasms of opinion' he writes, 'When we speak of "public opinion" under Louis XV, we mean first and foremost the humours of Parisians. The capital was the privileged observatory of the court and government, and a receptacle for all kinds of lies and misinformation.'[54] In 1772, the humours of Parisians, amidst all the 'lies' and 'misinformation', could be very shrewd indeed ...

In any case, whether or not it is a question of moods, the Parisians seem to have been so anxious about the new situation of the *parlements*, and the resulting disturbances, that they could scarcely find the time to take any interest in the illness of Louis XV, despite the government's attempts to spur them into prayer and devotion. Not that they were really short of time; they simply lacked the motivation to work up any emotion about an event to which they were virtually indifferent ... Hardy sorrowfully tells us so, finding the Parisians disrespectful and their expression of hatred when the king's death was announced on 10 May 1774 'very shocking'. On the other hand, when it was announced shortly afterwards that Maupeou was to be exiled, there were uncontrollable demonstrations of joy. But the spring of 1775 brought other troubles: high bread prices, explosions of popular feeling in the kingdom, the Flour War of July 1775. Public opinion was turning wrathfully towards new preoccupations.

In prison

The reader will have realized by now that the Bastille was not a cheerful place. Those who spent a long time there were gravely affected in body, and sometimes in spirit – all the more because there were no fixed rules to govern their detention, and their situation depended on circumstances and on the regular discussions about them which took place between the governor of the Bastille and the police authorities. These discussions decided whether they would be allowed visits, correspondence, clean linen, walks on the terrace and, of course, the day and hour when they would be set free.

Whether a prisoner was to be freed or sent into exile depended on the highest authorities of State, especially during troubled times such as the Jansenist disturbances or Damiens' assault. In certain cases, the king was personally consulted by the *lieutenant criminel*, the lieutenant general of police or even the first secretary of state, to decide whether or not a prisoner could be freed. The time spent in prison would have given his jailers an idea of their prisoner: whether he had repented of his crimes, how old he was, whether his nearest and dearest had made representations on his behalf; an intervention from his parish priest would carry a good deal of weight. More surprising are annotations which give an idea of the measure of punishment: certain reports from the governor state that such and such a prisoner has been 'well punished', so that another future could now be contemplated for him. 'Well punished' was a subjective criterion with an element of pity, or even compassion, for those who had fallen ill in their damp dungeons; but it could be something quite different, a real awareness that the Bastille was a truly dreadful place for individuals who were paying the price for acts which might not, after all, have been so terrible, but who had been made an example of.

'To calm people's minds', 'to eliminate the number of troublemakers', 'to make an example before the people': such were the reasons given by the police, who, as I have already emphasized, were more interested in the details of single, disturbing events than in analysing a general situation whose causes might be wide-ranging. Proofs were often insubstantial; the authorities admitted this, but they still preferred to lock people up, if they were suspected of contaminating the political atmosphere, rather than leave them at large. Their perception of the accused often stopped at a description of his personality, without any attempt to fit his behaviour into a wider story, that of the society of which he was part. Thus prisoners were most often described as 'monsters' or 'mad': talking sedition, dreaming of the king's death or carrying pamphlets on one's person were proofs of a deviancy that only madness – or diabolical wickedness – could explain. However, as the years went by we see a gradual change in police attitudes, prompted by a massive increase in the expression of popular opinion, the vigour of critical attitudes and the increased persecution of the seditious speakers who were growing like asparagus in May. Commissioners of police (especially Rochebrune) and governors began to notice that a diagnosis of monstrousness or madness was no longer sufficient to explain those rebellious spirits who expressed themselves so eagerly and so fluently on current events. In 1764, Pauquet,[55] a confectioner who lived in a furnished room in Paris, was noticed by an informer who followed him throughout the day. He was curious and 'was always walking about the city and was amused by the slightest thing' (nothing extraordinary about that!); from time to time he dropped in at an inn, where he would tell how he occasionally wrote to the king, having a secret to reveal to the Marquise de Pompadour which, he said, he had learned on his journeys to England and Ireland. These assertions put him into the Bastille, where, as usual, he was interrogated by Commissioner Rochebrune, who thought he was 'hot-headed almost to the point of fanaticism'. Later on, when in prison at Charenton, he was again interrogated by Rochebrune, who noted in the margin of his dossier, 'He talks nonsense with a presence of mind which amazes me.' The phrase is striking: what, indeed, was sense, and what nonsense, in those minds so excited by events? Madness could not explain everything when prisoners were found to be possessed of presence of mind and a lively critical spirit. The authorities were gripped by a vague feeling of uncertainty, though they did not wonder very much more about it.

There was reason to be astonished, nonetheless. Between 1757 and 1765, quite a number of people were at work within the walls, demanding from the governor their share of the meagre rations of pencils and paper. Writing, to the authorities' minds, was dangerous. Writing could save one from sickness and despair, thought the prisoners who spent their time writing long correspondences, memoirs, mathematical or geometrical theorems, political treatises full of reforms and visions of the future. Others more self-centred drew up lengthy addresses justifying their conduct and their ideas, and wrote voluminous letters in which new ideas rubbed shoulders with respectful addresses to the monarchy. Many suggested improvements in the budget, writing out reforms to the state finances and compiling miniature treatises: from the darkness of their confinement they reflected on the reasons which kept them there and exercised their intellectual daring in conceptual systems, often obscure ones, fighting by any means possible against secrecy and secrets. Several managed to have their writings made known or even published: for instance, there was Le Prévôt de Beaumont,[56] who in a dozen or so manuscripts managed to produce a respectable treatise of 272 pages entitled 'The Cries and Moans of the Oppressed French Subject in the State Prisons'; it was addressed to Louis XV and aimed against his ministers, lieutenant of police and prison governors. The manuscript was written in 1778, published shortly afterwards and proved very influential.

There is room for an exhaustive study of work done in prison under the Ancien Régime and of the impact on the public of this activity, a product of inner conviction, literary or scientific inspiration or the attempt to forestall a descent into madness. From de Sade[57] to Beaumarchais, via a great number of lesser-known names, one would discover an activity as feverish as the activity outside the walls which the police was striving to eradicate. Perusing some of these works, one can still feel the harshness of the imprisonment and its dire effects on even the liveliest minds: some prisoners slowly succumbed to physical and moral collapse, and their writings bear the mark of it. The writing becomes shapeless, the style breaks out in noisy and disordered phrases, entire passages look like howls of lamentation. In the course of time some texts even become indecipherable, peppered with cabbalistic signs or flights of musical notes. These pathetic relics of individuals struggling with their own toppling reason bear laconic marginal annotations from the police – 'His mind is quite deranged', 'He is very sick in the head', 'The blood is coming from his chest and his mind is disordered' – which often justify keeping the victim in prison and support the original diagnosis of madness at the time of the arrest.

And meanwhile, outside the walls, people were also claiming the 'right to write and speak about any matter of State'.

Conclusion

They have spoken; I have written. What I have done, basically, is to deploy their words – or word – under a series of headings which help us to see how it emerged, established its authority and founded its legitimacy. I have tried to show its coherence as well as its contradictions, dwelling as much on its archaisms as on its eagerness to cross new frontiers. I have not sought to integrate it into any kind of global discourse, but to grasp certain moments of emergent meaning; to seize a glimpse of its liveliest expressions; to mark the places where it stamped its desire for legitimacy.

We have seen how it was fashioned by space and time and twisted into multiple forms of expression clinging to the single instant, and to a will to know which was proof against all discouragement. We have not sought to divine whether it was a word of truth or not, but to show how it developed within a context of probability which gave it enough strength and motion to cause disquiet among those it addressed. I have crossed the threads of official anxiety with those of individuals, the better to show the new constructs which could produce morsels of truth. We have not witnessed the birth of a certain opinion nor tried to measure it, for, accepting the attendant risks, I set aside the idea of seeking its origins, which I considered too cramping. The words within the word we have fitted into interpretive networks so that the resulting events and 'operations of thought' could be built into recognizable outlines. Sometimes we have read in this word a multiplicity of strategies in which defiance and cunning co-existed with assent to exemplary kingship. Sometimes we have seen how its apostrophes and interjections stand alone, distanced from news overheard or eagerly sought;

distanced from information given by others or by the monarchy itself, with its austere rhetoric and its alliance-seeking ceremonial. We have seen legendary and traditional themes spring back to life even as different practices of thought were emerging, meeting the earlier ones and sometimes thrusting them aside, sometimes linking with them in a curious amalgam. We have taken note of trifling incidents upon which effects and emotions formed themselves into new convictions; we have discerned great events which merely reinforced indifference or irritation. We have seen (for the source material left us little choice) that the king was a privileged locus of words; we have seen his imposing presence; we have uncovered the successive configurations of his person and function; we have glimpsed the way in which he shrugged off his subjects' expectations, and grasped at new gestures which his subjects summarily rejected. We have perceived moments in which an individual affirmed his own identity even while his mind was troubled by political and monarchic policies which were ejecting him from his former positions.

Where we have seen the emergence of critical attitudes and the ordering of opinions caught between assent and transgression, we have tried to understand what forms of understanding and emotion they used in order to exist – and later, cease to exist. We have looked for their would-be points of anchorage, but we have tried not to construct an order which smoothed over all the discontinuities and singularities of time.

I may be accused of having created overall *dis*order; but, reflecting on the motives which triggered thoughts and actions, I think we have brought out several points.

1 The people of Paris were eager to keep up with current events: it was part of their way of life, a habit which was both reflective and emotional. The city was an informational sphere whose inhabitants organized themselves so as to *know* more and unravel the secrets of king and monarchy. Public curiosity was not a character trait, but an act which brought each and every individual into politics.

2 A taste for information and the practices necessary to acquire it emerged as much from a certain structuring of the urban sphere as from the attitude of a monarchy which was disinclined to consider popular opinion as a worthwhile adjunct.

3 Knowledge of public affairs began with a knowledge of other people's business: the sort of knowledge that the city and its configuration obliged everyone to acquire. There is a strong connection between the private attitudes of the Parisian towards his neighbour and the attitudes he might assume towards an event. Information about other people and news of current affairs were means of existing fully in a

milieu where no one was ever alone. The urban sphere shaped individuals and put them in a position of knowing about the Other, being known and recognized by the Other; this was the only way of finding a place in that uncertain jungle of inescapable and unforeseeable relationships. The affairs of one's own neighbourhood dictated the very forms of knowledge of, and in, the city, while the monarchy, as part of its policy, repeatedly attempted gestures of oneness with its capital. The king made himself into a spectacle for his cities, conveying information in a way which demanded admiration or sympathy. But, by reason of a curious twist in the productive effects of that ritual, the people were receptive to the outward forms, but not to the message. They would turn out for the ceremonial, but looked elsewhere for their sources of information.

4   The people lived, and knew that they lived, between truth and falsehood, things possible and things unverifiable. The feelings of uncertainty provoked by the manipulations of police and politics strengthened the taste for knowledge which fed on widespread and variegated pieces of news. It was a morass; but public opinion, far from sinking into it, became ever sharper and stronger.

5   Contemporaries, like historians, often asked themselves if the flood of news of all kinds had swept the people into disaffection from their king. With due caution, one might suggest that the opinions of individuals did not always closely follow the exaggerations of the news, or even its content. From time to time we must stop considering the one as the cause or consequence of the other, for in between opinions and news many other views or practices might be insinuated, and start new views circulating within an urban sphere.

6   The immersion of the people in an informational sphere containing more probability than truth did not, as politicians persisted in believing, accentuate the credulity and instinctual passions of the lower orders. At the heart of that chaotic anthill of disconnected information something was emerging, something firm and solid: quite simply, the right to know and to judge, the right to expect the king to divulge his secrets. Gossip and rumours might still feed people's natural taste for novelties and marvels, but this did nothing to prevent the establishment of a feeling that political knowledge was legitimate, and could properly be claimed.

7   The fear of the authorities at this outbreak of the word is a thread which runs through the whole of the eighteenth century, organizing repression, multiplying sources of information and arousing, quite unintentionally, a lively determination to speak out which wove itself round the very desire to eradicate it. The anxieties of the monarchy did in fact accomplish a *tour de force*: they created archives which limpidly

reflect that anxiety – and then give clear expression to the very state of opinion which the monarchy pursued and persecuted.

8 If eighteenth-century opinion seems 'relevant' to us today, it may be for the following reason: by expressing themselves, men and women became, and organized, the present. What they said rocked the old certainties, overturned the old situations; above all, it bore on the event, and in so doing, in turning away from that same event, it created new forms of alterity.

Notes

Foreword

1 Gilles Deleuze, *Pourparlers* (Minuit, 1990), ch. 3, p. 119.
2 Nathalie Sarraute, 'Conversation et sous-conversation', in *L'Ere du soupçon* (Gallimard, 'Folios Essais'), pp. 83–122.
3 Pascal Quignard, *Albucius* (POL, 1990), p. 44.

Introduction

1 Jürgen Habermas, *The Structural Transformation of the Public Sphere*, tr. T. Burger and F. Lawrence (Cambridge, Mass., 1989), p. xviii.
2 Keith Baker, 'Politique et opinion publique sous l'Ancien Régime', *Annales Economies Sociétés Civilisations* (hereafter *Annales ESC*), January–February 1987, pp. 41–7. Sarah Maza, 'Le tribunal de la nation: les mémoires judiciaires et l'opinion publique à la fin de l'Ancien Régime', ibid., pp. 73–90. Mona Ozouf, 'Le concept d'opinion publique du XVIII siècle', in *L'Homme régénéré. Essais sur la Révolution française* (Gallimard, 1989), pp. 21–53. Roger Chartier, *Les Origines culturelles de la Révolution française* (Editions du Seuil, 1990).
3 Patrick Champagne, *Faire l'opinion* (Minuit, 1990), p. 41.
4 'Tentons l'expérience', *Annales ESC*, November–December 1989, special number *Histoire et sciences sociales, un tournant critique*, pp. 1317–23.
5 Pierre Charron, *De la sagesse*, lst edn (Bordeaux, 1601), reprinted in series Oeuvres de Langue Française (1986), quoted by C. Jouhaud in 'Révoltes et contestations d'Ancien Régime', in A. Burguière and J. Revel, eds, *Histoire de la France. L'Etat et les conflits* (Editions du Seuil, 1990), p. 71.
6 Luc Boltanski, *L'Amour et la Justice comme compétences* (A.-M. Métailié, 1990), p. 54.

Chapter 1 Words scorned and persecuted

1 Jean Buvat, *Journal de la Régence, 1715–23* (Plon, 1865). Mathieu Marais, *Journal et Mémoires, 1715–1737,* ed. Lescure, 4 vols (Didot, 1863). Edmond-Jean Barbier, *Journal historique et anecdotique du règne de Louis XV,* 4 vols (Renouard, 1847).

2 *Gazetins de la police secrète, 1726–1741,* Bibliothèque de l'Arsenal, archives de la Bastille, MSS 10155–10170.

3 Pierre Rétat, ed., *L'attentat de Damiens, Discours sur l'événement du XVIIIe siècle* (Presses Universitaires de Lyon, 1979); Dale Van Kley, *The Damiens Affair and the Unraveling of the Ancien Régime, 1750–1770* (Princeton University Press, 1984); Arlette Farge and Jacques Revel, *The Rules of Rebellion* (Polity, 1991); Roger Chartier, *Origines culturelles de la Révolution française.*

4 Ch. Carrière, M. Courdurié and F. Rebuffat, *Marseille ville morte. La peste de 1720* (Maurice Garçon, 1968).

5 Charles Aubertin, *L'Esprit public au XVIIIe siècle. Etude sur les mémoires et les correspondances politiques des contemporains, 1715–1789* (Didier, 1873), p. 2.

6 Ibid., p. 27.

7 On these executions and their ritual, see Michel Foucault, *Discipline and Punish. The Birth of the Prison,* tr. A. Sheridan (London, Allen Lane, 1977); Arlette Farge, *Fragile Lives: Violence, Power and Solidarity in Eighteenth-Century Paris* (Polity, 1993).

8 *Mémoires du Président Hénault,* new edn corrected by F. Rousseau (Paris, 1911), p. 290, on the *parlement*'s move to Pontoise.

9 Bibliothèque de l'Arsenal, AB 10155–10170, *Gazetins de la police secrète,* edited by the lieutenant general of police, together with some handwritten notes of day-to-day gossip in the court, the city, in gardens, salons and cafés. The whole is a diary of public opinion from 1724 to 1781.

10 AB 10156, February 1726, fol. 70.

11 AB 10156, 11 December 1726, letter from Verdain.

12 As a comparison, readers 200 years from now may have trouble in understanding the commentaries in the Resistance journal *Libération*!

13 AB 10158, September 1728.

Chapter 2 Words caught in flight: government, information and resistance

1 Catherine-Laurence Maire, *Les Convulsionnaires de Saint-Médard. Miracles, convulsions et prophéties à Paris au XVIIIe siècle* (Gallimard/Juillard, 'Archives', 1985).

2 AB 10164, July 1733.

3 F. Ravaisson-Mollien, *Les Archives de la Bastille, 1866–1904,* 19 vols, vol. XIV (1726–1737), letter from Fleury to Hérault, 23 April 1733.

4 Rétat, *Attentat de Damiens.*

5 AB 10161, 30 January 1732.

6   *Lettres du commissaire Dubuisson au marquis de Caumont, 1735–1741* (A. Rouxel, Paris, April 1736), letter III.

7   Louis-Sébastien Mercier, *Tableau de Paris*, revised and enlarged edn (Amsterdam, 1782–83), vol. V, *Liseurs de gazettes.*

8   Mercier, *Tableau*, vol. II, *Nouvellistes*, p. 97.

9   *Journal des nouvelles de Paris de 1734 à 1738*, Bibliothèque Nationale MS 13694. Collection of unsigned autograph letters addressed to Poulletier, intendant of Lyon. In a note they are attributed to Bergès, a correspondent of Voltaire. This is not certain, and it is also doubtful that they were really addressed to Poulletier. These are in fact ephemeral, unsigned news-sheets, and it is hard to tell for whom they are intended.

10   AB 10838, fol. 155, police note from 1724.

11   Frantz Funck-Brentano, *Figaro et ses devanciers*, assisted by Paul d'Estrée (Hachette, 1909); *Les Nouvellistes* (Hachette, 1905).

12   *Chevrier, nouvelliste pamphlétaire*, Bibliothèque Nationale MS français 22085.

13   The gazettes of Utrecht and Amsterdam, for example, were very well known.

14   Her husband kept an office with which Bachaumont was later associated.

15   AB 12385, private register on Lavely and his accomplices, 20 October 1770.

16   Christian Jouhaud, *Mazarinades. La Fronde des mots* (Aubier, 1985).

17   AB 11544, surreptitious newsmongers, 1743–51.

18   AB 11544, fol. 135, note by Maurepas.

19   AB 11544, fol. 427, note by Inspector Poussot, 12 January 1745.

20   Mercier, *Tableau*, vol. V, *Liseurs de gazettes.*

21   Orléans, Bibliothèque Municipale, manuscripts of Lenoir, lieutenant of police, MS 1422.

22   Mercier, *Tableau*, vol. II, *Nouvellistes.*

23   Ibid.

24   *Lettres du commissaire Dubuisson*, VII, 1735.

25   *Anecdotes galantes et secrètes de la Cour de France sous Louis XV* (no date).

26   Mercier, *Tableau*, vol. II, *Brochures.*

27   See especially: Daniel Mornet, *Les Origines intellectuelles de la Révolution française 1715–1787* (Armand Colin, 1967, first edn 1933); Robert Darnton, *The Literary Underground of the Old Régime* (Cambridge, MA, 1982) and *Edition et sédition* (Gallimard, 1991); Roger Chartier, *Origines culturelles*; Jean Sgard, *Lumières et lueurs du XVIIIe siècle, 1715–1789. Histoire de France à travers les journaux du temps passé* (L'Arbre Verdoyant, 1966); Jean Sgard, ed., *Dictionnaire des journaux, 1600–1789*, 2 vols (Universitas, 1991). See also the studies by P. Rétat and Dale Van Kley and the unpublished thesis by Myoncheol Jou (supervised by Daniel Roche), 'Les Gens du livre embastillés, 1750–1789'.

28   Funck-Brentano, *Figaro*, p. 126.

29   Chartier, *Origines culturelles*, p. 108.

30   Mercier, *Tableau*, vol. IV, *Les Affiches*, p. 28.

31   Mercier, *Tableau*, vol. II, *Liseurs de gazettes.*

32   *Nouvelles ecclésiastiques ou Mémoires pour servir à l'histoire de la Constitution Unigenitus*, 1728.

33   Barbier, *Journal historique*, vol. I, November 1731, p. 73.

34   Catherine-Laurence Maire, 'Agonie religieuse et transfiguration politique du jansénisme', in *Jansénisme et Révolution, actes du colloque de Versailles des 13–14 octobre 1989*, Chroniques de Port-Royal (Bibliothèque Mazarine, 1990), pp. 103–14.

35   Catherine-Laurence Maire is now preparing a thesis on 'Figurisme et jansénisme' under the supervision of Jacques Revel. In March 1991, in a seminar led by Revel at the Ecole des Hautes Etudes en Sciences Sociales, she gave a paper on the *Nouvelles ecclésiastiques*.

36   *Nouvelles ecclésiastiques*, vol. I, *1728–1729–1730*, 3rd edn, Utrecht, 'aux dépens de la Compagnie', 1735.

37   AB 10158, 16 October 1728.

38   Barbier, *Journal*, vol. I, November 1731.

39   AB 10160, 26 October 1729.

40   *Nouvelles ecclésiastiques*, vol. I, 3 December 1728, pp. 45–6.

41   The phrase is from Boltanski, *L'Amour et la Justice*.

42   *Nouvelles ecclésiastiques*, 28 October 1728.

43   Ibid.

44   Ibid., 2 April 1730.

45   Ibid.

46   Ibid.

47   'The General Hospital is composed of eight houses: the Salpêtrière, the Pitié, Bicêtre, the Saint-Esprit, the Enfants-Rouges, Scipion and the Enfants Trouvés [foundlings] of the Rue Notre-Dame and the Rue Saint-Antoine. There are over 12,000 mouths to feed, not counting almost 6000 infants out to nurse in the current year. Of the 12,000, 800 are licentious women and madwomen in the House of Confinement; there are between 700 and 800 licentious men at Bicêtre, some healthy and others with unmentionable diseases, and a great number of beggars of both classes.' Ibid., 20 March 1850.

48   Christophe de Beaumont became archbishop of Paris in 1746.

49   *Nouvelles ecclésiastiques*, 9 July 1748.

50   Ibid., 7 August 1749.

51   Ibid., 4 September 1749.

52   Ibid., 13 November 1751 (vol. VII, *1751–1755*).

53   Edmond-Jean Barbier and the *Nouvelles ecclésiastiques* give a good deal of detail on this. See also: Félix Rocquain, *L'Esprit révolutionnaire avant la Révolution, 1715–1789* (Plon, 1878); Jean Egret, *Louis XV et l'opposition parlementaire* (Armand Colin, 1970); Patrice Allio, 'Querelle des refus de sacrements durant le Parlement de Paris, 1749–59', MA thesis, 1988; M. Foisil and P. Chaunu, extracts in *L'Emoi de l'Histoire 6–7* (1990), pp. 137–53.

Part II

1   Daniel Roche, *Le Peuple de Paris* (Aubier, 1981).

2   S. Hardy, 'Mes loisirs, 1764–1789', Bibliothèque Nationale, MS français 6680–87.

Chapter 3 Mobility and fragmentation

1 Norbert Elias, *The Court Society*, tr. E. Jephcott (Oxford, 1953).
2 R. Chartier, preface to 1985 Flammarion edn of Elias, *La Société de Cour* (Neuwied & Berlin, 1969; Calmann Lévy, 1974; Flammarion, 1985, with preface by Roger Chartier), p. xxi.
3 Hardy, 'Mes loisirs', 9 November 1768.
4 Ibid., 7 December 1770.
5 Chevrier, *Almanach des gens d'esprit*, 3 vols (1774), vol. I, p. 297.
6 Jean-Claude Lavie, 'Les mots en jeu', preface to new French edition of Freud, *Le Mot d'esprit et sa relation à l'inconscient* (Gallimard, 1988).
7 Mercier, *Tableau de Paris*.
8 Jean Starobinski, *Le Remède dans le mal. Critique et légitimation de l'artifice à l'âge des Lumières* (Gallimard, 1989), ch. 2, 'Flatterie', pp. 61–90.
9 AB 10158, *Gazetins de la police secrète*, October 1728.
10 Ibid.
11 Maire, *Les Convulsionnaires*.
12 AB 10159.
13 AB 10162, 24–5 August 1732.
14 AB 10164, 12 September 1773.
15 AB 10164, 2 February 1735.
16 Claudio Melanesi, *Mort apparente, mort imparfaite. Médecins et mentalités au XVIIIe siècle* (Payot, 1991).
17 AB 10161, 24 January 1732.
18 Robert Favre, *La Mort au siècle des Lumières* (Lyon, Presses Universitaires de Lyon, 1978).
19 AB 10160, 4 September 1729.
20 Farge, *Fragile Lives*.
21 AB 10160, 4 September 1729.
22 Ibid., 12 September 1729.
23 AB 12170, denunciation of an invented plot. Dossier of P. R. du Touche de La Chaux, of the king's bodyguard, 10 January 1762.
24 Archives Nationales, documents of the procureur Gueulette, AD III 18, decree of the court of the *parlement*, 1 February 1762.
25 AB 12170, 10 January 1762.

Chapter 4 Motifs

1 Buvat, *Journal*, April 1716.
2 Barbier, *Journal*, 20 October 1726.
3 Hardy, *Mes loisirs*, 17 July 1771.
4 Ibid., 15 May 1773.
5 Buvat, *Journal*, 12 December 1722.
6 *Nouvelles à la main. Lettres de Paris du 24 mai 1777 au 2 juillet 1997*, Bibliothèque de l'Arsenal, MS 7083.
7 Jean-Marie Goulemot, 'Démons, merveilles et philosophie à l'âge classique', *Annales ESC*, November–December 1980.

8   Pierre Ricoeur, article on belief ('Croyance') in *Encyclopaedia universalis*.

9   Steve L. Kaplan, 'Religion, Subsistence and Social Control: The Uses of Sainte Geneviève', *Eighteenth-Century Studies* XVIII (winter 1979/80), pp. 142–68.

10   Abbé Amiet, *Le Culte liturgique de sainte Geneviève* (Editions de la Ville de Paris, 1984).

11   Nicolas-Toussaint Delamare, *Traité de la police*, II, sect. X, 'Des processions', ch. 3, 'Procession de la châsse de sainte Geneviève'.

12   The Le Senne documents in the Bibliothèque Nationale contain many details of the statutes and ordinances concerning the ceremonial processions for Saint Geneviève. *Inter alia* we have: 4° Z Le Senne 14616, *Recueil des documents relatifs à la confrérie des porteurs de sainte Geneviève*; 4° Z Le Senne 11328, *Statuts et règlements de la compagnie des porteurs*, 1731, in-4°; 4° Le Senne 3009 (15), *Les Antiquités et cérémonies qui s'observent avant et au jour de la descente et procession de la châsse de sainte Geneviève avec les jours et les années qu'elle a été portée depuis 1206 jusqu'à 1725*, in-4°, 8 pp.; 4° Z Le Senne 3009 (13), *Relation de ce qui s'est passé à la découverte de la descente et la procession de la châsse de sainte Geneviève en 1725 et de ce qui a suivi*, Paris, in-4°, 22 pp.

13   Archives Nationales, K 1014.

14   Barbier, *Journal*, vol. I, pp. 221–2.

15   Bachaumont, *Mémoires secrets pour servir à l'histoire de la république des Lettres en France depuis 1762 jusqu'à nos jours ou Journal d'un observateur* (London, Adamson), vol. VII, p. 182.

16   AB 10167, *Gazetins de la police secrète*, 3 May 1740.

17   Mercier, *Tableau de Paris*, vol. II, *L'église Sainte-Geneviève*, p. 151.

18   Bachaumont, *Mémoires secrets*, vol. III, 15 April 1770.

19   Ricoeur, 'Croyance'. (Collins English Dictionary defines superstition as 'false worship or religion; an ignorant and irrational belief in supernatural agency, omens, divination, sorcery, etc.; a deep-rooted but unfounded general belief.' *Tr*.)

20   Robert Mandrou, *Magistrats et sorciers en France au XVIIe siècle. La fin des bûchers de sorcellerie* (Plon, 1968), p. 482.

21   Ravaisson-Mollien, *Archives de la Bastille*, vol. XIV, 1749–1757, *Chercheurs de trésors*. There is an excellent book on this subject by Jean-Michel Sallmann: *Chercheurs de trésors et jeteurs de sorts. La quête du surnaturel à Naples au XVIe siècle* (Aubier, 1986).

22   AB 10545, Marie Gueneau, wife of Gueule l'Amour, public scribe, aged fifty-one, accused of calling on devils to reveal treasure, 1773.

23   AB 10590, sorcery and looking for the philosopher's stone. Dossier of Marie-Madeleine du Colombier, widow of J. Gaillard, in the Bastille from 26 March to 29 December 1710. She peddled 'secrets' to help in love and gambling.

24   AB 10577, Gobert de Mainville, priest, 12 November 1705. A self-styled sorcerer, he called on spirits to discover buried treasure, prepared horoscopes and told fortunes.

25   AB 10577, espionage and spell-working.

26   AB 11855, three private persons passing themselves off as sorcerers, 1754.

27   Bibliothèque de l'Arsenal, MS 4824, fol. 377. Examination of the possession in Landes, 1735.

28 The recipe for living to the age of 500 is a simple one. It was supplied by Forcassy, a clock-maker, and is included in Ravaisson-Mollien, *Archives*, vol. XIV, p. 317: (1) take the elixir of the *Magnum Opus* once every twenty-five years; (2) choose a house at a distance from the city; (3) a room on the third floor; (4) four windows to admit air; (5) no company of cat or dog; (6) be bled from the right wrist; (7) fast on broth once a fortnight; (8) sleep on a mattress of wool between two blankets of wool with a bonnet on the head, three days and three nights without being awakened; (9) take a bath in warm water lasting three hours; (10) then the skin will be renewed. Forcassy was to spend a month in the Bastille; his dissatisfied customer had swallowed quicksilver on his recommendation and had scarcely any skin left at all.

29 Bibliothèque de l'Arsenal, MS 7581. Collection entitled *Diversité*. Evreux, 1774. Many treatises were published which denounced popular errors. Here is an example: 'p. 217. Popular errors. It has taken a very long time to efface the majority of popular errors. A good many remain today: (1) the rose of Jericho flowers every year on Christmas Eve; (2) many people believe that the elephant has no joints and is obliged to sleep standing up, or leaning against a tree; (3) pigeons have no liver; (4) the she-bear licks her cubs into shape; (5) ostriches can digest iron; (6) swans sing melodiously as they die; (7) ants bite off the ends of the seeds they collect to stop them germinating and rotting; (8) men weigh more after death than when alive; (9) Jews naturally have a bad smell; (10) years 7, 14, 21 and 63 (made up of 7 x 9 or 9 x 7) are unlucky.'

30 AB 10156, 30 March 1726.

31 AB 10156, 18 May 1726.

32 AB 10157, 31 May 1729.

33 Letters from Commissioner Dubuisson, September 1738, letter XI; June 1739, letter VI, peace celebrations.

34 Hardy, *Mes loisirs*, 31 October 1768.

35 Ibid., 11 September 1770.

36 Steve L. Kaplan, *The Famine Plot Persuasion in Eighteenth-century France* (Philadelphia, 1982).

37 AB 10167, 23 and 24 September 1740.

38 Hardy, *Mes loisirs*, 23 November 1772.

39 Marais, *Journal et mémoires*, 11 June 1723, case of For-l'Evêque.

40 On this point, Michel Foucault's analysis of the popular literature concerning criminals and thieves (in *Discipline and Punish*) is most enlightening.

41 This interpretation would not have been possible without the perusal of the following studies: H. J. Lüsebrink, ed., *Histoires curieuses et véritables de Cartouche et de Mandrin*, 'Bibliothèque Bleue' (Montalba, 1984); Patrice Péveri, 'Pour une étude de la pègre parisienne au XVIIIe siècle: le procès de Louis-Dominique Cartouche' (unpublished thesis in preparation under the supervision of Jean-Louis Flandrin); Isabelle Foucher, 'Deux bandes de voleurs du XVIIIe siècle', thesis for diploma, Ecole des Hautes Etudes en Sciences Sociales, under the supervision of Jacques Revel.

42 Bibliothèque de l'Arsenal, MS 7557, 'La Vie de Cartouche', declaration by twenty defendants, fol. 9, 2 December 1721, evidence of Jean-Pierre Balagny.

43 Foucault, *Discipline and Punish*.

44   Mercier, *Tableau de Paris*, vol. IX, *De la Cour*, p. 6.

45   Ibid., vol. I, *Le Monarque*.

46   Duclos, perpetual secretary to the Académie Française, *Mémoires secrets sur le règne de Louis XIV, la Régence et le règne de Louis XV*, first published in the eighteenth century with notes by Voltaire, republished in two volumes in 1764.

47   AB 10156, July 1726.

48   Mercier, *Tableau de Paris*, vol. II, *Les j'ai vu et les je n'ai point vu* ('The I-saw-thises and the I-didn't-see-thats').

49   AB 10029, Journal of the Chevalier de Mouchy, 1744–48.

50   Paul d'Estrée, 'Un journaliste policier, le chevalier de Mouchy', *Revue d'Histoire Littéraire* (1898), p. 195; Funck-Brentano, *Figaro et ses devanciers*, ch. 14, 'Le chevalier de Mouchy'; Bastille Archives, dossiers no. AB 11491 (1741) and AB 11571 (1745).

51   The king's confessor was a Jesuit called Père Pérusseau. Bishop Fitzjames, who replaced him at this point, was the bishop of Soissons and the primary confessor. Georges Minois, *Le Confesseur du roi. Les directeurs de conscience sous la monarchie* (Fayard, 1988).

52   Barbier, *Journal*, vol. II, pp. 406–7 (August 1744).

53   AB 11582, *Tanastès* affair, 1745, fol. 20.

54   AB 11582, interrogation of 29 August 1745, fol. 20.

55   Yves-Marie Bercé, *Révoltes et révolution dans l'Europe moderne, XVIe–XVIIIe siècle*, 1980; *Fête et révolte. Des mentalités populaires du XVIe au XVIIIe siècle* (Hachette, 1976); Robert Mandrou, 'Vingt ans après, ou une direction de recherches féconde: les révoltes populaires en France au XVIIIe siècle', *Revue Historique* 242 (1969), pp. 29–40; Georges Rudé, *The Crowd in the French Revolution* (Westport, Conn., 1986); Edward P. Thompson, *The Making of the English Working Class* (London, Gollancz, 1963); Christine Jouhaud, 'Révoltes et contestations d'Ancien Régime', in A. Burguière and J. Revel, eds, *Histoire de la France: L'Etat et les conflits* (Editions de Seuil, 1990), pp. 21–99; Jean Nicolas, preface to *Mouvements populaires et conscience sociale XVIe–XIXe siècle* (Maloine, 1985); *Révolte et société*, 2 vols, series 'Histoire du Présent' (Publications de la Sorbonne, 1989).

56   Saint-Simon, *Mémoires*, Collection 'J'ai lu', p. 488.

57   Archives Nationales, U 363, 'Recueil de Lisle, Conseil secret du Parlement de 1687 à 1774'.

58   Buvat, *Journal*, vol. II, p. 40.

59   Bibliothèque Nationale, Actes Royaux, F 23622 (164–281), item 245.

60   Farge and Revel, *The Rules of Rebellion*.

61   Edgar Faure, *La Banqueroute de Law, 17 juillet 1720* (Gallimard, 1977); Ernest Lavisse, *Histoire de France. Le règne de Louis XV*, bk I, ch. 2, pp. 24–5.

62   Mme Dunoyer, *Lettres historiques et galantes* (Paris, 1723).

63   I shall not look in detail at the rationale of this uprising, since it is the subject of the aforementioned Farge and Revel, *The Rules of Rebellion*.

64   Kaplan, *The Famine Plot Persuasion*.

65   On the role of women in uprisings see Arlette Farge, 'Evidences émeutières', in Natalie Z. Davis and Arlette Farge, *Histoire des femmes*, vol. III (Plon, 1991).

66 AB 10155, Saturday 25 August 1725, café Détienne.
67 AB 10023–7, papers from Duval, first secretary of the lieutenancy of police. See especially AB 10027, year 1725.
68 Métra, *Correspondance secrète, politique et littéraire ou Mémoires pour servir à l'histoire des cours, des sociétés et de la littérature en France depuis la mort de Louis XV* (London, 1787); Hardy, *Mes loisirs*; *Mémoires* of the Abbé Terray, comptroller general of finance, with an account of the uprising in Paris in 1775, followed by fourteen letters from a shareholder in the East India Company (London, 1776); Ernest Lavisse, *Histoire de France*, vol. IX, part I, 'Louis XVI, 1774–1789'. Georges Rudé, 'La taxation populaire de mai 1775 à Paris et dans la région parisienne', *Annales de l'Histoire de la Révolution française* 143 (April/June 1956), pp. 139ff.; Robert Darnton, 'Le lieutenant général de police J. P. Lenoir, la guerre des farines et l'approvisionnement de Paris à la veille de la Révolution', *Revue d'Histoire Moderne et Contemporaine* XVI (1969); V. P. S. Ljublinski, *La Guerre des Farines. Contribution à l'histoire de la lutte des classes en France à la veille de la Révolution* (Presses Universitaires de Grenoble, 1979). Manuscript sources: Archives Nationales Y 10558, riots of 3 May 1775; Archives Nationales Y 12791A, archives of Commissioner Roland; Bibliothèque de l'Arsenal AB 12441–7; Archives Nationales K 1022, no. 25.
69 Métra, *Correspondance*, vol. I, p. 338.
70 Condorcet, *Oeuvres*, vol. V (Paris, 1867), p. 101: Life of Turgot, written in 1783.
71 Abbé Terray, *Mémoires*. Historical account of the riot in Paris on 3 May 1775, and what preceded and followed it.
72 Hardy, *Mes loisirs*, for Wednesday 3 May 1775.
73 AB 12447, 'Corn' affair, fol. 63.
74 Rudé, 'Taxation populaire'.

Part III

1 Rétat, *Attentat de Damiens*, ch. 8, 'Le mobile de Damiens, fanatisme et folie', p. 220.
2 Jacques Revel, 'Marie-Antoinette', in François Furet and Mona Ozouf, eds, *Dictionnaire critique de la Révolution française* (Flammarion, 1988), pp. 286–97; Jean-Marie Goulemot, *Ces livres qu'on ne lit que d'une main. Lecture et lecteur de livres pornographiques du XVIIIe siècle* (Aix-en-Provence: Alinéa, 1991); Darnton, *Edition et sédition*.
3 Pierre Laborie, 'Histoire politique et histoire des représentations mentales', *Cahiers de l'IHTP* 18 (June 1991), *Histoire Politique et Sciences Sociales*, eds D. Perschanski, M. Pollack and H. Rousso. This article is very illuminating for our purposes; it was followed by an equally important rejoinder from Nicole Loraux, 'Questions antiques sur l'opinion. En guise de réponse à P. Laborie'. See also Pierre Laborie, *L'Opinion française sous Vichy* (Editions du Seuil, 1990).
4 Arlette Farge, *Le Goût de l'archive*, series 'Librairie du XXe siècle' (Editions du Seuil, 1989), p. 146.
5 Bibliothèque Nationale, Fonds Joly de Fleury, MSS 2072–2077. Seditious talk connected with the Damiens affair, 1757–60.

6 Maire, *Les Convulsionnaires*; Darnton, *Edition et sédition*; Goulemeot, *Ces livres . . .*
7 Note that the dossiers do not extend to the rioters arrested during the most serious uprisings of the eighteenth century, or those suspected or suppressed by the *Chambre Ardente* during the Poisons Affair of 1679–82.
8 See the police inspectors' reports in the Bibliothèque de l'Arsenal, notably those of Inspectors Roussel (AB 10028), Damotte (AB 10123) and Poussot (AB 10139–10141), 1738–54.
9 In the Y Series of the Archives Nationales.
10 Bearing in mind that women were more seldom arrested by the police than were men, being considered less civilly and criminally responsible.
11 Michael Walzer, *Regicide and Revolution. The Trial of Louis XVI* (Cambridge University Press, 1984).

Chapter 5 'Who is to stop me killing the king?'

1 AB 10319, 30 March 1684, threats against the king.
2 Walzer, *Regicide and Revolution*, p. 1.
3 Ernst Kantorowicz, *The King's Two Bodies: A Study in Medieval Political Theology* (Princeton, 1957).
4 Cangé collection, vol. LXVI (quarto, 1719); cited in A. Babeau, *Les Préambules des ordonnances royales et l'opinion publique* (Picard, 1896), p. 23.
5 Ibid., p. 29.
6 In 1724 and 1764 there were a number of requests for imprisonment, addressed by families to the king, which can be interpreted along these lines. The families bypassed the normal judicial process and asked the king to 'touch' them and remove from their midst, by imprisonment, the diseased member who had betrayed the family honour. See Arlette Farge and Michel Foucault, *Le Désordre des familles. Lettres de cachet des archives de la Bastille* (Gallimard, 'Archives' collection, 1982).
7 AB 10419, February 1684, Marie-Geneviève de Saint-André, suspected of evil designs on the king's life.
8 Ravaisson-Mollien, *Archives de la Bastille*, vol. XVIII, p. 268.
9 AB 10419.
10 Cangé collection, preamble to the decree exiling the Maréchal de Villeroi in 1722.
11 Maza, 'Tribunal de la nation'.
12 AB 10363, case of Nicolas Martin, 1678.
13 AB 10528, dossier of François Henry de Bardy of Villeclerc, lackey, March 1701.
14 Georges Mongrédien, *Mme de Montespan et l'Affaire des poisons* (Hachette, 1953); Frantz Funck-Brentano, *Le Drame des poisons* (Paris, 1899, reprint 1928); Dr Masson, *La Sorcellerie et la science des poisons au XVIIe siècle* (Paris, 1904); Jean-Claude Petitfils, *L'Affaire des poisons: alchimistes et sorciers sous Louis XIV* (Albin Michel, 1977); Marie-Claude Olivier and Jacques Solé, 'Affaire des poisons et mentalité magique', Actes du 3ᵉ Colloque XVII Siècle, Marseilles, series 3, no. 95 (1973); Arlette Lebigre, *L'Affaire des poisons, 1679–1682* (Complexe, 1989).

15 Robert Mandrou, *Magistrats et sorciers en France au XVIIe siècle* (Plon, 1968).

16 These practices were not imaginary; to be clear about what was really happening in society at the time, we need only look at the archives. The dossiers of crimes of poisoning at this period are very revealing. They deserve to be studied for themselves, purged of all the more or less sensational literature which has accumulated around them. The sources are: AB 10338–59 (twenty-one bundles containing all the interrogations and trials of poisoners); Bibliothèque Nationale, Collection Clairambault 161–463 (papers of La Reynie, lieutenant general of police, concerning the Poisons Affair); Bibliothèque Nationale MS français 7608 (collection of original documents concerning the trials and summary of secret interrogations destroyed in 1709); Bibliothèque Nationale, MS français 7630 (trial of La Joly).

17 Lebigre, *Affaire des poisons*, p. 67.

18 Ravaisson-Mollien, *Archives*, vol. VI, p. 437.

19 AB 10388, 3 October 1683.

20 AB 10731: Catherine Gaudron 'says that she found a ball of thread which contained several packets of poison addressed to persons of the first rank, very close to the person of the king'. She was put in the Bastille in April 1721 and remained there for so long that all trace of her was lost.

21 AB 12023, year 1758, a dangerous madman: the Thorin case.

22 On this exact point see Farge, *Goût de l'archive*, pp. 76–7.

23 On the Thorin affair, and for a different and more detailed analysis, see Arlette Farge, 'La mort du Roi et l'imaginaire collectif, affaire Thorin (visions et crédulité), 1758', in *Le Père. Métaphore paternelle et fonctions du père: l'Interdit, la Filiation, la Transmission*, introduction by Marc Augé, series L'Espace Analytique (Denoël), pp. 325–37.

24 On this theme of loyalty to the king see the interesting paper given at the EHESS seminar (led by Jacques Revel) on 8 March 1991 by Lisa J. Graham of John Hopkins University: 'Entre bon discours et mauvais discours: le langage de la fidélité sous le règne de Louis XV'. Lisa Graham is completing a PhD on public opinion in the eighteenth century, and I am grateful for the chance of exchanging views with her.

25 Ravaisson-Mollien, *Archives*, vol. VII, pp. 349–50.

26 AB 10501, Jacques Vigier, 2 March 1694.

27 AB 10558, Robert Laurent, 14 October 1705.

28 AB 10438, Benjamin Crutz-Crosnier, year 1687.

Chapter 6 'Your worthy subjects deserve a king who shall surpass them.'

1 Bibliothèque de l'Arsenal, MS 6608 (composite), fol. 107, 'La Convalescence du Roy', 1744.

2 Barbier, *Journal*, November 1744.

3 Ravaisson-Mollien, *Archives*, vol. XIV. The editor says in his preface: 'The repression of Jansenism and the surveillance of public morals constitute almost all the matter of volume XIV. The cases are easy to understand, and a lengthy commentary would be superfluous.'

4   Félix Rocquain, *L'Esprit révolutionnaire avant la Révolution, 1715–1789*, p. 115.
5   AB 11547, Modeste Brunet, 23 August 1744, inquiry by Inspector Poussot and interrogation by Commissioner Rochebrune.
6   AB 11548, Jean-François Cagnen, priest, 21 March 1744.
7   D'Argenson, *Journal*, vol. VI, p. 7.
8   Ibid., vol. V, p. 362.
9   Bernard and Monique Cottret, 'Les chansons du mal aimé: raison d'Etat et rumeur publique, 1748–1750', in *Mélanges Robert Mandrou. Histoire sociale, sensibilités collectives et mentalités* (PUF, 1985), pp. 303–15.
10 AB 11658, fol. 143, 16 July 1748.
11 Barbier, *Journal*, December 1748.
12 Ravaisson-Mollien, *Archives*, vol. XV, p. 446, affair of Prince [Charles] Edward; vol. XII, pp. 300ff., affair of the pamphlets and '14 lines against the king after the arrest of Stuart'.
13 Ibid., vol. XV, p. 446.
14 Ibid., vol. XII, p. 300.
15 AB 11664, dossier of the Chevalier de Bellerive, 18 April 1749.
16 Dufort de Cheverny, *Mémoires, La Cour de Louis XV*, introduction and notes by Jean-Pierre Guicciardi (Perrin, 1990), p. 97.
17 AB 11733, Clément-Jérôme de Rességuier, ensign in the French Guards, 8 December 1750.
18 AB 11729, A. Allègre, November 1749.
19 Ibid., fol. 412.
20 Bibliothèque Nationale, fonds Joly de Fleury, procurator general to the Paris *parlement*, MSS 2072–2077, years 1757–65.
21 Ibid., MS 2073.
22 Ibid., MS 2075, 9 July 1757, prévôté of Mitry, arrest of François Lépine.
23 Ravaisson-Mollien, *Archives de la Bastille*, vol. XVI, p. 43.
24 Fleury archives, MS 2072.
25 Ibid., MS 2073.
26 Ibid., MS 2075, 17 February 1770.
27 Ibid., 24 July 1762.
28 Ibid., February 1770.
29 AB 11986, Mme Hatte de Vauné, 4 July 1758.
30 AB 11989, Mme de Sénac, 26 July 1758.
31 AB 11990, Cadot de Condé, 12 February 1758.
32 AB 12002, Moriceau de la Motte, July 1758.
32 Barbier, *Journal*, p. 289.
34 AB 12058, Tavernier, 1759–89.
35 Michel Antoine, *Louis XV* (Fayard, 1989), p. 735.
36 AB 12107, Michel Mitre-Touche, 23 February 1760.
37 AB 12094, Constans, 24 February 1760.
38 Ravaisson-Mollien, *Archives*, vol. XIX, p. 210.
39 AB 12164, Jacques Ringuet, 30 September 1762.
40 AB 12514, Pierre Dayrivier, 30 September 1762.
41 For further details see the exhaustive study by C. Aubertin in *L'Esprit public du XVIIIe siècle*, 3ième époque, ch. II, 'Mémoires de Bachaumont', pp. 373–99.
42 Barbier, *Journal*, vol. VIII, p. 75.

43   AB 12057, Effer de Sybourg, July 1759.
44   AB 13292, Anne Apoline Josèphe Chevalier, wife of Nicolas Renard, 2 January 1766.
45   Marc Chassaigne, *Le Procès du chevalier de La Barre* (Paris, 1920); Eric Walter, 'L'affaire La Barre et le concept d'opinion publique', in *Le Journalisme d'Ancien Régime* (PUL, 1981).
46   Voltaire, Corréspondence générale, XII, 16–18.
47   Hardy, *Mes loisirs*, Bibliothèque Nationale, MS français 6680–7.
48   Ibid., 29 January 1771.
49   Ibid., 1 March 1772.
50   I shall not pay close attention to this point. For one thing, the story is very well known; for another, Dale Van Kley is about to publish a detailed study of the pamphleteering activity caused by Chancellor Maupeou's reforms.
51   AB 12433, Louis Laporte, 6 February 1773.
52   AB 12390, Abbé d'Iharse, 7 April 1771.
53   AB 12401, Monsieur Lombard, 14 March 1772.
54   Antoine, *Louis XV*, pp. 595–6.
55   AB 12227, Pauquet, 1 February 1764.
56   AB 12351, Le Prévôt de Beaumont, 12 November 1768, denunciation of the 'pact of famine'. He was not freed until September 1789. He had published seditious pamphlets accusing those in authority of 'exercising a monopoly of the corn and exciting the people to rebellion by making them die of hunger'.
57   Maurice Lever, *Donatien Alphonse François, marquis de Sade* (Fayard, 1991). See ch. 16, 'Le temps immobile, 1778–90', for a detailed account of the relationship between de Sade's imprisonment and his writings.

Index